Keepers of the American Dream:
A Study of Staff Development
and Multicultural Education

D1565955

Keepers of the American Dream:
A Study of Staff Development and Multicultural Education

Christine E. Sleeter

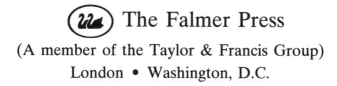 The Falmer Press

(A member of the Taylor & Francis Group)
London • Washington, D.C.

USA The Falmer Press, Taylor & Francis Inc., 1900 Frost Road, Suite 101,
Bristol, PA 19007

UK The Falmer Press, 4 John Street, London WC1N 2ET

First published in 1992

A catalogue record for this book is available from the British Library

Library of Congress Cataloging-in-Publication Data are available on request

ISBN 0 75070 0807 cased
ISBN 0 75070 0815 paperback.

Cover design by Caroline Archer

Typeset in 10/12pt Times by
Graphicraft Typesetters Ltd., Hong Kong

Printed in Great Britain by Burgess Science Press, Basingstoke on paper which has a specified pH value on final paper manufacture of not less than 7.5 and is therefore 'acid free'.

Contents

Acknowledgments

I owe a debt of gratitude to many people for their help with this book. Without the support of the Joyce Foundation, the project reported here would not have been possible, nor would I have had the time and resources to document and evaluate it. William McKersie and Angel Zapata at the Joyce Foundation, in particular, were encouraging and supportive throughout.

Susan Gould of the Regional Staff Development Center and Tom LoGuidice of the University of Wisconsin-Platteville (formerly of Carthage College) deserve much thanks for their partnership throughout this project, for their feedback on earlier drafts of this manuscript and for their patience and good humor in the development, conduct and criticism of the project. I also thank Esther Letven, Director of the Regional Staff Development Center, for her support.

Margaret Oliver assisted in much of the data collection; her skill, insights, and professionalism attest to the potential of undergraduate students to serve as valuable research assistants. I also thank former students Pamela Beach and Craig Matheus for analyzing portions of the data that were collected.

Several people gave helpful feedback on drafts of the manuscript while it was in progress, or on ideas directly related to it. Sincere thanks go to John Buenker, Carl Grant, Ozetta Kirby, Dwayne Olsen, Jackson Parker, Lana Rakow, Barbara Shade, Barry Troyna and Melvin Williams.

The teachers who participated in the study, who are given pseudonyms in the manuscript, deserve hearty gratitude for putting up with my intrusions into their lives and work, and for giving time and thought in the interviews. A qualitative study generates a considerable amount of tape recorded material that requires transcription, and the following people transcribed tapes with patience and efficiency: Roma Cesario, Shelley Danzer, Judy Gaal, Elzy Hill, Diane Montour and Marilyn Timm. Sharon Eaves' fine work on the index was greatly appreciated.

I would also like to thank individuals in my own professional past who 'developed' me through staff development programs similar to the one reported here. While this book questions the degree to which most staff development in multicultural education actually changes people, it has been one of the factors that helped me grow. My rather belated thanks go to the Urban Education pre-service education program of Central Washington State College (now University) in the early 1970s, to the former staff of the Ethnic Cultural Heritage Program in Seattle, to those who conducted Human Relations workshops for teachers in Seattle Public Schools during the mid-1970s and to Carl Grant who directed the Teacher Corps Associates Program in which I participated as a graduate assistant, and who mentored much of my own professional growth.

Malcolm Clarkson, Managing Director of Falmer Press, has my gratitude for his enthusiastic support of this project. Finally I appreciate the support and encouragement of friends and colleagues at the University of Wisconsin-Parkside who cheered me on as I scurried out to schools, tape recorder in hand and as I labored over my word processer while endeavoring to bring order to the reams of paper and tapes I had generated.

Foreword

Keepers of the American Dream: A Study of Staff Development and Multi-cultural Education provides educators with a rare opportunity to have an insider's view of the culture, context and social dynamics of a staff development project concerned with multicultural education. Professor Christine E. Sleeter chronicles with great clarity and engaging, reflective thought how the teachers and the project staff were affected personally and professionally by this dynamic in-service experience. Beginning with a search for funds with which to begin the project and concluding with a critique of what happened and why it happened during the life of the project, Professor Sleeter critically examines each phase of this staff development experience. Problems and issues primary to the raging national multicultural debate are addressed. Collaboration efforts that take into account ideological and instructional issues that occur between and among teachers, school administrators and the project staff are also discussed in relation to multicultural education.

Professor Sleeter has provided the educational community with a text on staff development that should keep us intellectually engaged for years to come. Readers will leave this volume greatly informed about both the theoretical and practical aspects of staff development from a multicultural perspective. Also, given the importance of educational reform *and* staff development, *Keepers of the American Dream* will become an indispensable resource for schools undergoing educational change and for professors who teach staff development courses.

Fundamental to the integrity of the writing and the analyses present in this book is how Professor Sleeter situates herself as a storyteller. *Keepers of the American Dream* is her narrative — as she tells how she, too, learned and grew — as well as her research account of this project and its participants. By keeping a narrative, Cooper (1991) reminds us, 'We literally become teachers and researchers in our own lives empowering ourselves in the process' (p. 98). *Keepers of the American Dream* will empower all who read and learn from it.

The Wisconsin Series on Teacher Education is pleased to include Professor Sleeter's outstanding work *Keepers of the American Dream: A Study of Staff Development and Multicultural Education* in its growing collection of books that critically examine various aspects of teacher education.

Carl A. Grant
Series Editor
University of Wisconsin-Madison

Introduction

Over the past ten years, I have received an increasing number of requests to come 'do' a workshop for teachers and/or administrators on some aspect of cultural pluralism or multicultural education. I have always approached the task with some ambivalence, and with experience that ambivalence has grown rather than diminished. At first I attributed it to nervousness about speaking before a group of people and about being a White person talking about race-related issues. But as I gained experience in addressing such issues before an audience, a larger source of ambivalence developed, which led ultimately to this book.

As I have become increasingly cognizant of the depth of the issues surrounding inequality in society and schools, and of resistances to change, I have become increasingly pessimistic about the potential for workshops in multicultural education to accomplish very much. Usually they represent a compromise between conflicting interests. Often they are initiated by teachers or sometimes parents, usually of color, who want *something* to happen that will improve education and life chances for children of color. Or they may be initiated by administrators and teachers who experience on a daily basis conflict among students or concern about low achievement levels. (Too often, however, educators take low achievement as given when they should be looking for ways to address it.) Administrators may generate requests for help with 'multicultural issues', but do so within the context of requests for help on a variety of fronts, most of which they perceive as being unrelated to multi-culturalism. So, in a given school or school district, time and resources are divided in a tug of war between, for example, a new reading program, new computer software, a new discipline program, a testing program and multi-cultural education. Multicultural education thus takes the form of a 'program' to add on, preferably in one all-day or half-day session. Those who have a sense of the depth of the issues involved in multicultural education, and those who view it as a way to do the whole of education rather than a program to add on, are aware that such a workshop only begins to scratch the surface, but hope it will lead to continued learning and work. Those who know fairly little about multicultural education, on the other hand, often regard the matter as 'taken care of' once a workshop has been completed, and mentally (and sometimes literally) check it off their list of problems to address.

I no longer participate in one-shot 'flash and dash' workshops. But as a teacher educator, I do still participate in longer education efforts, packaged in the form of university courses. And I do still participate in long-term staff development projects if they appear to be reasonably well thought-out. What impact do long-term courses of study in multicultural education have on teachers, and on the instruction children experience? The professional literature, which I review in chapter 2, gives very little indication. Having participated in such courses of study as a teacher, my sense was that their impact lies somewhere between no impact and significant change.

So I decided to find out. The staff development project examined here was born one morning in my office in a discussion with Susan Gould from a local staff development centre. Both of us are White women and former teachers. We had been involved for a year with a group of teachers who felt that 'something' needed to be done in the schools to address their growing racial diversity. Periodically someone would suggest that their staff needed a workshop. While neither of us viewed a workshop as useful, we wondered what we could accomplish by offering an ongoing course of study, and building it into teachers' workday.

At the time we sought funding for a staff development project, neither district was offering much staff development on multicultural education nor had they plans to do so. But both of us had contact with teachers and administrators who believed it was needed. Neither of us was employed within either district; working through a staff development center and a university, we would be offering a program that would supplement what the districts were (or weren't) doing.

The staff development project was originally conceptualized and funded for one year; later a second year of funding was obtained. The foundation that funded it was particularly interested in programs to improve the achievement of children from low-income and racial minority backgrounds. Thus, the project was to serve schools with concentrations of such students, and focus mainly on improving classroom instruction.

As soon as we were notified that it had been funded, we sent advertisements to schools in which at least one-third of the students were racial minority and/or low-income. The advertisement stated that the purpose of the program would be to prepare teachers 'to work more successfully with the culturally diverse student population as found in our schools today'. Nine full release days would be provided for sessions spaced throughout the school year, and teachers would also be expected to participate in four after-school sessions.[1] Teachers were invited to apply on a form attached to the advertisement. The form mainly asked for a statement of how the teacher believed he/she, his/her students and his/her school would benefit. This book examines what happened.

Chapter 1 situates the staff development project within a broader social context. Here I outline three theoretical perspectives about social inequality — conservatism, liberalism and radical structuralism — and discuss the field of multicultural education in relation to them. Then I review the social climate prior to and during the 1980s, when this project took place, focusing on the history and conditions of the communities in which the schools were located.

In chapter 2 I review literature on staff development and on staff development for multicultural education. I then introduce the school districts and the staff development project and describe the research process I used to study it.

In chapter 3 I present a portrait of the thirty participating teachers in their classrooms at the beginning of the staff development project. The portrait is organized around themes that are explored over the two years in subsequent chapters. Chapter 4 describes the staff development sessions during the first year, and examines what teachers reported learning from them. In chapter 5 we step back into their classrooms to assess the extent to which their participation in the staff development project was affecting their teaching. In chapter 6 a second year of the project is examined: the sessions that were held, what teachers reported learning, and what impact it had on their classroom teaching.

In chapter 7 I analyze why things happened (or did not happen) as they did. Here I examine the staff development project itself, the teachers' position in the social structure (most were White women) and the structure of their workplaces. In chapter 8 I suggest future activities in which multicultural educators should engage to change schools to make them more equitable and just.

Readers may wonder about the title of this book, *Keepers of the American Dream*. This phrase appeared on the nametags we used during the staff development project. Susan and I intended it to suggest that the teachers would promote a progressive definition of the American dream, one that strives toward equality across social groups, open democracy and active pride in diverse Americans as fellow-citizens. As the two years of staff development progressed, however, I began to appreciate the degree to which many Americans hold a much more conservative version of the dream than I do: one that champions competition among individuals for gain and upward mobility. Still others view the American dream in terms of interpersonal relationships much more than social standing or social justice.

Martin Carnoy (1989) described schools as enormously complex institutions in which two different and in many ways opposing charges are played out: the reproduction of a stratified labor force and the inculcation of democratic ideals. How one conceptualizes the American dream and the role of schooling depends partly on how much weight one gives to each of these two charges. Thus, as I probed what teachers believed they should be doing, and what they believed multicultural education and the issues it addresses are about, I began to construct their interpretations of what the American dream is. They did not all hold the same views, but in their approaches to teaching and learning, they all tried to promote their own beliefs about America and what it stands for. In this sense, this is much more than a book about staff development: it is also a book about how teachers view diversity and inequality in America and the school's role in addressing these.

Note

1 The grant was funded for ten days, but we used only nine for full-day sessions. Funding for the tenth day was used for a dinner meeting in August before the next school year.

Chapter 1

The American Dream in the 1980s

By 8.30 a.m., most of the teachers had arrived for the first session of what would become a two-year staff development project. Some chatted amiably, others sat and waited for the session to begin. When all thirty had assembled, Susan and I, the project directors, greeted them and provided a brief overview of the project. In the process, we directed their attention to their nametags: printed under their names stood the caption: 'Keepers of the American Dream'. As participants in a staff development project for multicultural education, these teachers were designated not only as keepers of the American dream, but also as conveyers and interpreters of it to the diverse population of children in their classrooms.

In this book I examine the impact on classroom teachers of a staff development project in multicultural education. Hundreds of school districts have engaged in staff development for multicultural education since the 1960s, but only a few have systematically examined its impact: I was able to locate only four published studies reporting the impact of such a project on teachers (Grant and Grant, 1986; King, 1980; Redman, 1977; Washington, 1981).

Keepers of the American Dream, however, is more than a study of staff development. It is an examination of social relations and social meanings about cultural and racial diversity at a particular time in the history of the United States. The late 1980s witnessed the rapid diversification of student populations at the same time the United States was undergoing a crisis of national identity and international status. Competing discourses about cultural diversity and social justice raged. For example, *Time* magazine's 1990 cover story 'Beyond the Melting Pot' announced that, 'In the 21st century — and that's not far off — racial and ethnic groups in the US will outnumber whites for the first time' (Henry, 1990, p. 28), and many college campuses instituted requirements that students study the histories and cultural productions of Americans of color and women. At the same time, however, Americans bought and read thousands of copies of Bloom's *The Closing of the American Mind* (1987) and E.D. Hirsch's *Cultural Literacy* (1987), and several states passed 'English only' legislation. How did teachers process participation in a staff development project that addressed these kinds of issues as they relate to school? How did they construct and reconstruct their understanding of cultural diversity and social stratification in the context of the 1980s?

In this chapter I provide a framework for analyzing the staff development project and the sense teachers made of it. First, I discuss what the American dream means and contextualize it within three theoretical perspectives about society. Next I briefly review what I mean by multicultural education, relating it to those theoretical perspectives. I then provide a historic overview of the cities in which this staff development project was located, and examine the discourse about society and schooling that teachers in the 1980s would be familiar with.

Theoretical Perspectives on the American Dream

In *The Immigrant* (1977), Howard Fast wrote of his main character, Dan Lavette:

> He was 40 years old, and if anyone ever had, he had surely dreamed the American dream. . . . He had come out of nothing, and he had made himself a king, a veritable emperor. He ruled a fleet of great passenger liners, an airline, a majestic department store, a splendid resort hotel, property, land, and he dispensed the food of life to hundreds of men and women who labored at his will. . . . It was of his own making and his own doing that he controlled twenty million dollars of property. (p. 252)

For generations, Americans — particularly White Americans — have grown up believing they can achieve the American dream. Dan Lavette's success epitomizes that dream, and while very few achieve it in such grandiose fashion, most Americans strive to attain some version of the American dream.

Studs Terkel explored what the American dream means to Americans from different walks of life. Although their own particular dreams differed widely, they shared a common desire to catch the 'brass ring' (1980, p. xxiii). For example,

> (*Company president*): The American Dream is to be better off than you are. How much money is 'enough money'? 'Enough money' is always a little bit more than you have. There's never enough of anything. This is why people go on. If there was enough, everybody would stop. You always go for the brass ring that's always out there about a hundred yards farther. It's like a mirage in the desert; it always stays about a hundred yards ahead of you. (*ibid*, p. 38)

> (*Former Miss USA*): There're always gonna be girls who want to enter the beauty pageant. That's the fantasy: the American Dream. (*ibid*, p. 6)

(*18-year-old boy*): I wanna be my own person. Maybe own my own business one day. I feel that's what America is. Getting your own business and prospering from that will make it easy when you get older. You can just sit back and rest. (Terkel, 1988, p. 410)

The term 'American dream' was coined during the Great Depression of the 1930s. At its root it has always held 'a promise of a society in which individuals have the opportunity to improve their relative position, regardless of their race, creed or class. It represented a vision of opportunity and possibility' (Roper Organization, 1987, p. 3). Based on a survey consisting of telephone interviews with a sample of 1506 adults, the Roper Organization found most Americans to adhere to one of two broad interpretations of the American dream:

The first focuses on economic opportunity and progress. It is a dream of affluence and material comfort, of doing better than previous generations. . . . The second definition is more spiritual. It is America, home of freedom and justice. It is our Puritan fathers 'City on a Hill', a shining moral light to the rest of the world. (p. 8)

Most Americans are optimistic about their own prospects for attaining their dreams. James Kluegel and Eliot Smith (1986) summarized their findings of interviews with 2212 Americans as follows:

A clear majority of the American population subscribes, largely unreservedly, to the characterization of America as the land of opportunity. . . . On the one hand, Americans do express some doubts about equality of opportunity. . . . On the other hand, Americans express little doubt about their chances as individuals to make economic advancement. On the whole, they believe that no limits have or will impede their opportunity to make the most of themselves. The American public expects to have work careers characterized by steady advancement. The average American considers him or herself 'better than average' in terms of his or her prospects to get ahead. (p. 52)

For analytical purposes, I wish to examine the American dream through the lenses of three theoretical perspectives: conservatism, liberalism, and radical structuralism.[1] I have chosen these three perspectives because they offer the greatest help in examining the beliefs of the teachers in this study.

Assumptions Conservatism and Liberalism Share

Most citizens of the United States and other Western capitalist countries share a core of beliefs that Michael Parenti (1978) termed 'Lockean ideology'

(p. 43). Key elements of these beliefs are individualism and civic rights. As John Locke conceptualized the ideal state of nature,

> First, it is a 'state of perfect freedom', in which men do as they choose within the limits imposed by the law of nature. Second, it is a state of equality for its inhabitants. No one has any more right, authority, or jurisdiction than does anyone else. Men are born equal in this way — not equal in capacity but equal in the rights they possess. (Harmon, 1964, pp. 246–7)

In the best possible world, individuals would be free to pursue their desires and compete with one another for self-advancement. This emphasis on the individual supports a valuing of privatism.

People differ; what they attain will differ because individuals vary in abilities and effort. Therefore it is viewed as natural while rights should be equal, attainments would not. A class system would naturally result, but it should allow for individuals to move up or down. As Parenti (1978) put it, 'The center (liberalism) and right (conservatism) share a common commitment to the capitalist system and the ongoing class structure and institutional hierarchy' (p. 48).

People are also assumed rational to some degree. Because their unregulated pursuit of happiness would lead to a state of war, it is in their best interests to establish consensus regarding laws that regulate their exercise of individual rights. When it is functioning properly, the larger society is viewed as a self-regulatory system in which individuals share consensus on its governing rules and everyone is able to attain a fair degree of happiness in accordance with his or her effort and abilities. This is an idea basic to structural functionalism, a theoretical perspective conservatism and liberalism share.

> The structural functionalist is preoccupied with social integration based on shared values — that is with consensus — and he (she) conducts his (her) analysis solely in terms of the motivated actions of individuals. For him (her), therefore, education is a means of motivating individuals to behave in ways appropriate to maintain the society in a state of equilibrium. (Floud and Halsey, 1958, p. 171)

Education prepares young people to fill the varied roles that exist in society, which is viewed as an organic whole to which the various parts contribute: 'In keeping with the functional perspective in general, the needs of society are seen as determining the behavior and the rewards of the individuals within it' (Collins, 1977, p. 122).

One has only to look around oneself to see wide discrepancies in the degree to which individuals actually attain their dreams. Americans who adhere to the 'Lockean ideology' divide into conservatives or liberals based on their view of human nature, their explanations for inequality, and their belief in the legitimacy of collective claims against the workings of the political economy.

The American Dream from a Conservative Perspective

From a conservative perspective, the good society and its government places as few restrictions as necessary on individuals, allowing them to strive for whatever they want. The American dream symbolizes the goals and desires of individuals and the opportunity for relatively unrestricted striving. All individuals, except those who are unfit (such as law-breakers or mentally ill people), should have an equal opportunity to compete with each other to attain their desires. Government should restrict individual competition minimally, but at the same time traditional institutions such as the family, the church, and various private associations should 'instill a sense of personal discipline, courage, and motivation' into people and curb or control 'the mistakes that people make' (Hoover, 1987, p. 33). Humans by nature are viewed as flawed and subject to immoral temptations, which are regulated best by institutions that preserve tradition, which in turn are best controlled by 'good people: by the natural aristocracy of talent, breeding, and, very likely, wealth' (*ibid*, p. 34).

Inequality is viewed as a natural result of individual differences in natural endowment and effort. Society's diverse roles are best played by those whose nature equips them for particular kinds of roles; 'many conservatives see this differentiation of roles as biologically determined' (*ibid*, p. 33). Cornell West (1987) described three conservative explanations for the low status of African Americans, which can also be applied to other groups: the sociobiology, culturalist and market explanations. The sociobiology explanation holds that racial minority groups and women are genetically distinct in some respects, and therefore tend not to compete successfully in intellectual and technological endeavors with men of European descent. The culturalist explanation holds that 'the character and contents of Afro-American culture inhibits Black people (or other low-status groups) from competing with other people in American society' (*ibid*, p. 76). The habits, values, language, and lifestyle that people who are poor, people in inner-cities, or Indians on reservations learn at home, for example, are perceived as inherently inferior or undeveloped. According to the culturalist version of conservatism, schools need to replace the culture of a 'disadvantaged' group with one more suited to successful competition in public institutions. However, state intervention to remediate effects of 'cultural deprivation' should be minimal so as not to reduce individual initiative.

Natural inequality rooted in genetics or culture may also be exacerbated by discriminatory behavior of biased individuals who hinder the efforts of other individuals. The market explanation holds that employers and other members of dominant groups discriminate against individuals on the basis of tastes or prejudices, such as aversion to Black people, stereotypes, or a belief that lower class people are not very bright. This dysfunction of the social system can be corrected by modifying people's tastes and prejudices to make them more inclusive and less stereotypic. If people learn to interact with others as individuals based on personal characteristics they actually exhibit, society will work fairly.

The purpose of schools is to 'instill the traditional wisdom of the society' (Hoover, 1987, p. 34). Schools should develop character and morality, which would include personal integrity as well as ability to judge others as individuals based on their character. It is also viewed as appropriate for schools to identify the social roles for which various children are best suited and to prepare them accordingly.

The American Dream from a Liberal Perspective

Like conservatism, liberalism defines the American dream in terms of the opportunity for individuals to strive and compete for their desires. But it diverges from conservatism in its optimism about human nature. Liberals place more emphasis on rationality than do conservatives and are less concerned about rationality being undermined by genetic differences in capacity or moral depravity. As a result, liberals tend to reject sociobiological explanations for inequality and the conception of a 'natural aristocracy'.

Contemporary liberal thinking is more reformist than classical.

> Classical liberalism (emphasizing individualism regulated by the marketplace and only minimally by government) has one great flaw: to celebrate individualism is to accept extremes of economic inequality that leave some people far ahead of others in even the most basic prerequisites for a decent life. (*ibid*, p. 63)

Reform liberals champion individualism but have some sympathy with claims that social institutions do not work fairly for some groups, and therefore support a limited degree of state intervention on behalf of them as groups. Writing about feminist theories, for example, Alison Jaggar (1983) explained that,

> Liberal feminists believe that the treatment of women in contemporary society violates, in one way or another, all of liberalism's political values, the values of equality, liberty, and justice. Their most frequent complaint is that women in contemporary society suffer discrimination on the basis of sex. By this, they mean that certain restrictions are placed on women as a group, without regard to their individual wishes, interests, abilities or merits. (pp. 175–6)

Some people find this mixing of individualism and collective concern confusing, but Harmon (1964) explained:

> The confusion [in their thinking] is evidenced by the fact that liberals with profoundly humanitarian instincts were simultaneously arguing for more collectivism on the one hand and more individualism on the other. Such a situation may appear contradictory in theory, but in practical terms it need not be contradictory at all. It is perfectly logical, for example, to demand a greater degree of governmental intervention to provide for social welfare, and at the same time to demand greater freedom of speech for the individual. (pp. 379–80)

Reform liberals support state interventions that attempt to ensure that people will be treated as individuals without regard to group membership. They also support state interventions such as affirmative action, which attempt to remediate effects of past discrimination, believing that at some point in the future they will no longer be needed and individuals will be able to complete as equals. Educational programs such as Head Start, transitional bilingual education and English as a Second Language, and social policies such as desegregation and child care are viewed as helping to equalize the playing field. Liberals share conservatives' view that 'disadvantaged' groups are hindered by cultures that do not enable them to compete well in the marketplace, but unlike conservatives, endorse strong state efforts to remediate effects of 'dysfunctional' cultures. 'Reform liberals do not set out to abolish the marketplace, but rather to use governmental power to remedy the inequalities of opportunity that it produces' (Hoover, 1987, p. 62). Ultimately, liberals believe that cultural, attitudinal, and institutional dysfunctions that block the strivings of individuals can be corrected.

Radical Structuralist Perspectives on the American Dream[2]

Radical structuralists share a sense of optimism for cooperation and collective living that they believe is thwarted by individualism and competition (*ibid*, pp. 83–4). The good life should be found in a synthesis of the welfare of individuals and the welfare of the collective. Mudimbe (1988), for example, contrasted Western with African philosophy:

> Western philosophy accepts as its starting point the notion of an unconstrained and uncontextualized 'I' — that is, an 'I' defined in relation to the self and its inner being rather than in relation to others. The African mode, however, seems more communal and emphasizes an 'I' that is always connected to and in relationship with others. (p. 1)

He found Marxism and feminism, like African thought, to identify the good of the individual with the good of the collective, rather than divorcing the two and elevating the individual. Justice, liberty and equality, which are fundamental to the American dream that both conservatives and liberals champion, ought to characterize the lives of all people; justice and equality ought to prevail across groups and include material conditions and political power. If the world were organized around collective equality, each person would be able to channel her or his energies into the uniquely human drive to create and express (Hoover, 1987, pp. 83–5).

Radical structuralists characterize society as involving struggle among competing groups. The group rather than the individual is the focus of attention. Martin Carnoy (1989) explained:

> In the social conflict theory, the struggle of dominated groups to change the conditions that oppress them and the attempts of dominant groups to reproduce the conditions of their dominance are the key to understanding changes in the economy, in social relations, and in the culture. These changes, in turn, are reflected in state policies and in public schooling, both prime targets of conflict. (pp. 6–7)

Struggle among groups is continuous; 'there is no ultimately good society, only a continual struggle to overcome specific obstacles to human fulfillment as these become apparent' (Jaggar, 1983, p. 208).

Radical structuralists argue that the ideology of the American dream obscures group conflict and human fulfillment within a collective context by focusing on the individual. For example, in his analysis of modern social movements, Carl Boggs (1986) remarked that liberalism and the spirit of the American dream,

> depended in great measure upon a self-regulating market, abundant territorial space and natural resources, dynamic community life, and later, prospective for seemingly endless material growth. (p. 6)

As I will argue shortly, these conditions were never present for many groups of Americans. But even for the White middle class,

> By the 1960s, . . . none of these conditions prevailed any longer, with the result that liberalism was finally transformed into a ritualized belief system barely masking a highly centralized and expansionist corporate system. In economic terms liberalism failed to generate any new priorities that could encourage a shift away from outmoded patterns of production, work, and consumption. (*ibid*, p. 6)

Radical structuralists maintain that inequality cannot be addressed effectively through solutions that focus on altering chances for individuals. Speaking about racial inequality, for example, Joyce King and Thomasyne Lightfoote Wilson (1990) wrote:

> We recognize the need to challenge societal illusions of inclusion and individualistic progress as did our enslaved ancestors who, when confronted with a slave system that denied their humanity and threatened Black existence, affirmed their human worth and value. (p. 21)

Theorists debate the central causes of oppression, but agree that they are structured into the major institutions of the society and require collective actions that aim toward equality across groups. Further, most powerful organizations, and particularly the state and corporate world, are structured primarily by groups with the most power and operate to their benefit. Thus, the state cannot be relied upon as an instrument to serve the interests of oppressed groups; oppressed groups themselves must mobilize to challenge and restructure specific institutions that thwart their own interests.

The American dream itself needs to be reconstructed to emphasize public welfare and quality of life over privatism. For example, Ruth Sidel (1990), after studying the dreams of contemporary young women, criticized conventional conceptions of the American dream for their inability to serve women, and called for a new dream structured around very different rules:

> The fundamental components of the American Dream — an almost devout reliance on individualism; the notion that American society, particularly at the end of the twentieth century and the beginning of the twenty-first, is fluid enough to permit substantial upward mobility; the belief that hard work will lead to economic rewards, even for women, a group that has always been at the margins of the labor force; and the determined optimism in the face of massive social and economic problems — will not serve women well. (p. 239)

Education becomes a crucial process for bringing about a more equal society, since through education young citizens can examine social relations as they exist currently, examine alternative social arrangements and learn to act collectively as change agents. However, as a state controlled institution, public schooling rarely accomplishes this.

Race, Class and Gender as Axes of Inequality

Much has been written recently about intersections of race, social class, and gender as axes of inequality and forms of difference (for example, Allen, 1986; Chan, 1989; Grant and Sleeter, 1986a; hooks, 1990; McCarthy, 1990). It is quite possible for an individual to profess one theoretical perspective regarding one axis of inequality, such as gender and another regarding other axes of inequality. For example, bell hooks (1990) criticizes avant-garde Whites who take a radical position on gender and/or social class, but accept implicitly more conservative beliefs about race; or African American men who view racism from a radical perspective but regard women, including African American women, as their inferiors. In analyzing a person's beliefs about the social structure and inequality, it is important not to assume consistency.

Multicultural Education

Debates rage among these three theoretical perspectives regarding the extent to which schools either serve as avenues for equality or reproduce an unequal society. For example, all children in the US must attend school until they are at least 16; school itself is not reserved for a privileged elite. But once in school, students are grouped and tracked in ways that reproduce existing patterns of social stratification. Knowledge and skills such as reading can promote thought and open doors to investigation; but they can also persuade children to think in prescribed ways, and the process of being taught can convince some children that they are incapable of learning. Joel Spring (1989) articulated this dichotomy well:

> Education can be for freedom or slavery.... On the one side, it can
> be used to give future citizens the knowledge and ability to protect
> and advance their political rights and beliefs. On the other side, it
> can be used to enslave citizens by shaping behavior and beliefs to
> conform to the needs of political power. (p. vii)

Multicultural education challenges school processes that reproduce inequality. But multicultural education has been articulated by a multiplicity of voices and perspectives, and it is difficult to identify which theoretical perspective informs the field most strongly. Suzuki (1984) pointed out that,

> many widely differing conceptualizations of multicultural education
> have been formulated. As a consequence, the various programs in
> the field often appear to have conflicting purposes and priorities.
> Many educators have come to view multicultural education as ill
> defined, lacking in substance, and just another educational fad. (p. 294)

Often to the uninitiated, multicultural education simply means teaching children from different cultural backgrounds (or even from any single background that is not White American) in one school or classroom. To others, it means teaching about people in other countries; those who assume that America is (or should be) basically a White nation often confuse international education with multicultural education. Many educators think they know what multicultural education is all about; in the discussion below, I will refer to those who have been actively involved for years with multicultural education and have helped formulate its directions and practices.

Multicultural education advocates reject conservatism; on that most of them agree. However, it is more difficult to disentangle the influences of liberalism versus radical structuralism, especially in the United States. In England, multiculturalists, who hold a liberal position debate with antiracists, who hold a radical structural position. Antiracist writers,

> criticize multiculturalists for defining the educational difficulties stemming from a multiracial society as problems resulting from the presence, per se, of black children. These include 'underachievement', lack of motivation, indiscipline and alienation, low self-esteem, damaged personal identities and cultural differences. Antiracist theorists, on the other hand, define white racism as the main problem. This is said to manifest itself in racist ideologies, racialist practices and structural inequalities. From this perspective then, the alienation of black students, for example, is not pathological but a rational response to racism in the education system. . . . Antiracists adhere to the view that racism is an integral feature of the education system and that it manifests itself habitually in institutional forms. (Troyna and Williams, 1986, p. 46)

In the US, the debate is not so clearly demarcated. Those who have been involved for years in multicultural education and broader social struggles see it as challenging oppression, but divide somewhat on how schools should work toward that goal or what the 'good society' would look like. The division stems partly from the limited power of the language of liberalism, which many multicultural education advocates use, to address radical structuralist concerns; it is aggravated by the fact that advocates are almost always working with limited time and resources, and need to focus their energies. Multicultural education in the US has been criticized as growing out of a liberal perspective (McCarthy, 1988; Olneck, 1989), but a brief examination of its history refutes this claim (Sleeter, 1989a).

Multicultural education in the US originated in the racial debates and protests of the 1960s. Michael Omi and Howard Winant (1986) argued that racial minority groups shifted during that period from a war of maneuver, in which an oppressed group tries to 'ward off violent assault, and to develop an internal society as an alternative to the repressive social system they confront', to a war of position, in which 'oppositional political projects can be mounted, and upon which the racial state can be confronted' (p. 74). At that time, ethnicity theory as an explanation for race relations was challenged. Ethnicity theory is based on analysis of the experience of European ethnic groups in the United States; it focuses mainly on the extent to which groups can retain a distinct culture while becoming structurally assimilated into the dominant society. It holds that the removal of legal barriers to progress will allow African Americans and other racial minority groups gradually to attain economic parity with Whites, just as White ethnic groups did, which is a conservative as well as a liberal position. Omi and Winant argued that racial challenges to ethnicity theory demonstrated that it does not fit the experience of visibly identifiable racial minorities. Racial minority group intellectuals developed alternative radical structuralist theories that dealt more effectively with race; Omi and Winant reviewed class-based and nation-based theories, and West (1987) reviewed left-liberal, Marxist, and genealogical materialist theories of racial oppression. However, 'none of the challenging viewpoints could achieve hegemonic status . . . in part because . . . of their reduction of race to another phenomenon and the "partial" nature of their analysis' (Omi and Winant, 1986, p. 91).

In its inception, multicultural education was clearly connected with a broad social and political racial struggle that was rooted in a radical structuralist understanding of oppression. Multicultural education addressed school practices, with the understanding that reform of schools was linked with other movements outside education.

> A major goal of most ethnic revival movements is to attain equality for the excluded ethnic group. . . . Since the school is viewed by ethnic reformers as an important institution in their oppression, they attempt to reform it because they believe that it can be a pivotal vehicle in their liberation. (Banks, 1984, p. 58)

Geneva Gay (1983), one of the main proponents and developers of multicultural education, provided a useful discussion of its history. She noted that in the mid-1960s, 'The ideological and strategic focus of the (Civil Rights) movement shifted from passivity and perseverance in the face of adversity to aggression, self-determination, cultural consciousness, and political power' (p. 560). Multicultural education

> originated in a socio-political milieu and is to some extent a product of its times. Concerns about the treatment of ethnic groups in school curricula and instructional materials directly reflected concerns about their social, political, and economic plight in the society at large. (*ibid*)

As members of racial minority groups gained access to White schools, they actively confronted racism within those schools, especially all-White curricula and low expectations of students' ability to learn. On college campuses students demanded ethnic studies courses and elimination of stereotypic and derogatory treatment; in public schools, racial minority groups challenged curricula and the 'ethnic distortions, stereotypes, omissions, and misinformation' in textbooks (p. 561). Social science research challenged cultural deprivation theories legitimating low expectations of racial minority group children and suggested that 'the academic failure of minority youths was due more to the conflicting expectations of school and home and to the schools' devaluation of minority group cultures' (*ibid*).

Gay described the 1970s as 'prime times for multiethnic education, during which "an avalanche of revisionist materials — including pedagogies, psychologies, ethnographies, histories, and sociologies" were created in the forms of "a wide variety of ethnic books, films and filmstrips, recordings, audio-visual packets, course outlines, and study guides"'(p. 562). Conferences, workshops, and policies such as the Ethnic Heritage Act and the NCATE standards for accreditation supported this activity. However, Gay cautioned that, while 'theory was advancing, emerging and evolving with apparent continuity . . . multiethnic practice remained largely fragmentary, sporadic, unarticulated, and unsystematic' (p. 562).

The political climate of the late 1960s and early 1970s supported the development of multicultural education. In the late 1970s and 1980s the climate changed. The left lost considerable visibility and momentum, and some oppressed groups shifted from confronting and trying to change the system to working within it. Carlos Muñoz (1987), for example, described the shift in Chicano politics 'that took place during the 1970s from a politics of militant protest to a politics focused on the electoral process and the two-party system' (p. 43). Racial minority groups competed vigorously against each other, and many Latinos rejected race as the main factor in their oppression, adopting ethnicity theory with renewed vigor. African Americans split into various opposing camps, leaving no agreed-upon and coherent strategy for advancement (Marable, 1987). Multicultural education advocates found themselves expending energy defending, and at times even rediscovering, ideas that had been more obvious in the late 1960s, and defending against conservative attacks by couching analyses of problems and recommendations for reform in the language of liberalism.

One difference among advocates of multicultural education is the relative importance of race, ethnicity, language, gender, social class, religion and other forms of diversity or oppression. Another difference is the main goal advocates believe multicultural education ought to be aiming toward and the relative importance of cultural difference versus inequality, individuals versus collectives, and the need to repair society versus radically changing it. Carl Grant and I have distinguished among five different approaches to multicultural education on the basis of the main goals they try to accomplish and the theories and practices that help to achieve those goals (Grant and Sleeter, 1985a; Grant, Sleeter and Anderson, 1986; Sleeter and Grant, 1987 and 1988).

The first three approaches generally assume that society will eventually change if we change individuals (children). Developing positive self-concepts and intergroup relations is the main goal of the Human Relations approach, which appeals to both liberals and conservatives because of its stress on individual attitudes. Social psychology research on the formation of prejudice, stereotyping and social segregation informs it. Its advocates believe that interpersonal prejudice and hatred thwart the attempts of individuals to pursue the American dream; if people learn to get along and appreciate each other, hostility and tension will diminish.

The next two approaches are neither clearly liberal nor radical structuralist; they can be worked through either perspective. Raising the achievement of students from oppressed racial groups is the main goal of the Teaching the Culturally Different approach. It draws heavily on learning theories in psychology, sociolinguistics and anthropological concepts of cultural compatibility. Its proponents believe that if children from racial and language minority groups achieve well in school, they will be able to negotiate barriers in later life that hinder their pursuit of the American dream. But to enable children to achieve well, school processes need to be changed so they build on and work with, rather than replacing, cultural strengths racial and language minority group children bring from home. While some believe successful individual mobility alone will achieve group equality, others who do not share this view argue that oppressed groups at least need well-educated leadership to advance their struggles.

Changing society by educating children about cultural pluralism and diversity, as well as making sure all achieve well, are the main goals of the Multicultural Education approach. It draws on the same theories as the first two approaches, as well as curriculum theory and anthropological theories about cultural transmission and cultural contact. Its advocates assume that if students experience success, equality and pluralism in their education, they will be prepared not only to pursue their own dreams in the wider society but also to bring about changes that are needed to make society more open.

The other two approaches emphasize collective action to change social structures, and are rooted in radical structuralism. Single Group Studies attempt to mobilize future citizens to bring about structural and cultural changes in society for the benefit of a particular oppressed group. This approach includes such programs as Black Studies, Chicano Studies or Women's Studies; it explicitly teaches students about the history of the group's oppression, how oppression works today, and the culture the group developed within oppressive circumstances. Finally, Education that is Multicultural and Social Reconstructionist aims to confront all forms of oppression in the wider society by preparing future citizens to examine and change political and economic structures. It draws on sociological theories of oppression and culture. The advocates of these two approaches believe that the American dream will remain open to only a minority of citizens until the citizenry, and especially members of oppressed groups, learn to use on their own behalf skills of political analysis and collective social action.

Much of the language and conceptual work in multicultural education is drawn from ethnicity theory, even though its main connections have been with racial struggle rather than White ethnic issues. Discussion often revolves around cultural pluralism versus assimilation, ethnic identity and prejudice, which are themes in ethnicity theory. While these themes are relevant to

racial struggle, the theory itself deflects attention away from structural inequalities in the distribution of power and wealth. One reason advocates of
multicultural education continue to use language of ethnicity theory is that
Whites will listen to it. Jacqueline Wade (1987) pointed out that, 'Blacks often
couch their complaints which point to overt and covert acts of white supremacy
in words that are more or less acceptable to whites' (p. 36). Similarly, Sara
Delamont (1989) analyzed women's use of conservative vocabulary to advance
their own relatively radical interests, arguing that 'muted groups' often cloak
their aims in 'acceptable' language, which can be quite effective as long as the
oppressed group does not lose sight of its aims after initial gains have been
made.

But many people, and particularly Whites, avoid examining structural
inequality issues that gave rise to multicultural education in the first place,
and assume it has to do only with preserving historic group cultures, reducing
tension, or cultivating tolerant White attitudes. This leaves the field open to
cooptation by those who seek to use knowledge about cultural differences to
control members of oppressed groups more effectively. For example, when
educators request multicultural education workshops to quell interracial
tensions and get resistant students of color to conform to teacher directives,
control is often the main goal being sought. Rather than asking how schools
are serving the interests of dominant groups better than those of oppressed
groups, educators ask how schools can continue to do more smoothly what
they have always done. Defining multiculturalism as individual differences
epitomizes this cooptation, since it not only rules out inequality as a concern,
but it also divorces culture from its origins in collective experiences and
collective histories.

The most effective way to distinguish whether any given advocate is
working from a liberal or a radical structuralist position is to ask the following
questions about his or her work: Is he or she working in concert mainly with
social movements originating in, and led by, oppressed groups, or mainly
with White middle class established interests? Does he or she advocate mainly
for individual rights or for collective interests? Does he or she view the
perspectives and cultures of oppressed people as dysfunctional or as healthy
responses to oppression?

Historic Context of the Study

The staff development project involved teachers from two contiguous school
districts serving cities which will be called New Denmark and Gelegenheit.
The history of the cities illustrates patterns in the structuring of racial, ethnic
and social class relations that many northern cities have experienced. Since
the project attempted to challenge taken-for-granted understandings the
teachers constructed in this particular community context, its history will be
briefly examined.

New Denmark's population was about 84,000, and Gelegenheit's was about 80,000; they are located between two large cities in the Rust Belt of the Midwest. The 1990 US Census data found New Denmark's population to be about 76 per cent White, 18 per cent African American, 8 per cent Latino, 1 per cent American Indian, Asian and Pacific Islander and 4 per cent 'other'. Gelegenheit's population was about 90 per cent White, 6 per cent African American, 6 per cent Latino, 1 per cent American Indian, Asian and Pacific Islander and 3 per cent 'other'.[3] The proportion of both cities' populations that was racial minority had grown steadily over the preceding two decades.

Both cities had developed as industrial manufacturing centers. Gelegenheit's economy had centered mainly around a large manufacturing plant which had just closed, leaving many people unemployed. Service industries were beginning to grow, absorbing workers slowly for lower wages. New Denmark boasted a more diversified economic base made up of several smaller industries than was the case in Gelegenheit; it also housed the world headquarters of a major corporation that produced chemical products. The history of these cities supported fairly conservative conceptions of the American dream, particularly for their White male inhabitants. A brief sketch will illustrate very different experiences diverse groups had.

Since White people arrived in the Americas, they have systematically decimated and pushed American Indians off their land so it could be used to advance White interests (Cornell, 1988). The Miami, Potowatomi, Kickapoo, Sauk and Fox Indians had inhabited the land on which New Denmark and Gelegenheigt were built. Two waves of European ethnic groups immigrated to the area in the 1800s, pushing them out. The Potawatomi were the last to leave, losing their territory in the Treaty of Chicago in 1833. By the 1900s, very few Indians remained in the area, although by the 1980s, elsewhere in the state Indian tribes (including a band of Potawatomi who had moved north) were engaged in active resistance to White attempts to limit and renegotiate their treaty rights.

In the latter half of the 1880s, 'Old Immigrants' from Northern and Western Europe and the British Isles, as well as Yankees from New England, came to the area for a mixture of economic and political reasons. They found land to be cheap, taxes low, provisions plentiful, and political equality to exist across blurred social class distinctions (Buenker, 1976 and 1977). For them, this was the land of golden opportunity where hard work was the main vehicle needed to attain their dreams. These were the people Ron Takaki (1979) has termed the 'virtuous men' who structured much of the economic and political life into which later arrivals were integrated, and who saw themselves as virtuous because of the work ethic and individualism they cultivated to pursue their own material gain.

Between 1900 and 1930, a second wave of immigration brought large numbers of people to the area from countries in Southern and Eastern Europe, including Russia, Italy, Poland, Lithuania, Czechslovakia, Hungary, Armenia, Greece, Austria and Yugoslavia. Immigrants came to both towns as well as the surrounding countryside; Gelegenheit in particular experienced a population explosion, subsequently becoming a more blue-collar industrial manufacturing town than New Denmark. Like the first wave of immigrants, the 'New Immigrants' came in search of better economic opportunities than those available to them in Europe; however, the opportunities open in New Denmark and Gelegenheit were different from those open to the Old Immigrants. Cheap, abundant land for farming was no longer available; instead, descendants of Yankees and Old Immigrants needed cheap, unskilled labor to work in their expanding industries.

Each successive wave of newcomers found opportunities increasingly restricted. Comparing the opportunities open to the two groups of immigrants in this area, John Buenker (1977) concluded that,

> Each successive immigrant group found its choice of occupations increasingly limited by the disappearance of cheap labor, the increasing amount of capital and skill required, the continuous centralization of business and industry, and the greater advantages in education and inheritance enjoyed by the decendants of earlier settlers. (p. 79)

The earliest immigrants had the first choice of available land and they established patterns of economic growth; later immigrants had to integrate themselves into patterns established and to some extent controlled by descendants of earlier immigrants. The Yankees and Old Immigrants 'generally enjoyed a good deal of social mobility in the rapidly expanding economy of the late nineteenth century', with British immigrants and Yankees faring best (*ibid*, p. 81).

The New Immigrants improved on the standard of living they had in Europe but did not experience the degree and speed of social mobility the earlier immigrants had experienced. They worked mainly as factory laborers and were able to raise their living standard through strong unionization. Besides factory work, the main other economic opportunity open to those who could afford it was to establish small businesses that catered 'to the needs of their fellow countrymen' and countrywomen (*ibid*, p. 82). During the depression, 'Immigrant and second generation workers together made up nearly two-thirds of the unemployed' (*ibid*, p. 83). New Immigrants experienced strong prejudice from the older immigrant groups, who restricted where they could live and pressured them to become 'Americanized' as quickly as possible.

Whatever dreams for a better life the New Immigrants brought with them were important to factory owners only insofar as they motivated immigrants to work, and were unwelcome when they led workers to organize to demand higher wages and better working conditions. William Greenbaum (1974) explained,

> why so many immigrants learned so fast, asked so few questions, and rose so rapidly during the first decades of this century. Most important

is the fact that the main fuel for the American melting pot was *shame*. The immigrants were best instructed in how to repulse themselves; millions of people were taught to be ashamed of their own faces, their family names, their parents and grandparents, and their class patterns, histories, and life outlooks. This shame had incredible power to make us learn, especially when coupled with *hope*, the other main energy source for the melting pot — hope about becoming modern, about being secure, about escaping the wars and depressions of the old country, and about being equal with the old Americans. (p. 431)

Both New Denmark and Gelegenheit established similar patterns of dealing with ethnic diversity, into which they later expected African Americans and Mexican Americans to fit. One pattern was simply to work one's way up the job ladder as the economy expanded, then to control access to increasingly better jobs so that fellow countrymen could benefit as well. Another pattern was to use schooling as an avenue for social mobility, but also to supplement or replace public schooling with alternatives designed to preserve the Old World language, culture and religious values. Yankees and English immigrants tried to 'Americanize' the newer immigrants, but the newer immigrants resisted through community organizations; both towns had experienced a history of conflict between pressures to assimilate and actions of individual groups to preserve their ethnic heritage. A third pattern was to use fraternal, benevolent and cultural societies to perform many roles to help the survival of immigrant groups, including 'finding jobs for new arrivals . . . and providing food and clothing to the victims of fires or natural disasters' (Buenker, 1976, p. 103); government agencies at that time did not perform these functions.

By the time African Americans and Mexican Americans arrived in significant numbers, most White ethnic groups had been structurally assimilated into the economy and political life, and the preservation of ethnic identity and ethnic traditions had become largely a matter of individual choice. Ethnic organizations still flourished, and by the 1970s some descendants of immigrants were experiencing a renewed interest in their 'Old World' heritage. To many residents, multicultural education meant studying the traditions of different European ethnic groups.

Nationally, over a period of about 200 years, the descendants of White immigrants had increasingly distinguished themselves from racial minorities, in the process solidifying race itself as a social construct. Omi and Winant (1986) pointed out that, 'A period of indentured servitude which was not rooted in racial logic preceded the consolidation of racial slavery' (p. 64). The development of slavery strengthened black and white as racial categories. European immigrants in the late nineteenth and early twentieth century had to struggle to be classified as White; eventually they succeeded in drawing 'the color line around, rather than within, Europe' (p. 65). Eventually many White immigrants were able to take advantage of the doors white skin could open in order to pursue the American dream, and a few achieved that dream in grandiose proportions.

Americans whose origins were not European were, for the most part, excluded from pursuit of the American dream and were used as either slave or cheap labor throughout much of US history. In both the North and the South during and after slavery, African Americans were excluded from work Whites wanted and paid so little that White workers often were forced to accept low wages themselves or be replaced by lower-paid African American, Mexican or Asian workers. Denied the right to vote, opportunities for an education, and access to White institutions, and terrorized through lynchings, African Americans were locked 'into the bottom of the job market' (Comer, 1988, p. 213). Mexican workers also became a source of 'cheap labor' for White industrialists and agriculturalists, enabling them to expand their own profits and hold down wages. Rodolfo Acuña (1972) argued that,

> the conquest of the Southwest created a colonial situation in the traditional sense — with the Mexican land and population being controlled by an imperialistic United States. Further, . . . this colonization — with variations — is still with us today. . . . Anglo-Americans still exploit and manipulate Mexicans and still relegate them to a submerged caste. . . . The relationship between Anglos and Chicanos remains the same — that of master-servant. (pp. 3–4)

However great the prejudice New Immigrants experienced, African Americans and Latinos experienced greater prejudices as well as legalized denial of access to many social institutions and labor unions until 1954.

Because it had been a stop on the Underground Railroad, a small number of African Americans had lived in New Denmark since before the Civil War. In the industrial boom following World War II, many African Americans moved from the South to New Denmark to secure better jobs and take advantage of freedoms they believed they had advanced fighting in the war. The African American population of Gelegenheit was very small until the 1970s and 1980s, when poor families increasingly moved there from a major nearby city, looking for cheaper housing and better work opportunities. A small number of Mexican Americans had worked near New Denmark and Gelegenheit as migrant laborers since the late 1890s. During World War II braceros were imported to work on the railroad and some stayed. But large numbers of Mexican families did not begin to settle in the area until the 1960s, when they came mainly to secure blue collar employment.

African American and Mexican American residents encountered a much more restricted opportunity structure than had European immigrants. As industry became increasingly mechanized, the need for unskilled labor dwindled, and semi-skilled and skilled White laborers protected their jobs for people like themselves. The 'centralization of business and finance had lessened the possibility for small neighborhood business', which had served White immigrants in earlier generations (Buenker, 1977, p. 85). Housing was much more restricted; African American and Mexican American families were able to move mainly into run-down neighborhoods that had been adandoned by earlier immigrant groups, where they were often charged higher rent than White families were charged. Mobility out of the inner city was difficult because of both racial discrimination and the low wages most of these families were paid.

Because of combined effects of racial discrimination in housing, banking, unions and employment, the time of their arrival, and major changes in the job structure after the 1960s, the pattern of working one's way up the ladder of opportunity did not serve racial minority groups in New Denmark and Gelegenheit as well as it had served Whites. In both cities, Gelegenheit particularly, racism was rampant. Housing policies in Gelegenheit, for example, deliberately discouraged African American and Latino families from moving into the city, and from clustering in blocs large enough to elect representatives to local governing bodies; by 1990 the city council, school board, and county board had yet to elect and seat a person of color.

In the late 1980s, when manufacturing jobs were severely cut back and one of the largest manufacturing plants had closed, Whites had secured employment for themselves much more effectively than African Americans and Latinos. A survey in 1990 noted that 'Unemployment rates for blacks and Hispanics — 15 per cent and 22 per cent, respectively — are three to four times greater than the 5 per cent for whites' (Results of survey, 1990, p. A3).

Like European ethnic groups, African American and Mexican American citizens strongly viewed education as a means of social mobility, but they depended on the public schools more than had earlier groups. Mainly for financial reasons, African Americans and Mexican Americans established fewer supplements or alternatives to the public schools than had earlier arrivals and found parochial schools relatively expensive. Employers required new employees to have completed increasingly longer periods of schooling than they had earlier, with post-secondary education increasingly required for better-paying jobs; completing school by the 1980s had become virtually a requirement for employment.

African Americans and Mexican Americans established fraternal and church organizations as had earlier groups, but '(b)ecause so many of the welfare functions performed by the earlier immigrants' national societies had been replaced by government programs, and because the cost of sick and death benefits was so high, the more recent arrivals relied much more upon' government agencies (Buenker, 1977, p. 112). Nationally during the 1960s and early 1970s, racial minority groups had pressured the government to protect rights that Whites had secured for themselves. Social class interests in the US have never been articulated as effectively in national government politics as racial interests were at that time. Locally in New Denmark and Gelegenheit, many Whites felt that African Americans and Mexican Americans were playing unfairly, rather than adhering to the rules that had governed the advancement of their own ancestors. Especially as manufacturing jobs dwindled, average household earnings fell, and unions lost power in the 1980s, many Whites increasingly resented people with dark skins who they felt were encroaching on 'their' turf, and receiving 'special' help from the government; Whites often pointed out that their parents and grandparents had taken care of themselves in time of need. African Americans and Latinos, on the other hand, argued that not only had the rules Whites played by changed between the early 1900s and the 1980s, but people of color had always had to play by different rules than Whites set for themselves, anyway.

The Rise of Conservatism in the 1980s

By the 1980s many Americans were skeptical of their ability or that of their children to achieve the American dream. Studs Terkel listened to Americans describing their concerns and fears:

> The American Way, to me, has been one of chasing the dollar. You hear a labor leader say: 'What's good for the company is good for us, because if they make a profit, we get more wages'. That's bullshit. US Steel is making more profit. We're sure as hell not making more wages. . . . Buying a piece of land has always been the American Dream. Owning your own home. A kid, starting out today, it's beyond him. (1980, pp. 240–1)

> I think Reagan made it very accepted to be a white bigot. It's the most fashionable thing. Now they say: America is white. America isn't single women on welfare. Why should us taxpayers support these people who ride on our backs and bring this country down? I'm afraid of what's gonna happen to blacks in this country. There are a fortunate few who will get over. But for the many, no way. . . . The dividing line is becoming clear and the bitterness is growing. You can't help but wonder why. (1988, pp. 67–8)

> The middle class seems to be disappearing here. You have your working poor and your elite. No matter how well you do, you're never quite able to stay ahead. It's harder and harder for the average person to attain the average American dream. (*ibid*, p. 69)

During the late 1970s and 1980s Americans 'experienced defeat in war, the . . . resignation of a President, an inflationary peak of 22 per cent, peacetime shortages of oil and gas, and the fall of Keynesianism and the political alignment which it sustained' (Omi and Winant, 1986, p. 137). Increasingly Americans were offered a conservative portrait of its problems and the causes of those problems.

The dominant discourse of the 1980s was conservatism, in contrast to the liberal discourse of the early 1970s. It is important to critique it briefly because it is the discourse to which teachers were most strongly exposed. Teachers did not have to read professional journals to encounter it, although it was certainly prevalent there; all they had to do was pick up the newspaper or turn on their television sets. And while many teachers and other Americans did not accept the dominant discourse, they had to search harder to find alternative definitions of the state of America and the state of education.

Americans were told that the United States was falling behind other countries in the international battles that Ira Shor (1986) termed the 'Trade War and Cold War' (p. 119), and that much of its loss was due to schools. Many emphasized that action would need to be taken in order to retain international supremacy in not just trade and influence, but also living standard. For example, an article in *Science* magazine explained that, 'The proper test of competitiveness, then, is not simply the ability of a country to balance its trade, but its ability to do so while achieving an acceptable rate of improvement in its standard of living' (Hatsopoulos, Krugman and Summers, 1988, p. 299). Further, Americans were told that, 'The United States retains the highest standard of living of major nations', and that it 'should be able to maintain a living standard at least as high as that of other advanced countries' (p. 299).

A variety of causes were described as having produced this loss in international status and living standard. Americans were told that 'our society itself has become uncompetitive' (Lamm, 1988, p. 9). Too many resources had been diverted in the wrong direction: 'The US spends almost 12 per cent of the gross national product on health care — far more than any of our international competitors' (*ibid*). American laborers were being paid too much: 'A notably bad habit partly combed out of the American system during the upheaval of the eighties was the self-indulgence of pay increases unmatched by productivity gains' (Nasar, 1988, p. 48). Further, 'schools today [are] not preparing kids for jobs, they aren't even teaching them to read and write' (Perry, 1988, p. 70). Beginning with *A Nation at Risk* in 1983, a spate of education reform reports elaborated on the 'rising tide of mediocrity' presumed to be spreading from the schools to the rest of society. In order to ensure that American citizens would be able to continue to pursue their dreams, international supremacy must be restored and school reform was to be one of the main strategies for doing that.

A second problem Americans were told about was the growing diversity of its population. For example, a special issue of *Time* magazine (11 July 1988) placed actor Edward James Olmos's picture on the cover, under the caption 'Magnifico! Hispanic culture breaks out of the barrio'. Readers of *Time* magazine in April 1990, were told about problems confronting America as it moves 'Beyond the melting pot'; the main problem would be learning to 'maintain a distinct national identity' that builds on commonalities while embracing ethnic diversity (Henry, 1990, pp. 28–9). Most discourse centered around trying to identify what we have in common in order to promote national unity. While some argued that new commonalities could be forged from diverse cultural input, others insisted that all immigrants must be turned into 'Americans' who embrace traditional definitions of American culture.

Discussions of immigration usually publicized Asians as the 'model minority'.

> In recent years, articles have proliferated in news magazines and Sunday supplements, proclaiming that Asians are 'Outwhiting the whites', explaining 'Why Asians Are Going to the Head of the Class', and touting 'The Triumph of Asian Americans'. (Suzuki, 1989, p. 13)

The reason attributed to the supposed success of Asians was their embracing of traditional American culture and values:

> 'It's no wonder'. Reagan emphatically noted, 'that the median incomes of Asian and Pacific American families are much higher than the total American average'. Hailing Asian and Pacific Americans as examples for all Americans, Reagan conveyed his gratitude to them: We need 'your values, your hard work' expressed within 'our political system'. (Takaki, 1989, p. 10)

Many Americans agreed, believing that Asians proved that racism no longer exists and anyone can attain the American dream; other immigrants and racial minorities ought to follow their example.

A third group of problems Americans heard much about in the 1980s were domestic social problems which many regarded as outcomes of moral lassitude: drug use, teen pregnancy, and a growing underclass dependent on welfare. A panel issued a report in June 1990, that reviewed statistics on the state of youth in America, concluding that,

> America is raising a generation of adolescents plagued by pregnancies, illegal drug use, suicide and violence, . . . [Y]oung people are less healthy and less prepared to take their places in society than were their parents. (Teens less healthy, 1990, p. 1)

If uncorrected, the result would be 'a failing economy and social unrest' (p. 1). These problems were most concentrated among the growing underclass, which conservatives such as John Silber (1988) described as 'seemingly self-sustaining, limited primarily to blacks and Hispanics though including individuals and families of all ethnic backgrounds' (p. 215). Silber characterized the tragedy of the underclass: they 'no longer dream the American dream. They do not imagine working hard and moving from where they are to where they would like to be' (p. 215). Many Americans blamed the welfare system for the growth of an underclass; for example, Charles Murray (1984) argued that welfare policies and the expansion of welfare rolls during the liberal interventionist state of the late 1960s and 1970s had produced a growing generation of dependants for whom unemployment and welfare had become a 'logical' and comfortable lifestyle. Silber (1988) emphasized the decline in the American family brought about by women working increasingly outside the home, the sexual revolution inflicting adolescents who are 'so immature that they lack the knowledge and insight to protect themselves' (p. 216), and television which uncritically presents children 'with sex, with violence, the perverse and the sublime' (p. 217). He urged moral education and self-control as the solution to the growing underclass (echoing moral Reagan's solution to social structural problems: Just Say No).

Americans were urged to pull together and work harder in order to re-establish supremacy in the international economic arena; the US would be able to continue to manufacture some products if it improved technology and allowed domestic wages to continue to fall (Nasar, 1988). But the future of the US was to be in technological development and information management, not manufacturing. The US was to become the 'brains' of world economic production while much of the rest of the world, particularly the Third World, was to become the 'brawn'. The message was not usually explicitly stated this way; what Americans were told was that manufacturing jobs were being exported to nations where wages were much lower, and jobs in the US would increasingly require thinking and problem-solving skills. The American Hudson Institute predicted that the majority of new jobs in the 1990s 'will require some form of education beyond high school' (Perry, 1988, p. 71). The dominant discourse suggested that Americans would pursue their dreams increasingly in 'high-tech' careers.

The US was to consolidate an economically imperialistic relationship with Third World countries. Conservatives cultivated an interest in cultural diversity, redefining how it should be treated. Cultural differences at home were to be stripped of political content but harnessed to help US business abroad. Racial and ethnic minority students who conformed to the demands of revamped schools and identified with business interests could look forward to careers representing American business internationally. Those who did not had no place in the future society, and the at-risk ideology placed blame for their failure squarely on the families and neighborhoods of oppressed groups.

Education reforms of the 1980s were to provide more workers for this information economy: excellence became the main by-word. In the reform reports, excellence meant raising academic requirements for high school graduation; requiring more math, science, and computer literacy; teaching higher-order reasoning; lengthening the school day and year; demanding stricter discipline; making it harder to enter college (an interesting recommendation if most new jobs will require post-secondary education); and improving the quality of teachers (Shor, 1986, pp. 116–7). On the heels of these reform reports came a large volume of discourse about 'children at-risk' of failure in the revamped schools and economy. Although definitions of who they were varied, Richardson and her colleagues (1989) explained that, 'The 'risk factors' or predictors that are statistically most often associated with school failure or dropping out are student background characteristics such as minority status, poverty, and language difference' (p. 4); pregnancy, drug use, and child abuse were also often cited as predictors of risk.

Ira Shor (1986) and Michael Omi and Howard Winant (1986) provided useful critiques of the conservative reforms of the 1980s. Compared to the post-war economic boom, the 1970s were a time in which Americans had to learn to settle for less: fewer jobs were available, prices rose, real income of a large portion of the population fell, and White middle class families experienced some of the hard times poor families had always lived with. Further, Americans were less bound together by consensus than they had been in the recent past.

Commonly held concepts of nation, community and family were transformed, and no new principle of cohesion, no new cultural center, emerged to replace them. New collective identities, rooted in the 'new social movements', remained fragmented and politically disunited. (Omi and Winant, 1986, p. 119)

The strategy of containing discontent by appealing to patriotism was invoked with vigor.

Whites increasingly feared losing control over access to the best positions. Shor terms the 1983 reform agenda as 'a crisis in white mediocrity and as an elite reaction against minority advances' (p. 143). The decline in SAT scores had served as 'proof' that students were learning less in school, although much less publicized results of the National Assessment of Educational Progress did not support this claim. But while test scores of White students either declined or remained roughly the same over the 1970s, depending on which test or sub-test one examined, test scores of Black and Latino students rose on both the SAT and the NAEP. Further, in the early 1970s, college-going rates of students of color rose dramatically. The non-White population was growing faster than the White population; if education really brings social mobility, Americans of color may out-compete White Americans with growing success.

But Americans of color knew their own economic status had not improved in over two decades for a variety of reasons, despite gains in education. Even Asian Americans, held up as the model group who had 'made it' were not nearly as successful as the media suggested. The media spotlighted individual Asians who did well in school and attained good jobs; poverty-ridden urban Asian neighborhoods, for example, or extreme difficulties many Asian immigrants faced were rarely noted. Further, the fact that Asian Americans still had to attain more education and work longer hours than Whites in order to achieve comparable earnings was rarely mentioned. Some of the most outspoken critics of misinformation about Asian Americans have been Japanese

Americans, the group often touted as most successful (for example, Jiobu, 1988; Suzuki, 1989; Takaki, 1989).

To mask its attempts to reassert white dominance, conservatives used the language of fairness and equality: 'Its vision is that of a "colorblind" society where racial considerations are never entertained in the selection of leaders, in hiring decisions, and the distribution of goods and services in general' (Omi and Winant, 1986, pp. 113–4). The racial ideology was re-articulated in 'code words . . . which refer indirectly to racial themes, but do not directly challenge popular democratic or egalitarian ideals', such as 'busing', 'choice' and 'reverse discrimination' (p. 120). The principle of individuality was reasserted; group claims to equality were decried as unfair. In fact, 'most civil rights remedies and mechanisms for achieving racial inequality are now considered to discriminate against whites' (p. 132).

Conservatives implicitly blamed women for many of the nation's difficulties by blaming teachers, 'the women who teach the children who fail' (Grumet, 1988, p. 23), and mothers who had failed to perform 'their' role at home by entering the workplace. The suggestion that fathers engage in more active parenting received much less attention. Sidel (1986) quoted a study published in 1931: ' "Truancy, incorrigibility, robbery, teenage tantrums, and difficulty in managing the children" all stemmed from a "mother's absence at her job" ' (p. 55); the same sentiment was echoed in the 1980s in discussions of latchkey children. And teenage girls, especially African American girls, were implicitly blamed for the rise in adolescent pregnancy and the growth of the underclass.

While education reforms of the 1980s advertised the twin themes of excellence and equity, their mission was to reestablish the traditional social order. The reform movement helped the economic system 'not by the creation of more good jobs that deserved higher wages, but rather by the creation of fewer job seekers with credentials suitable for the limited number of high-paying jobs' (Shor, 1986, p. 97). At their best, reform reports simply maintained silence about school practices that reinforce inequality; at their worst, they championed those practices (Grant and Sleeter, 1986b). In discussions that followed, students of color and students from low-income backgrounds were deemed 'at-risk' of failure rather than successful closers of the education gap or 'at promise' (Swadener, 1990).

America in general, and New Denmark and Gelegenheit in particular, were caught in a contradiction that has characterized United States history. On the one hand, the idea of being able to pursue one's own dreams in a nation of plenty is very compelling. And for many Americans, this idea has proved to be very real. But on the other hand, the pursuit of dreams has always involved competition for resources, and social structures that reinforce inequality have been built upon oppression. Greenbaum (1974) discussed fundamental value contradictions surrounding the American dream that still have not been resolved. Some of these include:

equality and justice in tension with rights of private property; individualism mocked by two of its natural outcomes in a capitalist state — insecurity and conformity; . . . reliance on the strength of the American family and on high rates of social, occupational and residential mobility that tear families apart; respect for craft coupled with respect for high speed; . . . self-restraint offset by ravenous materialism; dependence on inquiry and self-criticism and sanctions against the same; . . . and faith in a republican form of government and legitimate usurpation coupled with the encouragement of broad expectations regarding democracy and equality of opportunity. (p. 427)

These are not just contradictions of values. The American dream itself contradicts social structures that trap millions in poverty, including Americans and those abroad who increasingly are tied economically and politically to the US, and structures that legitimate the power of a few to build empires. Schools, often viewed as a great equalizer and an institution dedicated to preparing citizens who will improve society, reflect these contradictions.

Within this context, how did teachers in the late 1980s interpret schooling and multicultural education? To White America, the absence of mass protest, the presence of a small number of Black, Latino and Asian women and men and White women in new positions (for example, administrative jobs), and passage of civil rights laws suggested that most past discrimination had been remedied. Most teachers during that time were White women who had been teaching for a number of years. Many had begun teaching in the 1960s and 1970s; they had witnessed desegregation, ethnic revival projects, the development of bilingual education, and the passage of Title IX. Then they had experienced the recession of the late 1970s and 1980s and the conservative discourse surrounding the nation and schooling. What did they believe schools ought to be doing in response to racial and ethnic diversity, and how did they process the discourse of multicultural education in the context of those beliefs and their daily work in schools? This is the focus of the remaining chapters of this book.

Notes

1 For further development of these theoretical perspectives, see Holtz, *et al.*, 1989; Hoover, 1987; Jaggar, 1983; and West, 1987.
2 Radical structuralism houses several competing schools of thought such as Marxism, cultural nationalism, radical feminism and socialist feminism. Assumptions they share are synthesized here to distinguish them from the Lockean ideology and structural functionalism.
3 The figures for both cities add up to over 100 per cent because the US Census Bureau does not count Latinos as a racial group; Latinos may identify themselves as White, Black or Indian.

Chapter 2

Staff Development for Multicultural Education

Many school districts across the US for the past twenty years, and particularly those that have undergone desegregation or changes in student population, have used staff development as a major strategy for addressing discrimination in schooling.[1] There is some logic to doing this. While demographic changes have altered the complexion of student bodies, the teaching profession has become increasingly White. In addition, the influx of new teachers had slowed by the 1980s, leaving school districts with a large proportion of their teaching staffs having little, or no, training in multicultural education, but working with growing numbers of low-income students and students from racial and ethnic minority backgrounds.

Both New Denmark and Gelegenheit had long histories of ethnic pluralism but short histories of racial pluralism. Both school districts had experienced a rapid diversification of their student populations, although they addressed that diversification somewhat differently. The literature on staff development for multicultural education provides some guidance for developing a program for teachers in cities like these. In this chapter I will review that literature, describe both school districts, and introduce the staff development project that was studied.

Multicultural Education and Staff Development

Since the early 1970s, educators involved in multicultural education have developed recommendations for staff development. I will review those recommendations, then consider the extent to which they are actually followed.

Recommendations

Multicultural educators agree that the field is complex and that staff development needs to be extensive and systematic. Teachers must develop a knowledge base about cultural diversity, acceptance of cultural differences and commitment to serve cultural minority communities and skills for translating multicultural education into action in the classroom. Some authors discuss stages of development: Baker (1983) discussed acquisition, development, and involvement; Grant and Melnick (1978) discussed awareness, acceptance, and affirmation; and Burstein and Cabello (1989) discussed awareness, knowledge, acquisition and application of skills and reflection. While teachers do not progress through the stages in a linear fashion (i.e., learning to implement multicultural teaching strategies can also help raise one's awareness), the stages provide guidance for structuring and sequencing staff development activities. Teachers must first become aware of basic issues that support a need for multicultural education, then acquire substantive knowledge and learn to use new strategies.

Geneva Gay (1977) provided extensive recommendations for the content of multicultural teacher education which other authors have supported (see Baker, 1977; Burstein and Cabello, 1989; Contreras and Terrell, 1981; Grant and Melnick, 1978; Mock, 1983; Nickolai-Mays and Davis, 1986). She recommended that teachers 'become literate about ethnic group experiences' (p. 34): they need a knowledge base about both the functional lifestyles of different ethnic groups and the 'debilitating experiences that are often inflicted upon them by external forces' (p. 35). This includes acquiring knowledge about cultural patterns, value systems, communication and learning styles, psychological and sociocultural processes of growth and development, historical experiences and cultural creations of various American groups. It also includes learning the basic concepts and philosophical underpinnings of multicultural education, as well as learning about various resource materials for both classroom use and their own continued professional learning. In addition, it includes knowledge about classroom dynamics so that teachers can accurately interpret cultural conflict in the classroom and assess their own instructional styles and verbal behaviors.

Gay also discussed attitudes that teachers should develop. They need to come to grips with the limits of their own understanding of cultural diversity, recognize that stereotyping is normal, differentiate between stereotypes and authentic cultural patterns, and recognize the legitimacy of diverse cultural patterns and perspectives. They should develop awareness of their own values and perspectives, accept children's culturally conditioned behavior without evaluting it as wrong, and develop a sense of security about teaching ethnic diversity.

In addition, teachers should develop many skills. Cross-cultural interaction skills require learning different verbal and non-verbal communication systems. Teachers must learn to evaluate and develop multicultural curricula; and they need to develop skill in using instructional techniques that are effective in diverse cultural settings (Gay, 1977). Teachers should develop sensitivity toward minority communities and skills in working with parents (Baker, 1977; Mock, 1983; Nickolai-Mays and Davis, 1986), knowledge of second langauge acquisition and skill in helping children develop a second language or dialect (Baker, 1983) and skill in classroom management and discipline techniques that prevent problems and help children learn to resolve problems constructively (Nickolai-Mays and Davis, 1986).

Recognizing the enormous amount of new learning that is recommended, authors have suggested manageable ways to focus instruction for teachers. Gay (1977) recommended organizing information around themes that are common to several cultural groups rather than bombarding teachers with information from many groups. Baker (1977) recommended that teachers specialize in the study of one group other than their own to develop depth in understanding cross-cultural differences and similarities.

Somewhat less attention has been given to the process of multicultural staff development than to the content. Some authors have linked characteristics of effective in-service education with multicultural education, emphasizing that teachers must be involved in planning and designing the in-service, attendance should be required, it should take place at the building level, it should be practical, it should be ongoing and the administration should be involved (for example, Nickolai-Mays and Davis, 1986). Grant and Melnick (1978) applied Chin and Benne's (1975) normative-reeducative change strategy to multicultural in-service education, recommending that teachers be involved in planning, change be supported by collaborative involvement of various role groups connected with education (for example, school administration, community), teachers engage in ongoing dialog in a non-threatening environment, and a wide range of resources from the behavioral sciences be brought to bear on instructional and curricular change.

These recommendations agree that teachers should help plan multicultural staff development, the administration should support it, teachers should engage in active learning processes and staff development should be ongoing in a planned fashion. To what extent have staff development programs for multicultural education used the above recommendations?

Research on Staff Development for Multicultural Education

Surprisingly little has been published about what is actually done. The following synthesis is based on the limited published research on staff development for multicultural education and for desegregation, and anecdotal information from consultants who have been involved in staff development projects.

Staff development projects that are short and crisis-oriented are typical. Nicelma King (1980) studied in-service education for desegregation in sixteen school districts; she found most staff development projects to be 'concentrated around the time of a desegregation plan's implementation'; further, projects 'were usually short, with 55 per cent lasting one day or less' (p. 56). Consultants participating in such projects describe additional problems, which stem mainly from the limited time and resources allocated to multicultural staff development and the lack of understanding school administrators tend to have of it. Sessions are often one-shot, attended on a voluntary basis, and involve bringing in an outside consultant to talk to teachers; some consultants describe these as 'hit and run', 'flash and dash', or 'spray and pray' projects. Sometimes districts offer extensive training, but for only one or two topics (such as learning styles or parent involvement); or they offer an array of courses, each on one topic and teachers choose between topics. Needs assessments are usually superficial, such as polling teachers to find out what topics they would sign up for. School district personnel who organize the staff development often do not understand multicultural education any better than the rest of the staff, which is why projects are so limited and piecemeal. Usually they perceive teacher attitudes and overt expressions of prejudice and stereotyping as the main problems needing to be addressed, and often they share teachers' beliefs about 'deficiencies' in students or their home backgrounds. As a result, most staff development projects have little or no long-range plan for changing what teachers do in the classroom. Afterward, many districts assume that problems have been solved, and that they can move on to something else. When the problems prompting the staff development project continue to exist, they assume either that either multicultural education does not work, or the problems are due to something else (Sleeter, 1990).

Typically research on staff development for third-generation desegregation or multicultural education assesses changes in participants' attitudes, usually 'measured by the perceptions of participants themselves' (Hawley *et al.*, 1983, p. 138); its impact on what they actually do in the classroom is rarely investigated. Rarely is the impact of training over time assessed. The scope of studies is usually a single school or district, making it difficult to generalize findings to another setting.

Findings of studies are mixed. In King's (1980) study, only two of the sixteen school districts conducted a systematic evaluation that was based on a needs assessment. When King surveyed teachers to find out what they believed they had gained from the staff development, they responded that it helped staff morale and intergroup relations; they did not find it particularly helpful in learning to teach students more effectively. Redman (1977) studied the impact of a 70-hour in-service project that included a field experience. He found it to increase teachers' empathy toward minority persons, as measured on the 'Identification with the Underdog Scale'; effects persisted in a follow-up assessment two-and-a-half months later. Washington (1981) investigated the impact of a five-day workshop on forty-nine elementary teachers, using an attitude scale and a self-report classroom behavior scale. She found the training to have negligible effect on either attitudes or behavior, although the administration was very enthusiastic about the in-service, and some teachers requested further help with classroom materials. Grant and Grant (1986) studied the impact of a two-week program on thirty teachers and administrators who had applied to participate; they used a Curriculum Analysis and

Modification pre- and post-assessment. They found participants to integrate many more multicultural concepts into curriculum after the program than before. Ortiz (1988) conducted a study in classrooms in which teachers had attended cultural awareness workshops and seminars. She did not directly study their impact, but she noted that they had little effect. The workshops were assessed using attitudinal instruments only; Ortiz saw no impact on teachers' behavior, and found that, 'in most cases, the in-service events served to provide stronger justification for the continuation of existing practices' (p. 75).

A major problem is that organizers of most staff development for de-segregation or multicultural education pay more attention to the content to be taught than to effective staff development processes (Hawley *et al.*, 1983). To that literature we now turn.

Effective Staff Development

The literature on staff development provides considerable support for the effectiveness of certain practices. Sparks and Loucks-Horsley (1989) summarized the effective practices emerging from research in the late 1970s and 1980s:

1 Programs were conducted in school settings and linked to school-wide efforts.
2 Teachers participated as helpers to each other and as planners, with administrators, of in-service activities.
3 Emphasis was on self instruction, with differentiated training opportunities.
4 Teachers were in active roles, choosing goals and activities for themselves.
5 Emphasis was on demonstration, supervised trials and feedback; training was concrete and ongoing over time.
6 Ongoing assistance and support was available on request. (p. 40)

After reviewing a large body of research on staff development, they added to this list, emphasizing that, 'The consensus of "expert opinion" is that school improvement is a systemic process' (p. 54). As such, it needs these additional characteristics:

7 Schools should have norms that support colleagiality and experi-mentation.
8 District and building administrators should work with staff to clarify goals and expectations, and actively commit to and support teach-ers' efforts to change their practice.
9 Efforts should be strongly focused on changes in curricular, instruc-

tional, and classroom management practices with improved student learning as the goal.

10   There should be follow-up assistance that continues long enough for new behaviors to be incorporated into ongoing practice. (p. 54)

Bruce Joyce and Beverly Showers (1988) described staff development structured according to these characteristics as a 'human resource development system' (p. 5), and student learning should be the 'bottom line' (p. 27). Joyce, Bennett and Rolheiser-Bennett (1990) emphasized that staff development *can* help teachers learn to implement new skills that can measurably affect student achievement, but that there must be sufficient follow-up activity 'to enable teachers to achieve a deep understanding of innovations and correspondingly high levels of skill in their use' (p. 32). After reviewing research on staff development projects that affected student achievement, Michael Fullan (1990a) observed that such 'initiatives required considerable sophistication, effort, skill, and persistence to accomplish what they did. Most staff development activities do not measure up to these standards' (p. 7).

These ten 'best practices' reinforce and extend processes recommended in the literature on multicultural education. But most staff development efforts for multicultural education do not come close to measuring up to these standards. Further, there are additional dilemmas and problems inherent in attempts to address multicultural education through staff development.

Is Staff Development the Best Strategy?

Multicultural education ultimately means changing schools as institutions so that they serve the interests of children from oppressed groups. Staff development by itself provides only limited help in working toward this mission. Thomas Fox (1981) provided a useful framework for thinking about staff development, distinguishing among three very different purposes for it: stimulation of professional growth among teachers, improvement of teacher use of a particular skill or innovation and implementation of a broad social policy. Most of the literature on staff development develops the first two purposes; the third purpose best fits multicultural education.

In their review of the literature on staff development, Sparks and Loucks-Horsley (1989) described five models. Three of them — Individually-guided staff development, Involvement in a development/improvement process, and Inquiry — aim mainly to promote growth in teachers. The Observation/assessment model aims mainly to develop teachers' use of particular skills in the classroom, and the Training model can have either aim. Both of these aims limit how one conceptualizes multicultural education, although they provide guidance toward achieving limited conceptions of it.

Models oriented around professional growth of teachers assume that, 'individuals can best judge their own learning needs and that they are capable of self direction and self-initiated learning' (*ibid*, p. 42). They further reflect 'a basic belief in teachers' ability to formulate valid questions about their own practice and to pursue objective answers to those questions' (p. 50). Applied to multicultural education, professional growth models stress helping individual teachers to formulate good questions about issues and problems related to diversity and social equality, investigate those questions, then apply that knowledge in whatever manner they see fit. Such models assume teachers will confront issues and moral questions surrounding inequality and cultural diversity, and persist in learning whatever helps them maximize success of students. Different teachers may be affected very differently; the models assume there is no single set of outcomes that teachers collectively should manifest.

The main problem is that these models assume that teachers, who are predominantly White, economically secure, and successful school achievers, will confront racism, classism, and sexism in an objective fashion. This is not possible to do; people always frame questions and choose among analytical frameworks from a position that reflects their own values. Consider academic researchers, who supposedly make their living conducting 'objective' inquiry: much research White male social scientists have conducted on race, oppressed minority groups, and women has tended to reaffirm oppressed groups' positions in an unequal society. Beverly Gordon (1985) pointed out that educators face

> the sticky dilemma of attempting to educate the masses in a way that allows them accessibility to high status knowledge and places them on an equal footing to compete. Most assuredly in time, they will compete with our children and ostensibly with us for a share of the power and the reallocation of resources. And while most people do have good intentions, when our social status is threatened, we tend to become even more conservative in order to protect our material gains. (p. 37)

This is not to deny the value of encouraging teachers to investigate problems or issues of interest to them, but it suggests limits of such models for multi-cultural education.

Models oriented around skill development assume that the main focus of improvement ought to be skills in instruction or management; the models stress helping teachers master or improve their use of specific classroom skills. Staff developers using these models stress that 'teachers can change their behaviors and learn to replicate behaviors in their classroom that were not previously in their repertoire' (Sparks and Loucks-Horsley, 1989, p. 48). Teachers can raise student achievement by participating in staff development programs designed to help them master teaching skills (Joyce and Showers, 1988). The skills to be mastered can be identified by either the teachers themselves or an outside 'expert'. Applied to multicultural education, skill development models stress identifying the specific skills that teachers should use, then helping teachers learn to use them successfully. Since skill development models do not depend on teachers themselves to select what to learn, the problem of teachers not selecting to learn what they 'should' from a multicultural perspective is not as great as in professional development models. In fact, Joyce, Bennett and Rolheiser Bennett (1990) argue that teachers can develop an interest in acquiring skills that had not interested them previously if they see a positive impact on their students.

The main problem with staff development oriented around skills is that multicultural education cannot be reduced to skills. Developing skills that improve the achievement of students is certainly important and part of multicultural education. Other skills, such as redesigning curriculum, are also a part of it. But multicultural education also involves awareness of broader social and educational issues, and developing a knowledge base about oppressed groups and commitment to work with them to further their interests (for example, Grant and Melnick, 1978). Awareness and knowledge acquisition need to be thought of as more than background for, or follow-up to, skill development. Further, new skills cannot simply be added into classrooms as they currently exist; schools as whole institutions are designed to produce class and race inequality. Skill-development models help us think about how to teach skills involved in multicultural education, but that is all they do.

The third purpose of staff development that Fox (1981) discussed is implementation of a broad social policy, such as desegregation. Fox wrote that, 'This reason for in-service education and training has seldom been stated, but often has been implied in recent international conferences and publications' (p. 35). It is based on theories of social reform; but while the purpose is attractive, it is also 'risky because of our ignorance of social theory and our corresponding inability to deal with fundamental political dissent' (*ibid*, p. 36). Staff development for implementation of a broad social policy describes multicultural education better than the previous two purposes, but fairly little in the staff development literature helps us understand what staff developers should do.

Staff development focuses mainly on changing teachers; multicultural education advocates changing institutions as well as teachers. Multicultural education advocates agree that schools need to be restructured holistically; multicultural education is not an innovation to add on to what is already there (Grant, 1978). Some of the main elements or processes that need to be restructured include the curriculum, tracking and grouping patterns that resegregate students within schools, testing practices that 'prove' the inferiority of lower class and racial minority students, instructional strategies, relationships between schools and the communities they serve, language policies and programs, and the race and sex composition of school staffs.

Research in the sociology of education emphasizes that an institution cannot be changed by trying to change individuals within it, since the institution itself provides a strong context within which teachers construct patterns of beliefs and behavior (for example, Connell, 1985; Lortie, 1975; Britzman,

1986). As Gordon (1985) put it, 'social structures within society have more to do with influencing or shaping societal attitudes than do attitudes with influencing and shaping social structures' (p. 40).

A growing body of literature on staff development does discuss the importance of changing schools as institutions. Michael Fullan (1990b), for example, based on a review of school improvement projects, argued strongly that,

> institutional reform should be the primary focus and will not be achieved unless we conceive of the school as the center of change. Most current educational reform initiatives fail to grasp the essence of this point, as they direct their attention to curriculum reform, testing of students and teachers, school-improvement plans, career ladders, principal training, and the like. (p. 250)

In the 1980s 'restructuring' became a loud buzzword. But literature on re-structuring schools focused mainly on changing structures that affect teacher growth and teacher power, such as isolation, lack of collegiality, and lack of teacher authority to make major decisions (for example, Barth, 1990). These are not exactly the same structures and processes that reproduce social inequality, which means that it provides limited help in addressing school change for multicultural education.

Some teacher educators involved in multicultural education or radical education have suggested a way to confront the teacher-structure dilemma: teaching teachers to engage in social critique and politically-informed teaching so they and their students will learn to change the structures in schools and the broader society that reproduce inequality. Giroux (1988) discussed pre-paring teachers to be 'transformative intellectuals' who engage in 'making the pedagogical more political and the political more pedagogical' (p. 127). Gordon (1985) discussed 'emancipatory pedagogy in teacher education' (p. 39), which would involve teachers in examining dominant discourse through lenses of their own experiences and that of oppressed groups. Banks (1988) developed the Enlightening Powerful Groups model, which recommends helping members of dominant groups recognize the nature of oppression and its consequences, recognize one's own participation in a system of institutional racism, and ultimately develop a willingness to share power with groups who differ from oneself (p. 184).

But perhaps the greatest difficulty in multicultural teacher education is helping teachers to want to challenge structures and processes that benefit themselves. Some educators appeal to teachers' desire to help children learn, minimizing race, ethnicity, social class or sex as essential considerations. But this directs them away from an analysis of social inequality. Since most teachers are female, some staff developers begin with a critique of sexism; others begin with White ethnicity to encourage White teachers to draw parallels between their own experiences and those of racial minorities. Carlson (1987) suggested beginning with a critique of the oppression of teachers as workers, arguing that teachers historically have engaged in political activity to further their own well-being, and can examine inequality and social change by examining their own history.

Teacher education with radical intentions can become misdirected and deflect attention away from real collective struggles for social justice. Gurnah (1984) and Sivanandon (1985) have criticized racism awareness training programs that dwell on White guilt and suggest that Whites are confronting racism when they examine their individual psyches rather than engaging in social action, and those that provide White officials with a way to manage racial tensions without actually changing how institutions reproduce inequality. Similarly, bell hooks (1990) reflected on the 'difference between that engagement with white culture which seeks to deconstruct, demystify, challenge, and transform (versus) gestures of collaboration and complicity' (p. 110). It is not always clear when actions are linked with transformative movements and when they are not; she discussed the need for continual reflection and self-monitoring.

Ultimately, teacher education programs that are rooted in a radical structuralist analysis of oppression should help teachers develop links with local collective actions aimed at challenging oppression and help teachers develop both teaching practices and organized pressure activities that will advance the interests of oppressed people. This is a point we will return to in chapter 8.

The School Districts

Since New Denmark's population became racially mixed before Gelegenheit's, the two cities' school districts developed somewhat different policies regarding race. New Denmark Unified School District was created in 1961, when twenty-six county school districts were merged. At that time boundaries for junior and senior high schools were drawn such that each secondary school served a racially mixed population. As the African American population grew, however, several elementary schools became predominantly Black. In 1975, the district began a voluntary desegregation plan that included busing and magnet schools. Its elementary schools involved the most extensive busing. Debates about the plan were heated but it was instituted quite peacefully. The district experienced some White flight to parochial and private schools, but no White flight to suburbs since district boundaries incorporated the suburbs.

After the elementary schools were desegregated, the district sponsored several activities 'to try to get teachers to be ready for culturally different kids', as an administrator explained it to me (3 March 1989).[2] Social events brought groups together. Home-school workers were hired as liaisons between minority students and the schools; this position was dropped after a few years to save money. A federally funded Multicultural Center was developed and run by an African American woman. Teams of teachers from schools all over the district attended three-day in-service programs at the Center that focused mainly on cultural awareness, instructional strategies, and multicultural materials. The Center made a large collection of library resources available to schools. It was disbanded in about 1985 and materials were boxed and sent out to the schools.

The main body that was created to address desegregation issues and still functioning at the time of this study was a committee made up primarily of African American, Latino and White teachers, administrators and counselors. Its main job was to monitor how the students of color were doing in the schools. It met regularly and made recommendations about various issues and problems. It adopted the following goal statement, which had been authored by an African American home-school worker:

> Our ultimate goal is to have classrooms and schools where students
> and staff live and learn together in a school climate of mutual respect
> for each other with acceptance of themselves as individuals in a
> multiethnic multiracial society, with pride in their racial and ethnic
> heritage, and with awareness of the promise such a climate of mutual
> trust and understanding has for the greater society in which we live.

Five task forces focused specifically on the following: upper level course enrollment and grading, dropout and discipline issues, extracurricular activities, guidance and counseling and exceptional education. The district also had summer programs for elementary and middle school students of color who, with help, could qualify for entry into accelerated courses at the secondary level, although an African American teacher commented to me that if students had not been tracked into accelerated classes by sixth grade, they were 'out'.

An administrator commented that there was 'a tendency to have Hispanic kids get submerged in all of this. . . . Hispanic kids, I think, don't get thought about in a real culturally significant way' (3 March 1989). Language needs of Spanish-dominant students were served by a very small staff of bilingual and ESL (English as a Second Language) teachers headed by a Director of Bilingual Education. The bilingual education program was clearly aimed at transitioning students into English as quickly as possible. A teacher explained how the ESL and bilingual program worked:

> ESL is low-level English. When they get to a certain level, which is
> fairly proficient in English, then they move into bilingual [if they are
> Hispanic]. You would be able to communicate with a student who is
> going into bilingual. . . . The bilingual program works on their English
> skills, but they're more advanced students. (17 November 1988)

At the time this study began, the average racial composition of New Denmark's schools was 69 per cent White and other, 22 per cent Black, and 9 per cent Latino; 19 per cent of the students were classified as low-income. The desegregation policy set acceptable ranges for the ratio of Black, White and other students in a building at 10 per cent over or under the district average. For example, a magnet elementary school in which White upper-middle class parents competed to enroll their children was 86 per cent White and other, and only 7 per cent low-income. At the same time, the elementary school with the highest Black population was 38 per cent Black; the one with the highest Latino population was 24 per cent Latino and also had the highest low-income population, which was 42 per cent.

The district had given gender less direct attention than race. In accordance with Title IX regulations, girls' athletic programs were strengthened and vocational electives were opened to both sexes. An administrator in the early 1980s had been concerned about gender equity and fostered several activities to raise awareness of gender equity issues. When he left, no one replaced his leadership in this area.

The state's main policy regarding social class was to equalize per pupil spending among schools by setting a minimum below which no school district would drop. Programs within the district that addressed social class were mainly compensatory. Most schools offered federally-funded Chapter I/Title I remedial courses. Students from low-income homes who scored low on basic skills tests but did not qualify for Chapter I/Title I were enrolled in the district's Standards program for remediation. An array of additional 'at risk' programs were available. An administrator commented that the district's main approach was to offer a 'shot-gun' array of programs for students 'at-risk'. A school board member described the proliferation of programs as a 'bandaid approach' rather than a holistic, comprehensive approach, that 'makes people think things are happening when things aren't happening' (18 July 1991).

New Denmark Unified School District had developed a reputation for rigor and liked to project that reputation. It had a large standardized testing program and a well-staffed office for conducting internal research; in addition, the district had a history of implementing innovative programs. A recent brochure about the district announced proudly that its students 'have reached an academic level that far surpasses the averages of school districts nation-wide'. It boasted three elementary magnet schools, two of which were open to anyone on a first-come, first-serve basis and one of which housed the Program for Gifted and Talented Students (and all three of which enrolled a higher proportion of White students from middle and upper-middle class backgrounds than did most other schools). Newspaper articles regularly reported how well students were doing on standardized tests compared with national and state averages.

Many students, however, were not faring well. Test and other data were coded by racial group, and examination of these data revealed that African American and Latino students were not doing nearly as well as White students.

For example, the drop-out rate for all racial groups had fallen between 1983 and 1987, but it was still over twice as high for racial minority students as for White students. High school grade point averages for seniors in 1987 averaged 2.22; White students averaged 2.39, Black students averaged 1.70 and Latino students averaged 1.72. (The few Native American and Asian students averaged 2.08 and 3.34 respectively.)

In 1990, a series of local newspaper articles jarred New Denmark, reporting on the numbers of Ds and Fs received by members of different racial groups. Essentially, the articles elaborated on these patterns:

> Starting in the sixth grade, black males received Fs more often than they received As. That happened at every grade and, starting in seventh grade, with only the exception of eighth grade, Hispanic males and black females failed more often than they excelled. By ninth grade, all students got Fs more often than they got As. Males and minorities also had more Ds and Fs than As and Bs. (Taylor, 1990, 4A)

White students received a progressively larger share of the As, from 87 per cent in sixth grade to 91 per cent in twelfth. By then, 'the percentage of Hispanic and Black students who received four or more Ds and Fs remained above 60 per cent. For majority students, that rate was 30 per cent' (p 5A).

This series of articles had not been written when the present study was being conducted, but the patterns it exposed existed and data indicating them were available. The district's policy had been to try to extend its programs to everyone in the district through desegregation and to provide various remedial programs for 'at-risk' students (who were generally low-income and racial minority). Otherwise, the district did not focus directly on race, ethnicity, culture, gender or socioeconomics; its leaders assumed that everyone would benefit if offered access to the same programs. But the district was becoming increasingly aware that something was not working. An African American teacher explained to me that many desegregation issues had never been addressed effectively:

> Schools were integrated and they tossed us all in there, and hoped that everybody would swim, but a lot of problems, you know, have developed over the years, and now we're starting to realize that, hey, looking back, we missed something. (16 May 1989)

Gelegenheit Unified School District had been created in 1967 when local county school districts merged. It had not developed a desegregation plan; it embraced the neighborhood school concept, although when attendance boundaries were redrawn from time to time, racial composition of schools was taken into consideration.

At the time of this study, the racial composition of the school district was 80 per cent White, 11 per cent African American, 8 per cent Latino and 1 per cent Asian, Pacific Islander or American Indian; about 17 per cent were classified as low-income. Since students attended neighborhood schools, the composition of individual schools varied widely. The elementary school with the largest Black population was 61 per cent Black, 16 per cent Latino, and 22 per cent White; the elementary school with the largest Latino population was 38 per cent Latino, 29 per cent African American and 32 per cent White. In contrast, one elementary school was 91 per cent White, its students of color being Latino and Asian.

Students from low-income backgrounds were concentrated in a few schools. The school with the highest percent of students from low-income backgrounds reported 75 per cent, while several other schools in the district reported less than 10 per cent of their students low SES. The principal at the school with the highest proportion of lower class students pointed out how overcrowded the school was:

> Our school was ranked number one in [Gelegenheit] as far as children that are at risk. Which is not surprising, I mean it's been brought up in a couple school board meetings we're busting at our seams, we're sitting with, some of the lower grades have 31–32 kids in the room, we've got six or seven aides in the building and that's all because of overcrowding, so I think facilities we have are terrible. We've got a very, very small playground. . . . We tried on the playground, we've put boys on one side and girls on one side, we've tried that for a couple of weeks, didn't feel it worked. (10 February 1988)

He also pointed out that the popular perception in the district was that 'crummy administrators and crummy teachers end up in the crummy schools, or the inner city schools' (10 February 1988)

The main program the district had for addressing cultural issues was a small bilingual education program, although the school board argued every year about whether to support it. The program was instituted under duress when the Latino community complained about a lack of language programming to the state and the US Office of Education. The program was state supported and did not cost the district anything, but school board members periodically argued in favor of immersion as an alternative to bilingual education, invoking their grandparent's experience with assimilation as support. The first bilingual education program had consisted of support services within the regular English-language classrooms. That was insufficient, so separate classes were established at two elementary schools and one junior high for LEP (Limited English Proficient) students.

The district had few policies or programs addressing racial, cultural or gender issues but, like New Denmark, it did have several federal and state programs to remediate students from low-income backgrounds. In addition to federally-funded Chapter I/Title I programs, Head Start was also housed under district auspices and was reputed to be a strong program. The district had acquired state funds for raising achievement in low-income urban schools which supported various programs in five low-income elementary schools; schools had considerable discretion over exactly how to use the funds, for example, two schools instituted a parent-child pre-school program, one school offered Spanish language instruction and another offered French language instruction. The secondary schools had remedial programs for 'at-risk' students, and an alternative high school housed a well-developed program for pregnant students and students with young children. The alternative high school had originally been designed to serve students from a wide range of academic abilities and backgrounds, although over the years it had evolved into a 'dumping ground' for students who were failing in the other high schools.

In contrast to New Denmark Unified School District, Gelegenheit Unified School District did not code standardized test data or other measures of achievement by student race. The district administrator in charge of testing mentioned that he had helped the principal of a predominantly Black elementary school to analyze some grades in her school by race and he believed these data should be kept and analyzed, but so far they were not. In addition, drop-out statistics by race were not available. Were Gelegenheit's students of color faring better or worse than New Denmark's? My guess would be that they were faring about the same, but data did not exist with which to make a comparison.

Since Gelegenheit had not instituted a desegregation policy, it also had not instituted a staff development program on multicultural issues. A district administrator mentioned that there had been some training sessions for support staff and administrators; attendance was voluntary, but several were well-attended. The district had one Puerto Rican and two African American principals who were very active and very knowledgable about multicultural education issues; they helped organize awareness sessions, but had to fight the stereotype that 'that's their thing, that's their cause' (16 February 1988). However, teachers had not been involved in staff development. Some schools had begun a conflict resolution program, the guidance staff were working on drug-prevention and self-esteem issues with students and two administrators conducted regular workshops and courses for teachers in TESA (Teacher Expectations and Student Achievement). This was as close to multicultural training as the district had come.

A district administrator commented that the major barrier to staff development involving teachers was that,

> Teachers are so locked into a teaching day, and we actually have one day a year for in-service. . . . To set a priority that all teachers are going to see and get some in-service, it's real, real tough to do that.

The only levels you can do it somewhat is staff meetings, but . . . there
is so much to be accomplished in a building that again, it's difficult
to do that. (16 February 1988)

In addition, he pointed out that the district's basic skills orientation and rigid
curriculum made it difficult for teachers to feel they had time to spend on
human-relations topics. He believed teachers saw the curriculum as too rigid,
but administrators were 'so into student achievement' in their own schools
that they supported a set curriculum and testing program and did not support
activities that might take time away from delivering the curriculum. The main
recognition schools gave to multicultural education was Black History Month;
when I asked about el Cinco de Mayo, he asked if that was a Hispanic
holiday, then commented that Hispanic issues did not receive as much attention
as Black.

The district had a community human relations committee, but its meetings were sporadic. A former member related that the superintendent had
started the committee as an initial response to racial conflict in one of the
high schools, but once the conflict was temporarily reduced, committee
meetings became less frequent. The superintendent controlled the committee's
agenda; this member felt the superintendent manipulated it to serve the
interests of other administrators. Deep racial conflicts in the community and
schools were not addressed.

The district seemed to lack much leadership in multicultural issues, except
for the African American and Puerto Rican administrators, who tended to be
ghettoized and perceived as trotting out 'their' pony when they spoke out on
such issues. On several occasions it was mentioned to me that community
pressure would be needed to get the district to take more action. However,
the African American and Latino communities in Gelegenheit were smaller
and not as well organized as in New Denmark. Middle class African Americans
and Latinos who came to the area tended to move to New Denmark where
a well-organized nucleus of middle-class African Americans had developed.
Most African Americans and Latinos who settled in Gelegenheit were fairly
poor and did not want to lose advantages they found there. There was a
tendency for White administrators in the district to view these communities
as satisfied, when African American and Latino community leaders had deep
concerns about how well their children were being served. One of the school
administrators commented that the community probably had 'that fear that
if you shake it too much you may lose more than you'll gain. No one's ever
even said that to me, but I just sense it' (16 February 1988). He went on to
say that a district the size of Gelegenheit's tends to use a fad approach to
issues.

It gets so complex, so many issues come up that you are working
with so many people in different units, you know, as you're trying to
impact a whole district. . . . And so I don't think we ever quite get it

through before we either get disillusioned, get burned out with the issue, or something more important comes along. (16 February 1988)

This being the nature of a large school district, strong and consistent pressure would need to come from somewhere to make the district focus attention consistently on a set of needs like multicultural education.

Both districts' policies for addressing race, ethnicity, language, gender and social class oppression were generally quite conservative, although New Denmark had implemented some liberal policies in connection with its desegregation plan. The policies of both districts assumed that schools as they currently exist are neutral with respect to social stratification. If some kinds of students gained more than others from going to school, this was presumed due to differences among students and their preparation for school, not to the school itself.

For example, the bilingual education programs rested on the premise that everyone should speak English, a second language is of no value, and those whose native language is not English pose a problem that should be 'corrected' as quickly as possible.

If [the students] know enough English to get along in the classroom, then it's not such a problem for the teacher. If . . . they can function but they can't do very well, the teacher can usually cope with that, but if they just really can't function, then it's a big problem for the teacher. (ESL teacher, 10 May 1989)

District policies did not support bilingualism in anyone, except high school students who might be going to college.

In chapter 3, we will take a closer look at structures and processes in schools and classrooms. But the main point here is that district policies generally supported the idea that membership in a racial, cultural, language, gender and social class group should not matter. Students should be differentiated by age and achievement level only and should otherwise be treated as much the same as possible; remedial or language programs should strive to make students homogeneous. New Denmark's desegregation policy tried to 'erase' race by distributing students of color somewhat evenly across schools; Gelegenheit's tried to do it by officially ignoring race altogether. But in the process of attempting not to 'see' students' memberships in social groups, the districts minimized their ability to examine group oppression and ignored the strengths of groups of color and low-income people.

Introducing the Staff Development Project

The staff development project I studied was funded by a private foundation. It was operated through a staff development center serving the two counties in which the two participating school districts were located. Housed on a university campus, the staff development center served twenty-six public school districts, a technical college, a liberal arts college and a state university. It was governed by a consortium made up of chief executive officers from the state and from participating school districts, teacher union representatives and representatives from local school boards. Its purpose was to supplement district and building level staff development needs, focusing particularly on the personal and professional development of teachers. Even though it was housed on a university campus, a visitor to the center would usually encounter mainly teachers; university professors served as collaborators on some projects.

The center sponsored a variety of programs and projects, including study committees and networks of teachers interested in specific concerns (such as early childhood education, foreign language instruction), assistance for first-year teachers, fellowships for teachers, recognition of excellent teachers at an annual banquet and a wide variety of staff development projects. Most of its projects were coordinated mainly by classroom teachers; the center had a small permanent staff and also employed classroom teachers who were released for one-year periods to serve as center associates. Projects sponsored by the center were funded from a variety of sources, such as grants from foundations and private industry, grants from the state, and monies from participating school districts.

As I noted in the introductory chapter, my colleague Susan (who was employed by the center) and I secured funding initially to work with thirty teachers for nine days over a one-year period. In conceptualizing the staff development project, we made several considerations. Given the districts' histories with staff development for multicultural education, we assumed that awareness level activities would be most appropriate (Grant and Melnick, 1978), although we also believed they should be closely tied to curricular and instructional practices that impact on students (Joyce and Showers, 1988; Sparks and Loucks-Horsley, 1989). We believed it would be important to invite the teachers to help select goals and activities, and if possible to share what they knew with each other, although we also recognized that people may avoid sensitive material this way. We decided to devote the first session to a needs assessment and future planning, to try to tie the training closely to needs teachers perceived. Teachers would help select from potential areas of study drawn from those Gay (1977) suggested. We also tried to encourage more than one teacher from each school to participate so teachers could help and support each other. The staff devlopment project was not school-based; operating through the staff development center, it would be structured to promote the professional growth of teachers as individuals. An advisory committee made up of local educators and community leaders (most of whom were African American and Latino) discussed with us local needs and resources both before and after the first session, and made suggestions.

Thirty-four teachers applied to participate; thirty were accepted.[3] They taught grade levels ranging from preschool through high school, and were from eighteen different schools. They had taught between four and twenty-nine years; the average was fourteen years. Twenty-six were White, three were Black, and one was Mexican-American; twenty-four were women and six were men. Eighteen of the teachers worked at the elementary or pre-school level: twelve taught in the general education program at grade levels ranging from kindergarten through sixth, three taught special education (learning disabilities, emotionally disturbed and pre-first grade for children at-risk), one taught music, one taught English as a Second Language and one taught in a parent-child preschool program for low-income families.

Six teachers taught at the junior high/middle school level: one taught English, one taught art, one taught home economics, one taught technical education and two taught special education (learning disabilities and emotionally disturbed). An ESL teacher taught both middle school and high school in two different buildings. Five teachers taught at the high school level: one taught math in an alternative school, one taught economics, one taught technical education, and two taught special education (learning disabilities, and social studies for low-achieving and special education students).

The first session was devoted mainly to giving teachers an overview of the staff development project, ascertaining what knowledge and experiences they believed would benefit them, and gathering information about their knowledge of multicultural education. After teachers were welcomed and introduced to each other with a name game, Susan and I talked briefly about the nature of the project and the research that would be involved. I explained the research process and provided copies of the first interview I would be conducting and the observation schedule on which I would be taking notes. Interested teachers were also invited to sign up for university credit that could be earned participating in the project; eventually about half of them did so. Teachers spent the next hour-and-a-half completing three paper-pencil assessment instruments described later in this chapter. As they finished, they were invited to examine a display of multicultural education books and sign up for one or two they would like us to purchase for them. (The book most teachers selected was *Multicultural Teaching*, by Tiedt and Tiedt (1986), which we subsequently ordered for the whole group. Later in the year each teacher also received her or his second request.)

When the group had completed the assessments, they reassembled and I introduced multicultural education by giving an overview of each of the five approaches Carl Grant and I have synthesized (Sleeter and Grant, 1988). My intent was to answer the question teachers were asking: What do you mean by multicultural education? I described each approach in terms of its main goals and emphases, and main classroom teaching practices. I also provided teachers with a booklet containing two lesson plans illustrating each approach, as well as a learning style inventory and a cultural literacy quiz (from Grant and Sleeter, 1989). Each approach was accompanied by some discussion; I tried to pace the presentation slowly enough that teachers could assimilate parameters of the terrain of multicultural education. I hoped this overview would stimulate discussion later in the day, on the basis of which the remaining sessions would be planned. This was my most active role in the sessions during the first year; after this introduction I tried to fade into the background in order to study the staff development process.

Next, Susan showed a filmstrip entitled 'A Tale of O', which discusses consequences of being perceived as different from the majority. The majority in any organization was illustrated by Xs, and one or a small number of minority group members by Os. The filmstrip illustrated patterns such as Os visibly standing out and feeling spotlighted, Xs boxing Os into limited roles, Xs expecting their one O to speak for all Os, and so forth. The filmstrip was followed by discussion in which Susan asked for personal experiences like those shown. Several White teachers volunteered experiences, such as standing out visibly because of having red hair.

The teachers were then divided into five small groups to discuss what they perceived their greatest learning needs to be. They were provided with newsprint on which to write, and encouraged to come to some consensus within each group on six main questions, problems, or needs, then if possible to rank-order those in importance. (One group developed an elaborate scheme for the design of the next nine sessions.) The small groups shared with the whole group the fruits of their discussion. Then each teacher was asked to indicate on a sheet containing twenty topics, the six he or she would be most interested in learning more about.

The day closed with a brief discussion of days of the week that would be best for the remaining sessions, and dates for the next two sessions were agreed upon.

Summary

The staff development project this book examines began with nine full days built into the teachers' workday and later was expanded by five more days. That is considerably more time than most staff development programs for multicultural or desegregation have, but still is far less than would be needed to develop the awareness, attitudes, knowledge base and skills that literature in multicultural education recommends.

Multicultural education can be thought of as a broad policy that involves institutional change. Staff developers, however, usually approach it as a process of changing teachers as individuals. Given the resources we had, we adopted the latter approach, hoping that we could educate teachers about at least some of the institutional changes that should happen in schools.

Research Design and Methodology

Ethnography is the most suitable research approach for exploring what the teachers learned and did in their classrooms.

> The purpose of educational ethnography is to provide rich, descriptive data about the contexts, activities, and beliefs of participants in educational settings. Typically, such data represent educational processes as they occur. (Goetz and LeCompte, 1984, p. 17)

Ethnography lends itself well to theory construction based on the case that was studied; it is much more useful than survey or experimental research for examining complexity and relationships among diverse aspects of a problem. The particular case that is studied is in some ways unique, and findings do not necessarily generalize to all other similar cases. In other words, the staff development project studied here was representative of many, but unique in some respects. However, Spindler (1982) argued that,

> ethnographers feel that an in-depth study that gives accurate knowledge of one setting not markedly dissimilar from other relevant settings is likely to be generalizable in substantial degree to these other settings. Ethnographers also usually feel that it is better to have in-depth, accurate knowledge of one setting than superficial and possibly skewed or misleading information about isolated relationships in many settings. (p. 8)

Multiple research techniques are normally used in ethnographic research 'so that data collected in one way be used to cross-check the accuracy of data gathered in another way' (Goetz and LeCompte, 1984, p. 11). The main research techniques used for this study included observation of the staff development process, interviews, and classroom observations.

I attended most of the staff development sessions and took notes, particularly during discussions. I limited my involvement in the staff development process itself so teachers would talk freely about the sessions. Most of the time I simply sat in the back of the room listening, writing and collecting handouts. I was also able to obtain a copy of extensive notes one teacher took during all sessions the first year.

The project lasted two years. The teachers were each observed in their classrooms and interviewed between three and five times.[4] During the first year, three one-hour observations were conducted in each teacher's classroom, spaced evenly over the year. During the second year, two one-hour observations were conducted in the classrooms of teachers agreeing to continue to participate.

Observation notes were recorded on an instrument developed for this study, based on observation schedules used in other research projects (Goodlad, 1984; Grant and Sleeter, 1986c). Notes were taken on the following: classroom lay-out and decorations, student composition and behavior, materials used, content of lesson, instructional strategies used, teacher-student interaction patterns, and decision-making patterns. During the classroom observations, various documents were examined and gathered. For example, textbooks in use were examined, extra copies of worksheets or notes teachers had sent home were collected, and some lesson and unit plans were collected. In addition, student work was observed to the extent this could be done without disrupting the lesson. In several classrooms, I was able to ask individual students to tell me about the assignment they were doing; in a few cases students volunteered to tell me about their work.

Each observation was accompanied by an interview in which the teacher was asked to talk about the lesson and his/her use of material from the staff development project. Questions were also asked about the teacher's perception of his/her students, why he/she was teaching a particular lesson in a particular way, what he/she was getting out of the project, what had been most and least helpful in the in-service, what he/she had been able to use in the classroom, the extent to which he/she had attempted to disseminate ideas from the project to other people in the building and barriers and facilitators to working with multicultural education. In addition, teachers were asked to talk about where they grew up, went to school, taught previously, and so forth. Most interview questions were open-ended, and probes were used to elicit clarification and elaboration (Spradley and McCurdy, 1972). The intent of most questions was to find out what teachers saw as important within specific domains, such as 'curriculum' or 'students', as well as to elicit specific information. Interviews usually lasted between one-half to one hour. All but three were tape recorded and transcribed; three were conducted in settings too far from an outlet to plug in the tape recorder, so I took key-word notes, then wrote up the interviews immediately afterward.

I conducted most of the observations and interviews myself, but during the first year an undergraduate student helped. I had trained her in interview techniques and in multicultural education in two university courses. We did the first few observations and interviews together, and compared observation notes. I checked her notes and taped interviews as the year progressed, offering suggestions on notetaking and use of probes. We analyzed notes from the first observation together, sharing perspectives about what we were seeing. In the early stages of the research process, our sharing of perspectives broadened what both of us saw, as well as bringing us more in line with each other.

Teachers signed up for observations and interviews at times that were convenient for them. They always knew when I or my assistant would be coming; we never arrived unannounced. This may introduce some bias in that they would plan special things; at times I felt this may have happened. However, I did not view it as ethical to intrude with surprise visits.

We tried to be as unobtrusive and non-threatening as possible. Teachers responded to our presence in different ways. Some were a bit nervous, one quite obviously so during all of the observations. On the other hand, some forgot one of us was to come and seemed oblivious to our presence until the interview. Some teachers encouraged us to talk with students; some classrooms did not lend themselves to that. Some teachers introduced us to the class, some did not. A few talked with me continuously during the lesson rather than waiting for the interview, although I did not encourage that since I wanted to disrupt their teaching as little as possible. During interviews I tried to listen actively to whatever the teacher wanted to say (as long as it did not stray too much from the interview questions), and to encourage the teacher to talk. I tried not to let my own biases intrude, nor to assume the role of instructor in multicultural education, although occasionally that did happen.

I administered three paper-pencil instruments at the first and last sessions of the first year. The first instrument gathered demographic information (such as grade level and subject area of present teaching assignment, number of years taught, where teacher grew up, racial composition of schools teacher attended). It also contained forty-two items asking teachers to indicate how often they do specific things in the classroom related to multicultural education, such as use multiracial materials, teach about sexism, and deliberately adapt teaching strategies to student learning styles (Sleeter, 1986b). The second instrument, a curriculum and instruction assessment, asked teachers to read a description of a hypothetical multicultural classroom, then describe any implications that seem relevant to teaching this class, and modify two lesson plans to make them multicultural and adapt them to the hypothetical class of students. The third instrument was an attitude scale that asked teachers to indicate on a Likert-type scale the extent to which they agreed with 100 statements about race, social class, gender and disability (see Grant and Sleeter, 1986c, p. 270). Data from these instruments proved far less rich than data from the classroom observations and interviews, so they will be referred to seldom.

The validity of findings was checked in several ways. I asked teachers to describe and discuss lessons I had observed, and checked for consistency between my observation and their discussion. I used the same observation schedule for all observations. I asked some of the same questions more than once in different interviews, and checked for similarity of responses. Following most of the teachers into a second year allowed me additional checks on the validity of patterns I was seeing in the data. During the second year, I asked some of the same questions I had asked the first year (for example, tell me about your students, tell me about your curriculum); I also conducted observations at about the same times both years in order to check seasonal patterns. I also let teachers examine my observation notes and transcribed interviews if they wished. A few did so, finding information accurate, although one was horrified to read transcribed natural speech. Finally, I invited some teachers to react to drafts of this manuscript; those who did mainly validated what was written and commented that they had been curious what the other teachers were learning and doing, being familiar mainly with their own experience.

During the month following the first session, I observed most of the teachers in their classrooms and interviewed them. Chapter 3 describes their work at the beginning of the study.

Notes

1 Although desegregation and multicultural education are complementary, historically they have had different foci. Desegregation began as a policy issue addressing assignments of students to buildings, while multicultural education began as a classroom issue addressing teacher practices in classrooms. According to Grant (1990) 'The literature on school desegregation suggests that schools have paid minimal attention, at best, to multicultural concerns' (p. 31). Desegregation Assistance Centers, however, are increasingly addressing many of the same issues as multicultural educators. For excellent discussions of the relationship between desegregation and multicultural education see the September 1990 issue of *Phi Delta Kappan*, special section on School Desegregation, editor Carl Grant.

2 Dates following interview quotations refer to the dates of the interviews. Names of people who were interviewed, where used, are fictitious.

3 One teacher dropped after the second session and was replaced by a teacher in the same school. The teacher who dropped was not included in this study. His replacement was included, although not in the first set of observations and interviews reported in chapter 3.

4 The numbers of teachers observed (O) and interviewed (I) over the five observations times are as follows:

1		2		3		4		5	
O	*I*	*O*	*I*	*O*	*I*	*O*	*I*	*O*	*I*
29	29	27	27	29	30	19	22	17	17

The second time, two teachers were missed through scheduling problems, one was not observed because a student teacher was in charge, and one interview was lost on a defective tape. The third time, George was interviewed but not observed because he had assumed a principalship. The fourth time, three who were interviewed were not observed because they had non-teaching responsibilities at that time.

Chapter 3

The Teachers in their Classrooms

A visitor entering the classroom is struck by a combination of life and order. The pale peach walls are covered with displays, including pictures of animals, student self-portraits, cut-outs of Santa Claus and his reindeer, a large calendar and a set of pictures of several presidents. Desks are in rows and the students are writing. The teacher, a White woman in her forties, looks up and smiles, motions to a desk in the back and continues walking about, helping this child with a math problem, checking that child's paper. About two-thirds of the children are White, about a fourth are African American and two are Latino. As the minutes tick by, they begin to whisper, move about in their seats, shuffle paper and look around. Finally, the teacher announces that it is time for recess; she lines them up, and they file out of the room. This scene is typical of the classrooms of the teachers who elected to participate in this project.

The Teachers at Work

This chapter paints a portrait of how the teachers taught and viewed their work when the staff development project began in order to examine the extent to which their participation in it changed their classroom instruction.[1] First, however, it is important to situate the individual classrooms within a larger institutional structure. Schools in both districts used various forms of homogeneous grouping. The high schools had a tracking system, all of the schools had special education programs, both districts had programs for gifted students, both had pull-out bilingual education and ESL programs and both had an array of other remedial programs, which were mainly pull-out. These various programs constituted a structure fundamental to both districts. Most teachers were assigned to a place within this structure; for example, one could be an LD teacher, a Chapter I teacher, or a general education fifth grade teacher. Both districts were in the process, however, of disbanding homogeneous ability grouping for elementary reading in general education classrooms.

Many critics of schooling have raised questions about access to knowledge, pointing out that these structures help sort students for different futures, and reproduce society's racial and social class structure (for example, Irvine, 1991; Oakes, 1985; Orfield, Monfort and Aaron, 1989; Sleeter, 1986). A staff development program targeted toward improving instruction *within* classrooms tends to take as given the structure of classrooms into which children are assigned, a problem which will be taken up in chapter 7.

The Students

I asked the teachers to describe their students. Most teachers in the general education program described them mainly in relationship to grade level norms and remedial programs. They used terms for students suggesting a continuum of achievement or ability and an array of special programs: they talked about slow kids, 'basic' kids (lower track), kids who are behind, bright kids, 'honors' kids, Chapter I kids, learning disabilities kids, Standards kids (a remedial reading program) and so forth. For example:

> I have a big gap in the class as far as readiness for [academic] skills, though I have a super group and I have a dull group, which seems to be getting larger and larger as years go by, and the gap in the middle is getting wider. (8 December 1987)

> In the past we used to offer another level called Basic Economics which is for the slow learner, and I taught that. But we decided to drop the Basic last year as an experiment and I objected to it because I like direct learning, I felt like with my Basic class, they were usually small and I could just sit down and just be real homey with them. (11 February 1988)

Few teachers gave negative descriptions of these kinds of kids, but most had several students, or even an entire class, who were below grade level, and their descriptions tended to focus mainly on this group. For example:

> They need lots of help with everything. They're Basic Level kids, so they're not at grade level, so they need help with just about anything you could help them with. (19 November 1987)

Descriptions such as these focused mainly on academic deficits and rarely included intellectual strengths that could be used as building blocks for academic development.

Nevertheless, several teachers commented on their students' desire to learn, even those who they perceived as 'behind'. Some described their students as 'eager', some described them as 'hard workers,' if most lacked ability, at least they tried. For example:

> They are looking for attention. A lot of them, when I say I need help
> with the bulletin board, I'm bombarded, I mean they all want to
> help. (1 December 1987)

The special education teachers were more likely than the general
education teachers to describe their students one at a time. For example,
when asked to describe students' strengths, a teacher in the emotionally
disturbed program found it difficult to talk about her class as a whole:

> Their strengths are — I have to go with individual kids 'cause I can't
> go with the whole group. [Proceeds to describe an individual student]
> (11 December 1987)

After commenting on academic characteristics, teachers described students
in terms of classroom behavior (for example, good workers), group dynamics
(for example, who the leaders are), and developmental level (for example,
characteristics of first graders). These descriptions often focused on positive
student characteristics. For example:

> They're good at working together and they're also good at helping
> one another. You'll find some classes are families and some classes
> aren't even close. (15 December 1987)

> This group has a mind of their own. . . . There are some very strong
> individuals in the group and they're a real tight group, and sometimes
> its really hard to deal with certain individuals, they can be very
> stubborn and a couple of bullies in the group. . . . Generally they're
> good workers. (6 December 1987)

> Their zest for life [is a strength]. They love each other and they want
> to get along and are very anxious to learn at this point. Middle school
> kids are like that. (11 December 1987)

> They get along with each other, they cooperate with each other, a
> little tattling, but that's first grade, you know. (17 December 1987)

It was not clear from this interview how high the teachers' expectations
were, nor how strong their sense of ability to teach their students. Patricia
Ashton and Rodman Webb (1986) differentiated between teachers with
a high and a low sense of efficacy in academic instruction, teacher-student
relationships and classroom management. Teachers with a low sense of efficacy
in academic instruction described students as lacking ability and motivation,
having poor behavior, and coming from poor home environments. Those
with a high sense of efficacy described student progress and what they are
doing to bring it about. Teachers with a low sense of efficacy in teacher-

student relationships formed impersonal relationships with students; those with a high sense of efficacy formed close relationships. Teachers with a low sense of efficacy in classroom management focused on the constant need to monitor behavior and 'keep things under control' (p. 77); those with a high sense of efficacy worried much less about student behavior.

The teachers' descriptions suggested that most felt capable of establishing personal relationships with students and managing their behavior. They talked warmly about class dynamics and personalities and chuckled at tattling or headstrong behavior. But many expressed concern about their students' ability to learn. Most general education teachers drew the interviewer's attention to the range of abilities and the large number of 'low-ability' students. But they felt they could learn to teach more effectively, which was why they had joined the project.

A few teachers mentioned students' family background. Most descriptions seemed to be based mainly on inference from observing the child in the classroom, and focused on presumed deficiencies:

A lot of them don't have a lot of self confidence. . . . we've got a lot of single parents, a lot of kids that have dads that aren't around or dads that are away at prison and stuff like that, so a lot of them are on their own, latch key, they go home by themselves. (1 December 1987)

A lot of them come from very deprived homes, and they don't get the attention that they really need. They need a lot of love and attention. (14 December 1987)

But a few rejected the home deficiency idea:

I don't understand where they're coming from because that was not my kind of lifestyle, but, hey, let's get these kids going. They can do nothing about it, they have to be able to deal with it, we can't make allowances for it. . . . I know education is important to the parents that I have talked with [but] they're doing the best they can. (4 December 1987)

The yardsticks teachers used to measure their students were derived from students of the same age or grade level, known either personally from teaching in previous years, from their own life experiences, or from test and textbook grade level norms. The language in which they described students reflected heavily the context in which teachers came to know them: the classroom. Very few teachers talked about their students' interests, everyday life experiences, personal goals, or cultural background; most were probably unaware of these other dimensions of their students' lives. The ESL teachers were the only two to talk at length about students' cultural backgrounds, and to describe these as interesting. It was obvious from listening to the teachers that they cared about their students, but their care was tempered with concern about learning problems and the perceived probability that many of the students would never catch up. Further, in this first interview, some of them attributed academic deficits to presumed deficits in students' family backgrounds. Virginia Richardson and her colleagues argued that teachers do this for lack of a better explanation for students' problems:

> Searching for the problem at home appeared to relieve (teachers) from the normatively inappropriate response of blaming the child, or the soul-searching attribution to their own classroom and school. (Richardson, Casanova, Placier and Guilfoyle, 1989, p. 121)

As we examine further the curriculum and instruction used, it will become clearer how the classroom constrained teachers' knowledge of their students.

Classroom Physical Environment

The physical environment of a classroom suggests who the room is for, what kinds of activities occur, and what its inhabitants are like. It also suggests how the teacher perceives teaching and learning. As John Goodlad (1984) put it:

> Schools and classrooms . . . are better understood as little villages in which individuals interact on a part-time basis, within a relatively constrained and confining setting. Many of the constraining elements are clearly visible even when the setting is vacated at the end of each day — those inherent in the confining space and arrangement of furniture. (p. 113)

Comparing the classroom to a stage for a theatrical production, Shirley Heck (1989) argued that,

> A creative environment does not necessarily teach a child what to think but rather assists him (her) in how to think; a stimulating environment provides the motivation for a child to become a miniature researcher through the process of reading, living, and recalling. (p. 214)

Barbara Shade (1989) emphasized that visual stimulation, including color, 'vividness and multiplicity of stimuli' is particularly appealing to African American students (p. 19).

When entering most of the teachers' classrooms, one would encounter a variety of seating patterns and an array of colorful displays and materials. Twenty classrooms looked lively and interesting, but teachers differed somewhat in style of decorating. Eight decorated their rooms mainly around function or subject matter. For example, the art teacher put art projects all over his room and had a bulletin board about artists and careers in art. A home economics classroom had posters and bulletin boards about sewing and a set of letter-shaped pillows on one wall spelled the name of the school. A first grade teacher put words, letters and numbers all over the walls and, in an effort to teach independence, taught her students to search their environment to find out how to spell words or construct sentences when writing:

> I've been told there is too much in here for them to see, they don't know where to look first, but they do know where to look. When we need a word and they know where we've put that word, its unbelievable, they know exactly where to find that word. (17 December 1987)

Two special education teachers favored pastel-colored walls and posters of animals and scenery. One of them described her intent:

> The standard way that I was instructed in terms of having and running an E.D. classroom was, don't make things look bright. These kids are not fools. If they come home to drab surroundings, they don't want to come to school in that kind of situation. . . . I don't try to do real cutesy types of things, I want to get a message . . . [that] has to do with emotional and behavioral expectations of you and of me, and those are the only messages that I want up in my room. So when you space out, you look out the window, you know it rejuvenates you, you look at a poster and it's something that . . . feeds back into the positive. (3 December 1987)

Three elementary teachers decorated their rooms mostly with student projects, especially student art projects; other posters and instructional materials clearly took a back seat. Two more elementary teachers fashioned fairly artistic, colorful bulletin boards with construction paper and commercial cut-outs; these were the main decorations in their classrooms. Six teachers (five elementary and one junior high) decorated their rooms with 'everything but the kitchen sink', and even that in some cases. Bulletin boards, posters, student work and various objects of interest were liberally displayed around these rooms.

Eight classrooms were dull by comparison, for a variety of reasons. For example, the music teacher was temporarily housed in a basement room, which she soon lost because it was needed for classroom space; anticipating her move, a few posters were on the walls and boxes of materials were stacked. An LD teacher shared her classroom with another special education teacher; it was divided by a portable divider and somewhat noisy and cramped. The beige walls sported a few posters, a calendar and a map. A fifth grade teacher's classroom contained a few maps, animal posters and pictures of early presidents; he was not very oriented toward decorating. Some teachers do not appear to tune in to the physical environment of the classroom, focusing their attention instead on relationships with students and auditory or tactile stimuli. But in addition, classroom communities for some students or teachers, particularly those in special programs or non-academic subject areas, are often designated by the bureaucracy as temporary and makeshift, despite the teacher's wishes.

Room displays were analyzed for their portrayal of diversity. Holiday themes were part of the decorations of seventeen classrooms. The first classroom I observed, in late November, had a Thanksgiving display of turkeys, pilgrims and cornucopias. Sixteen classrooms observed in December contained Christmas themes. In a few, only a Christmas tree or Santa poster quietly announced the season. In others, the decorations fairly shouted Christmas. For example, an elementary classroom had a bulletin board entitled 'A Time for Giving' with Santa and a tree, a 'Christmas Around the World' bulletin board constructed partly by the students and a commercially-made reindeer cut-out. Another elementary classroom had a decorated Christmas tree, a cardboard fireplace, a Santa bulletin board, paper candles on windows and a red and green paper chain across the ceiling. Two teachers tried to counter-balance attention to this Christian holiday by adding a few Hannukah artifacts.

In eight classrooms, people did not appear in decorations: either there were no decorations, or they consisted of things such as animal posters or subject-specific materials. In the other classrooms, most teachers had obviously attempted to make their decorations multiracial and non-sexist, although Whites and Blacks, males particularly, predominated. Seven classrooms had multiracial posters and commercially-produced multiracial teaching aids, which portrayed either heads smiling, or some facet of academics such as children climbing over letters. They usually contained equal numbers of different racial groups and both sexes, although in some cases it was difficult to discern the racial identity of 'brown' people. 'Famous American' posters, depicting for example famous men and women of a variety racial backgrounds, were used in three classrooms. Three classrooms displayed student self-portraits, which were multiracial.

White males appeared solo most often as Santa Claus, but also as early Presidents, clowns, pilgrims, workers, Peanuts characters and Mark Twain. African American males appeared solo on posters in three classrooms, all doing something related to academics or achievement, such as reading a book or having become a successful artist. Posters depicting African American children of both sexes appeared in two classrooms. Neither African American nor White females appeared alone in any displays. Six classrooms had posters containing both African American and White people, such as a school basketball calendar or a poster showing smiling faces of children. Native Americans appeared in several classrooms: Indian artwork or artifacts were on display in two classrooms, a historic Indian village project children had constructed for a social studies lesson was displayed in one and Indian faces (mostly male) appeared on posters in three classrooms. Aside from multiracial displays and a holiday bulletin board in the ESL classroom, no identifiable Latinos or Asians were pictured. One classroom, however, had a pinata. No people with disabilities appeared in decorations, nor did people who were identifiably not middle class. Finally, three classrooms (including the ESL classroom) displayed words and phrases written in languages other than English.

Some of the teachers pointed out posters depicting racial minorities. No one drew my attention to posters depicting Whites, suggesting these were viewed as 'given'. With the exception of the display of an Indian village, the decorations suggested little about the lives, culture, history, or viewpoints of the people represented. Much the same can be said of portrayals of the sexes: they suggested that the sexes are integrated (with males numerically dominant), that both sexes share similar roles and characteristics and that sexism is not an issue.

Seating arrangements varied. Twelve teachers, seven of whom taught general elementary grades, arranged desks in rows facing forward, and one elementary teacher arranged desks in a large square facing the center of the room. Two elementary special education teachers arranged desks in pairs facing each other. Five teachers — two elementary and three junior high/middle school — seated students in small groups around tables or in desks clustered together. Three teachers — pre-school, kindergarten and first grade — arranged the room in stations and children sat according to the activity they were to work on. The ESL teachers seated their students around a table. A special education teacher let students sit anywhere; they could choose between desks or tables. The high school math teacher arranged long tables in a large rectangle; students sat mainly around the outer sides. Finally, the home economics and high school technical education teachers had students moving between seats and equipment; they worked on equipment in pairs or small groups.

Students usually sat mixed by race and sex. In a few classrooms mixed seating was impossible because one sex or race predominated. Five classrooms were all-male: both technical education classes, both ESL classes and one special education class. None were all-female. Two special education classrooms had only one girl and several boys. In four classrooms that were roughly sex balanced, students helped decide where to sit and they tended to sit in a sex segregated pattern.

Three classrooms contained students of all one race: two special education classes were all-White and an ESL class had only one student. The other ESL class had an East Indian student and a Korean student. In seven racially-mixed classrooms students of color outnumbered White students; seating was racially mixed. In nineteen classrooms White students outnumbered students of color. In fifteen of these students of color were dispersed around the room; in the other four some students of color clustered together.

When the students, the teachers and the room displays are considered together, most classrooms conveyed an image of racial integration in which Christian Whites and African Americans are clearly most visible and Whites dominate. Further, some classes constituted male domains, particularly technical educational; in this study there was no female domain nor expression of feminism. Certainly there was no 'special place for ourselves' that Grumet (1988, p. 88) argued women need in order to mine and develop feminine potential and power. Other forms of diversity and oppression — that based on social class, disability, language, and dialect — were represented mainly in the students inhabiting classroom space but not the decor surrounding them. It was as if these differences do not count or are not legitimate; by failing to acknowledge them in the decor, treating them as deficiencies to be remediated in special classes, most classrooms did not seriously suggest that these forms of diversity can be seen positively, even proudly. But this inter- pretation would not be immediately obvious in most of the classrooms precisely because they appeared inviting, interesting, colorful, and reflective of diversity.

Curriculum and Materials

Children go to school to develop intellectual skills and to learn knowledge. Many people assume that the knowledge schools teach represents the best ideas of our culture and the most useful concepts for further learning and that it is factual and relatively unbiased. However, a growing body of scholar- ship contests this assumption, arguing that most curricula serve as instruments of social control. Rather than promoting thinking, questioning and investiga- tion, curricula mainly demand rote memorization. And the selection of content justifies social dominance of White wealthy males and the subordination of everybody else.

The socially constructed nature of the curriculum is rarely shared with students. Rather than being challenged to analyze and think about phenomena and to construct meaning that helps them understand the world better, students usually memorize predigested information; concepts, ideas, and interpretations of reality are presented as brute facts to be memorized in much the same fashion as multiplication tables (Cherryholmes, 1988; Goodlad, 1984). The knowledge offered to students is often so predigested that it seems trivial to them. Perceiving school knowledge as trivial, many students dismiss it, viewing life experience as a more reliable source of knowledge (McNeil, 1986).

School knowledge promotes social control when it makes particular images of society seem natural and inevitable without presenting alternative images seriously. Textbooks today, even though they have undergone changes since the 1960s, still present White wealthy or middle class males as the main doers and the focus of attention, and all other groups as either subsidiary — such as Blacks and White women, or as non-existent — such as poor people (Sleeter and Grant, 1991). Furthermore, the conceptual threads undergirding the curriculum and the canon for selecting ideas and knowledge are drawn from the experiences and perspectives of the dominant group; adding in heroes and contributions of other groups does not change this. For example, whites moving West in the 1800s are called settlers rather than immigrants or invaders, even when Indians are acknowledged to have been present. Heroes, heroines, or contributions of non-dominant groups that are included usually reinforce, rather than challenge, broad themes in the curriculum; for example, Sacajewea, who helped white explorers, is included much more often then Geronimo, who fought against white invaders (Banks, 1991). In addition, textbooks suggest that the American dream is open to all people in society equally, and do not teach about structural inequalities today, vested interests in social policy, or struggles of oppressed groups (Apple and Christian-Smith, 1991).

School knowledge alienates students when it neither relates to their lives or interests, nor invites students to become engaged in using it for a meaningful purpose. Henry Trueba (1989) argued that many minority children are never offered a good reason why they should invest energy in learning school knowledge because it is presented to them as alien and unconnected to what they know. Too often, 'the curriculum is not appealing to children because it escapes children's experience, and thus their interest and grasp of concepts' (p. 143). Confronted daily with decontextualized bits of knowledge that relate to a culture they do not know very well, many children experience stress and frustration, but are not helped to examine the roots of their alienation. As Paulo Freire (1973) argued,

> Our traditional curriculum, disconnected from life, centered on words emptied of the reality they are meant to represent, lacking in concrete activity, could never develop a critical consciousness. (p. 37)

Eight teachers taught reading lessons when they were observed. One class of first graders practiced words in workbooks and on computers as part of the 'Writing To Read' program (J.H. Martin, IBM, 1986), and another class practiced several phonics and syntactic skills (for example, 'ai' words; putting 's' at the end of plurals). Much of the work in both classrooms focused on skills in isolation of meaningful content, although children in the 'Writing to Read' program spent about fifteen minutes composing stories at word processors. Students in two fifth grade classrooms in different schools read orally the same story in the same textbook (Clymer *et al.*, 1985), about a coyote who comes to the city and adapts to this new environment, answering comprehension questions from the teacher's guide every few paragraphs. A junior high LD class read a story about an athlete who sustained an injury and became paralyzed, and a story about different kinds of phobias; both stories provoked student questions and discussion. A junior high ED class discussed *Johnny Tremain*; the teacher first asked comprehension questions, then compared Johnny's life in 1773 with the lives of 14-year-old boys, now, focusing mainly on family responsibilities (including babysitting) and career planning.

A junior high English teacher taught a reading lesson about a Puerto Rican family in New York that illustrates students' lack of practice in talking about race or ethnicity. She introduced the story by asking students to name their ethnic backgrounds; a few White students named European ethnic groups, two African American students said they were Indian, other students called out a variety of racial and ethnic groups (although no one said Black or African). Unsure where to go with this discussion, the teacher proceeded with the story and followed it with a discussion of differences in customs between Puerto Rico and New York. The last ten minutes were spent correcting punctuation errors in sentences. Afterward, the teacher commented on the lesson:

> None of our Black students said that they had any ancestors from Africa, and I was amazed, and I wasn't exactly sure what to say about that, but I thought that was so funny, they all said they had Indian [ancestors], I don't know if they thought it was so obvious that they didn't mention it. . . . I was really surprised, so I will pursue that at some other time. (19 November 1987)

With the exception of the junior high LD teacher who encouraged spontaneous discussion, teachers tightly controlled content in these reading lessons. Content was also highly controlled by the text materials in all of the classrooms except the two special education classes. Reading in the first grade classrooms consisted mainly of learning decoding skills; reading in the upper grades consisted of reading assigned stories and answering comprehension questions designed by the textbook authors.

Seven teachers taught math lessons. A class of pre-first graders practiced counting and number recognition, using workbooks and chalkboard. A class of first graders worked on 'math stories' (subtraction problems) for families of seven; then they completed a Christmas worksheet that practiced the word 'poinsettia'. A class of second graders also practiced subtraction families and word problems; then the teacher involved them in brainstorming how they could improve their subtraction skills. A class of both second and third graders worked problems at their individual skill levels in workbooks. The teacher in an elementary LD class worked with a group of primary grade students on fact families, addition and subtraction (for example, $6 + 5 = 11$; $9 + 3 = 12$); other students worked individually on either reading or math skills. A fifth grade ED class worked on individualized language arts and math assignments out of textbooks and workbooks. Finally, a class of high school students worked on individualized math assignments, mainly algebra, using either textbooks, worksheets, or the computer. Textbooks, workbooks and worksheets dominated six of the seven math lessons; manipulatives appeared in only one classroom. Math itself, as in the classrooms Goodlad (1984) studied, was presented 'as a body of fixed facts and skills to be acquired, not as a tool for developing a particular kind of intellectual power in the student' (p. 209).

Two special education teachers taught social studies. A high school LD class worked on packets of material assigned by other teachers, mostly related to geography; the LD teacher helped them complete the work. A high school ED teacher taught about geography for a history unit; her main objective was to address some misconceptions. First she had students draw what they thought a map of the world looks like, then discussed how most of us think ethnocentrically, putting the US in the center. She asked students to brainstorm what they know about China; students offered information about Japan and other Asian cultures in addition to China, several making remarks like, 'What's the difference?' The teacher emphasized that China and Japan are very distinct, pointing out which characteristics actually refer to China and which do not. She then lectured on China at the end of the nineteenth century, the Open Door Policy, the Boxer Rebellion and Teddy Roosevelt.

The other teachers taught lessons from various other subject areas. For example, a sixth grade teacher taught a science lesson about acids and bases, using litmus paper and common household products, preceded by a short 'Fat Albert and the Cosby Kids' cartoon. A home economics class practiced threading a sewing machine, then stitching forward and backward. An art class worked on one of three art projects: a picture of an animal using torn paper to show color and texture; drawing projects using magazine pictures to practice proportion, line, and color; or drawings for the Christmas card/winter scene contest. One technology education class practiced reading prints for drafting and another built wooden model cars to learn about aerodynamics and CO_2 propulsion and to practice using woodworking equipment. A fourth grade music class practiced rhythm, then sang songs, including a traditional Jewish song. A second grade music class listened to a story about the Nutcracker, then colored a picture of it. An ESL class discussed Christmas traditions and customs in America, learning new vocabulary words, such as wreath, Christmas trees, holly, exchange and presents; students compared American holiday celebrations with holiday celebrations in their home countries. An elementary class worked on a project constructing a coat of arms about themselves: they first wrote complimentary words about the person to their right, then practiced saying 'thank you' to compliments; they wrote words to put on their coat of arms that they would like someone to say about themselves; and they read orally stories they had written the previous day about things they do with the family for fun. A kindergarten class recited the 'Pledge of Allegiance', practiced letters of the alphabet, sang a Christmas song and listened to a Christmas story, practiced counting angels and Christmas trees, listened to another Christmas story, looked at a book about Hannukah, looked at a book about a pinata and sang a Christmas song in Spanish.

The curriculum was analyzed for its attention to diversity. Christianity was celebrated through Christmas themes in seven lessons. A few teachers mentioned having come to wonder about the appropriateness of celebrating Christmas at school, even though they had Christmas decorations in their own classrooms. For example, the art teacher said that he added 'winter scene' to the Christmas card contest because one year a student could not participate for religious reasons. Other teachers who viewed Christmas as an important part of American culture did not see this as a problem, since students who could not participate were few in number and excused from participation. For example:

> We just had a Christmas program, and there were Christian songs, Silent Night was sung, and Oh Little Town of Bethlehem, and a lot of the Christian-oriented songs. . . . We brought in a Mennorah and brought in some other cultures, you know, but most of the songs were just the universal songs that we've learned and heard. I don't know . . . if any [teachers] this year had any that were Jewish or any other nationality, I know we've had Muslims, [they] just have to be excused and leave, . . . there hasn't been any report of any flack as far as any celebrations being done in the classroom, you know, objections by any parents that I'm aware of. . . . Your heart goes out to those students because, you know, in our culture it just is so celebrated, it is so prevalent, I've never . . . been given any objections about celebrating any aspect of Christmas. (14 December 1987)

Textbooks in use were fairly multicultural and gender-balanced, although they were predominantly White, middle class and almost devoid of people with disabilities, as are most textbooks today (Sleeter and Grant, 1991). African Americans appeared quite often, although Whites outnumbered them. About equal numbers of both sexes appeared. In math and reading skill books, publishers appeared to have assigned roles to people almost at random. Field notes from a first grade class captured an impression most of these books conveyed:

> Kids pictured are different colors. You don't learn about cultural diversity by reading the book but you see different colored people in different roles. Gender — about 50–50. Class — middle (kids have new-looking toys and clothes) (15 December 1987)

White males were a significant part of the content in five lessons: the story about the paralyzed athlete, Johnny Tremain, Teddy Roosevelt, *The Nutcracker* and a Christmas movie showed in a fourth grade classroom. African Americans, mostly male, were a significant part of the content only in the movie about *The Cosby Kids*. Latinos were a significant part of the lesson in the story about a Puerto Rican family, which was also the only lesson to mention social class. Asian Americans were not part of the content in any lesson. Women were not the focus of any lesson, and females tended to appear in subservient roles. For example, in *The Nutcracker* story, the brother breaks a toy, the grandfather fixes things and the soldier saves the girl. In general, the curriculum was based on skills much more than on content about the social world.

When the teachers were asked to describe how they selected the content of these lessons, they responded mainly in terms of what is in the textbook or what is required. For example:

> The main objective for the reading lesson was to look at the adaptability of the coyote, and then also to make comparisons between the fiction and non-fiction account about the same, specifically zeroing in on adaptability and cleverness and certain traits of the coyote. It's part of our reading series and something that I'm supposed to teach, so that's probably why I selected it. (6 December 1987)

Teachers felt bound to follow the adopted textbooks, and knew other teachers would expect their students to have mastered content for that grade level.

A few teachers said they selected what to teach based on what kids need to know to function in society (referring mainly to jobs). This was a common determinant of curriculum for the ESL and the technical education teachers and to some extent the junior and senior high special education teachers. For example, a special education teacher described part of her content this way:

> Right now we're into the unit that focuses on job skills, and where I am in terms of my planning, in eighth grade the kids go through a four-year plan, they're planning for 9th to 12th grade, and if I get them right now, we start bombarding them with possibilities. . . . We went to [name of company] looking at the cheese industry and looking at the entry level jobs that they could come into. (13 December 1987)

Only a few teachers mentioned student interest or their own personal interests as determinants of what they teach. A special education teacher described her tendency to tune in to material she or the class finds of particular interest:

> That extra magazine, sometimes there'll be one article that's interesting that I really want to use, and this one has a bunch of them. . . . My lesson plans [for the week] are usually obsolete on Tuesday. We get so off track. . . . If they're interested and I think things are working, then I'll change (my plans). (20 November 1987)

Attention to students' or their own interests was not restricted to special education, but it was more prevalent there, partly because class sizes were small, and because special education curricula were more flexible than general education curricula.

Four teachers — all specialists — mentioned attempts to make their curriculum multicultural. For example, a special education teacher described her approach to social studies:

I do a lot of the time show movies, current movies, to reinforce what we [studied]. When we did the Indians, I videotaped a lot of stuff from PBS, that'll reinforce what I'm doing. There was a thing on Nova about three years ago about Indian health care in the country, and how bad it is. They watched that. There was also a movie called, 'I Will Fight No More Forever' about Chief Joseph. I showed that, and I will sometimes sacrifice them being aware of dates to get the essence of the feeling of what I'm trying to get across. (7 January 1988)

The music teacher had many Latino students in class, so she tried to teach bilingually:

In the kindergarten, the first week there are two Spanish songs in there, so when the English-speaking children have trouble with Spanish, the Spanish-speaking children have trouble with English, so it is kind of an even flop for them, like, Oh, I can't do those two songs, but I can do these two, and by the end of the second or third week, they do all the songs, so they have a bilingual knowledge of these songs, they don't even know it. (4 December 1987)

In summary, most teachers saw content as fairly prescribed and fixed; their job was to deliver it much more than to shape it. Both school districts had fairly prescribed curricula, although teachers also had some latitude to add to the curriculum or decide how long to spend on a topic. But the prescribed nature of the curriculum appeared to limit how much teachers experimented with it, and perceived requirements elsewhere further constrained their interest in experimenting with it. Most of the teachers appeared to be conscientiously concerned about preparing their students to fit in and meet the expectations of other teachers and, later, employers. This was not described as a problem; most of the teachers did not seem to expect to develop much of their curriculum, although one technology education teacher was bitter about the imposition of what he saw as an inappropriate curriculum that rendered his knowledge of the subject area useless.

As a result of adherence to a relatively prescribed curriculum much of what teachers taught consisted of skills and concepts that were decontextualized from students' lives or interests. Students spent much of their time practicing isolated math or phonics skills, answering comprehension questions, or filling in worksheets much like Goodlad (1984) described as 'painting-by-numbers' (p. 108). Some teachers tried consciously to relate their curriculum to student experiences or interests, such as the science lesson using household products and the rather unsuccessful discussion of ethnic heritage. A few teachers built some lessons directly around students' life experiences and interests, such as the coat of arms project. But overall, decontextualized knowledge and isolated skills dominated the curriculum.

This kind of curriculum can become meaningless and mind-numbing. Further, reducing student expression to answers to pre-determined questions or reactions to tasks placed before them restricts how teachers come to know their students, the extent to which they invite students' personal knowledge and the extent to which homework capitalizes on what parents may know (Delgado-Gaitan, 1990; Gitlin, 1983). Classroom interaction usually centered around the curriculum, rather than what teachers or students were interested in or experienced outside school. Excluding students' personal interests as a motivational basis for learning, teachers tried to motivate students by creating visually inviting classrooms and, as we shall see, cultivating warm personal relationships with them.

Teaching Strategies

Schools generally use only a few teaching strategies most of the time with most students. Based on a review of seven classroom observation studies, I concluded that,

> The two main teaching procedures teachers use are lecturing or explaining information to the whole class, and monitoring seatwork in which students either fill in worksheets or answer questions based on reading the textbook. . . . There is also relatively little individualization; classes are taught as whole group most of the time, with everyone in the classroom expected to complete the same work. (Sleeter, 1987, p. 75)

Predominant teaching strategies tend to serve white middle class children better than low-income children and children of color. Barbara Shade (1989) distinguished between analysts and synergists, arguing that different cultural styles and survival strategies produce these two different styles of approaching and processing information. Analysts prefer to process infomation analytically, receive and give elaborate verbal explanations, engage in cause-effect thinking, create structure, 'sit and attend for a long period of time to inanimate objects', manipulate ideas mentally, and focus on a limited number of stimuli at a time (*ibid*, p. 191). Synergists, on the other hand, prefer visual and kinesthetic/tactile learning, respond to their inner feelings and perceptions, 'construe the world in its totality, often ignoring specific parts', interpret facial and body language well, synthesize ideas, and engage in creative and intuitive thinking; they prefer a multiplicity of stimuli, among which they alternate attention rapidly (*ibid*, p. 192). She argued that while synergetic learners find school dull and unstimulating, teachers view them as having short attention spans and learning problems, and either refer them to special education or try to change them into analytic learners. Shade recommended:

Rather than inferiorize the cognitive and behavioral patterns of the synergists, perhaps a more equitable approach is to readjust the teaching-learning process to accommodate and bridge the differences synergists display. To accomplish this task requires the development of a culturally compatible classroom which addresses the perceptual, motivation, and behavioral style of both types of learners. (*ibid*, p. 192)

Advocates of cooperative learning approach the issue of diverse approaches to learning from a different vantage point, but make similar observations about schools catering to only a portion of students. Elizabeth Cohen (1986), for example, advocated the multi-ability classroom that uses heterogeneous groupwork as an alternative to the single-ability classroom:

For example, students can solve problems visually, spatially, by talking and arguing about solutions, or through imaginative role playing. There are also many different kinds of tasks: discussion, manipulation, visual representation, long-term projects, interaction with community members, dramatization construction, and experimentation. (p. 146)

Since cooperative learning turns diverse skills, talents and approaches to learning into a strength rather than a problem in the classroom, it has been found to raise most students' achievement and particularly that of students Shade describes as synergetic learners (for example, Slavin, 1983).

The teachers in this study perceived themselves as having more power to determine how to teach than what to teach. When asked to describe their instructional strategies and why they used those strategies, they indicated that their choice was constrained or influenced mainly by school district policies that mandated whole-class instruction for reading, the number of students they have, how much or what kind of content they feel they must cover, students' attention spans, students' range of skill or ability levels, their own comfort level with particular teaching strategies, and student responses. Most teachers discussed only one or two of these factors and indicated that they have flexibility to vary instructional strategies.

During the first observation, teachers organized their instructional time in different ways, but individual seatwork and whole-class recitation were by far the two main teaching strategies they used. In seven classrooms students spent at least half of the observed time in whole-class recitation, followed by individual seatwork or individual silent reading. This was a particularly common structure for teaching reading. In interviews, teachers expressed a range of opinions about whole-class instruction for reading:

I like it. We were to the point before (where we had) so many little groups that it was nutty, you know, I had two groups within my room and I had kids that were cross-grade levels, I had third graders into a fifth grade book and that was going to the point of being crazy. . . . I think I'm making just as good progress and we're not holding down the kids either. (6 December 1987)

I sometimes think it's easier to work in smaller group. The only problem with that is you always have to be sure the other group has something to do and can do, and oftentimes you give them the seatwork type of thing that probably doesn't pertain to what they are doing anyhow because its got to keep this group quiet to work with that other group. So, I don't know, it's six of one and half dozen of another. (4 December 1987)

I'll repeat this to you three times, I do not believe that, to put a child in a group that they do not belong yet, they're thinking I'm going to catch them up, but I have never yet seen that happen ... There are certain things they can do with the group, but I think there is still too much background work that has to be done at their level. (17 December 1987)

In two classrooms, both at the secondary level, the teacher lectured for about twenty minutes, the class engaged in recitation, and students did individual seatwork. A teacher explained that he preferred this structure to small group work because, 'I think with this whole class instruction you as a teacher have a little more control over the direction over who gets what accomplished' (30 November 1987). In two special education classes, students read orally for half the period, then had whole-class discussion or recitation, and individual seatwork.

In six classrooms students spent most of the observed time doing individual seatwork (worksheets or workbooks); most also spent part of this time individually or in small groups with the teacher, on the computer, or with another student. This was a common structure in special education classes, and some teachers also used it for math. Some teachers encouraged peer tutoring during individual seatwork and some prohibited it. Teachers explained their preference for individual work:

They have books at their desk that they do, and it's books that are mostly phonics and math books because it is something they can handle on their own. .... I like to have them individually do their assignments for the simple fact that I'm trying to force them into independence. .... As a general rule, that's what they're doing at their seat, they're doing the assignment of what we just had the lesson on. (4 December 1987)

I would have a math class with many, many students and they would be at all different levels, and then we had an attendance problem, which we also have now, so it was impossible to keep those kids together, so really it grew from the need to address individual skills and the fact that I would have one kid who could do geometry and another kid who couldn't do long division in the same classroom. (23 November 1987)

Two first grade classrooms were using mainly small group work. In one, groups moved from station to station every fifteen minutes, although students mainly worked by themselves. In another, small groups practiced a math concept after the teacher had presented it to the whole class.

In four elementary classrooms a variety of teaching strategies were used, none for more than about fifteen minutes; these included demonstration, oral reading or lecture by teacher, large group discussion, seatwork and kinesthetic or psychomotor activities (such as finger-play songs). These teachers varied teaching strategies often mainly to accommodate short attention spans or to control attention and activity levels. The two ESL classes had only one-two students each; students worked individually or as a pair with the teacher. Finally, in four classes students engaged in activities related directly to specific subject areas: pairs constructed projects in technical education, individuals worked on art projects in art, pairs worked at sewing machines in home economics and the whole class sang songs in music.

The number of minutes teachers spent using specific teaching strategies was recorded and totaled and the percentage of total teaching time for that strategy was calculated. (When multiple activities occurred simultaneously, the average amount of time each child spent on each activity was estimated so that the total number of minutes recorded was the same as the total number of minutes observed). Table 3.1 shows the preponderance of individual seatwork and recitation: 40 per cent of observed teaching time was spent using these two strategies. The third most-used strategy, small group discussion or project, was used in only four classrooms. Lecture was used mainly in two secondary level classrooms; in six elementary classrooms it was used to give directions or explain briefly a new concept. Psychomotor activities (for example, singing and sewing) occurred only in either preschool-kindergarten classrooms or subject-specific classrooms (i.e., singing and sewing). High-interest or high-activity strategies such as games and simulations were used very little. Even individual silent reading was not used much, a pattern which has been noted in other observational studies of classrooms (Goodlad, 1984).

The amount of time students spent working as part of a large group, alone, or as part of a small group, was calculated. Students spent 34 per cent of instructional time working as part of a large group (engaging in recitation, listening to a lecture, watching a demonstration, discussing with the whole class, watching films, or listening to the teacher read). Some of the recitation sessions clearly encouraged competition among students. For example, field notes in one classroom reported that:

Table 3.1: Teaching Strategies (December, 1987, 1351 minutes)

	Number of minutes	Percentage of time	Number of classrooms
Individual seatwork	285	21	14
Recitation	260	19	17
Small group project, discussion	100	7	4
Practice something psychomotor	90	7	4
Lecture	75	7	8
Organizing, non-academic activity	65	5	8
Individual work, not reading or seatwork	70	5	5
Oral reading by students	55	4	4
Seatwork in pairs	50	4	2
Individual work with teacher	58	4	2
Demonstration	45	3	5
Large group discussion	35	3	4
Individual silent reading	35	3	3
Socializing, confusion	33	2	6
Films	25	2	2
Work on computer	20	2	1
Oral reading by teacher	15	1	3
Game	10	1	2
Test	10	1	1
Simulation, role play	0	0	0

> Six kids put up hands most [often].... Hand-raising for recitation, and for Hangman frequently accompanied by O-o-o-o, o-o-o-o! (6 December 1987)

Students spent 31 per cent of instructional time working individually (doing seatwork, reading silently, working on the computer, taking a test, or completing other solitary projects). They spent 11 per cent of the time working in small groups with other students (discussion, completing projects, doing seatwork). In the only classroom in which students moved in small groups from station to station all period, however, much of the time was actually spent completing worksheets individually.

However, most teachers taught with enthusiasm, and were very well prepared. The following excerpts from field notes illustrate:

> *Minimal* time wasted. Teacher moves quickly from one song to next, has kids pass out and collect material. They seem used to this, help well. Teacher combines music with creative dramatics, body motion. Teacher appears to enjoy the kids — she looks enthusiastic, activities fun but kids must listen. (4 December 1987)

> Teacher talks with much enthusiasm, seems to like to make academics into games, looks as though all this is fun. Generates enthusiasm on part of kids. (17 December 1987)

Teacher well-organized — film, science materials already set up, so minimal time wasted in transitions. (1 December 1987)

In most classrooms very little teaching time was wasted or used for non-instructional purposes: only 5 per cent of the observed time was used for organizing or other non-academic activity (for example, passing out material, taking attendance, cleaning up) and only 2 per cent spent allowing students to talk without working, usually at the beginning or end of an instructional period.

The above describes what teachers were doing; how were students reacting? For the most part they were compliant and on-task, although in most classrooms there was also an undercurrent of peer group interaction or restlessness. Notes such as the following were taken during whole-class recitation, lecture, or oral reading:

Four boys on the west wall in single chairs do not participate very much in class and two of them seem not to be involved with the class at all. (5th grade, 4 December 1987)

Overall well behaved and quiet, very enthusiastic about answering questions [during recitation] — almost everyone raises hands when asked questions. (2nd grade, 4 December 1987)

Getting squirmy by 9.30 [reading lesson started at 8.35]; more boys than girls out of seat, one girl looking around, several kids scratching, moving things on desk, playing with pencil, etc. (1st grade, 4 December 1987)

During individual seatwork:

The kids stay on task very well and very little socializing is going on except to move in and out of the computer lab. (High school math, 23 November 1987)

A lot of students spent time waiting for their questions to be answered if their partner was not able to help them; after their help they returned to work and most seemed to remain on task. (2nd/3rd grade, 23 November 1987)

And during small group work:

2 white males, 1 black female. Larger boy takes over leadership, BF seems to have concept better. Kids take turns. Teacher circulates making sure they are taking turns telling math stories. Group gets more interested in quieter boy's watch, telling time. Back to math —

bigger boy keeping points based on getting it right. They aren't actually saying stories too well, their 'leader' gets them off track as much as keeping them on. (1st grade, 17 December 1987)

In summary, for the most part teaching strategies were fairly similar to what has been reported in other studies, and involved mainly strategies that would cater to analytic learners: students who prefer to work alone or to compete as individuals, respond well to print and step-by-step work (which is usually what worksheets and workbooks require), and can sit for long periods of time (Shade, 1989). Furthermore, students all did much the same thing in response to teacher direction. Teachers generally filled instructional time with instructional tasks; they spent very little time on non-instructional matters. Teachers indicated having flexibility to decide how they could teach, which suggests they perceived they could adopt alternative strategies if they viewed them as appropriate and understood how to implement them.

Most students complied with what they were to do, most of the time. To keep students interested and attentive, some teachers taught with obvious enthusiasm and some varied activities three or four times during an hour. Teachers also attempted to keep students motivated and engaged by developing a supportive style of interacting with them; to that we now turn.

Teacher-student Interaction

When teachers think about treating their students fairly, how they interact with students is often what they consider. Even so, there are biases across race and gender lines in teachers' interactions with students.

Over the past twenty years many educators have been sensitized to cross-cultural differences in communication patterns. For example, White listeners nod their heads and also give verbal responses such as 'uh-huh' while listening, while Black listeners do one or the other but not necessarily both, often with eyes averted (Erickson, 1979). Many White teachers have been taught that students of color may look down rather than at the teacher to signify respect; teachers in this project who had participated in prior courses or workshops commented on having learned this.

Teachers often interact differently with girls and boys of different races, calling on, praising and asking higher level questions to White males more often than other students and reprimanding Black males more than other students. Males as a group get more teacher attention than females; White males get more positive attention and Black males get more negative attention. Black girls who begin elementary school as assertive gradually become as invisible as White girls. Latino students of either sex seem to get disproportionately little attention (for example, Irvine, 1991; Jackson and Cosca, 1974; Ortiz, 1988). These differences in interaction patterns emanate from various factors, including differences in teacher expectations, teacher racial attitudes,

Table 3.2: Race and gender composition of 24 classrooms (per cents)

	Female %	Male %	Total %
White	29	36	65
African American	11	12	23
Latino	4	7	11
Asian	1	0	1
Total %	45	55	

gender differences among children in assertiveness and ability to command teacher attention, and teacher reactions to cultural differences in behavior and communication style.

In addition, the tone of teacher-student interaction is often more important for students of color than for White students (see, for example, Irvine, 1991; Ramirez and Castaneda, 1974). African Americans and Mexican Americans develop a finely-tuned ability to read social cues, as a survival skill. As a result, African American and Mexican American children sense the teacher's feelings about them and their academic ability more readily than White children, and react accordingly (Shade, 1989).

Most of the teachers in this study interacted with their students in a very warm and friendly manner; none were harsh or cold with students. Field notes contained descriptions of teacher-student interaction like the following:

Teacher interaction with children is very positive. Lots of praise used, teacher gives stickers for good work, answers questions students bring in patient and positive manner. (5 May 1987)

Boy bites tongue, starts crying. Teacher stops everyone [singing], and finds out what's wrong. Hugs him, he calms down, lesson starts again. (5 December 1987)

Whenever the children asked for help, he would not only give them clues, but would look at their other work and give them praise on things they had done correctly. (23 November 1987)

In only a few instances was the behavior of the teacher sharp or impersonal.

In each classroom in which whole-class instruction was used, a tally was kept for ten minutes of the race and sex of each child the teacher called on, praised, or reprimanded and the race and sex of each child who initiated a question. These data were compared with the racial and gender composition of the classrooms involved. Table 3.2 shows the percentage of students of each racial and gender group in these twenty-four classrooms. As this table shows, on the average, a little over half of the students were male and about two-thirds were white.

Table 3.3:   Teacher-student interaction patterns

WHO GETS CALLED ON

		Females %	Males %	Percentage %
Number	White:	52	75	62
of times	African American:	20	35	27
	Latino:	8	14	11
	Asian:	1	N/A	1
Percentage		39	61	—

WHO GETS PRAISED

		Females	Males	Percentage
Number	White:	5	18	49
of times	African American:	6	5	32
	Latino:	4	9	28
	Asian:	0	N/A	0
Percentage		31	68	—

WHO INITIATES QUESTIONS

		Females	Males	Percentage
Number	White:	6	23	56
of times	African American:	7	6	25
	Latino:	4	5	17
	Asian:	0	N/A	0
Percentage		35	65	—

Teachers called on students a total of 208 times during the ten-minute segments. As table 3.3 shows, they called disproportionately on males, but called on each racial group in rough proportion to their representation in the classroom. Teachers offered verbal praise for student responses a total of forty-seven times. (Responses such as 'Very good' or 'Good thinking' were counted as praise; responses such as repeating the student or mumbling 'uh, huh' were not.) Compared with the number of questions teachers asked students, they underpraised students by a large margin, although this varied widely among teachers. Girls and boys were praised in proportion to questions teachers asked of each sex, with boys getting more of both; white students were underpraised to a greater extent than black and Latino students.

Tally was also kept of the number of times teachers reprimanded or criticized students. Only nine reprimands or criticisms were noted during these ten-minute segments; all targets were White males. In most classrooms, this column was blank. Rather than reprimanding or criticizing, teachers occasionally redirected a child, reminded children of a rule, or quietly wrote the child's name on the board while continuing the lesson. (I later found out most buildings were using Assertive Discipline.) Field notes provide the following examples:

'Face front quietly' is a behavior teacher reminds kids to follow. (She says), 'Eyes up here', at one point seems to chart (names) of those that are obeying. (6 December 1987)

BF (Black female) found checkbook, gave another BF a check; she brought it to teacher, teacher nicely asked if someone found checks, explained what forgery is, took them away. (1 December 1987)

A kid calls someone a 'fag'. Teacher points to rule #5, 'No one has the right to put me down'. Has him read it, everyone read it, lesson keeps going. (5 December 1987)

Students initiated a total of fifty-two questions during these ten-minute segments; boys initiated about two-thirds of them. Whites initiated slightly fewer questions relative to their representation and Latinos slightly more.

In summary, racial groups were called on and praised roughly in proportion to their representation, although Latinos received a bit more attention than Whites. It seemed that teachers were making an effort to interact warmly and positively with students as much as possible and to distribute attention equitably across racial groups. It may be that they were particularly sensitive to distribution of attention while an observer was there; one teacher commented on this in a later interview.

There was, however, a gender bias in who teachers called on and praised and which students asked questions. Boys seemed to have a more visible presence in classrooms, regardless of their racial membership. A few teachers also used gender as a basis for dividing or organizing students, when other ways would have been just as effective. Two had students line up by sex to leave the room. Another asked first the girls, then the boys to sing a few passages; boys' voices had not yet changed, so this was not for vocal range. These practices may seem small and inconsequential, but they reinforce the assumption that gender matters in areas where it clearly does not. Reinforcing gender unnecessarily as a basis for dividing people can hinder efforts to help students question the extent to which gender matters in other areas (for example, strength) in which more people are likely to believe that it does.

Authority and Decision-making

Although Americans generally believe that schools are supposed to prepare students to live in a democracy, most classrooms are run like dictatorships and students learn little about the process of democracy by going to school. Freire (1973) argued that people,

could be helped to learn democracy through the exercise of democracy; for that knowledge, above all others, can only be assimilated experientially. More often than not, we have attempted to transfer that knowledge to the people verbally, as if we could give lessons in democracy while regarding popular participation in the exercise of power as 'absurd and immoral'. (p. 36)

Schools particularly teach students to acquiesce to authority rather than exercise it:

> The more hierarchical and rigid these (teacher-pupil) relationships are, and the more they are characterized by the concentration of decisions in the hands of the teacher and by a rigid control on the behavior of the pupils, the more easily will the latter acquire attitudes of docility and submission to authority. (Barbagli and Dei, 1977, p. 426)

Passivity and obedience schools demand are particularly a problem for students from low-income or racial minority backgrounds and for girls, who are members of groups that wield far less than their share of power in the broader society. They need to learn skills and dispositions for collective decision-making and action in order to articulate and further their own interests (for example, Banks, 1988; Freire, 1973; Shor, 1980).

For the most part, the teachers held a close rein on authority in their classrooms and shared fairly little of it with students. Where to sit was the main area in which students often had input. Twenty teachers were asked who decides where students sit. Ten allowed their students to select seats at the beginning of the year; teachers then moved students if they misbehaved, and some periodically reassigned seats so students would sit next to different peers over the year. Nine teachers assigned seats, frequently in alphabetical order. The teacher of the pre-school parent-teacher program did not use a fixed seating arrangement since children and their parents moved around the room frequently.

Most teachers controlled decision-making regarding how instructional time was to be spent. In twenty classrooms, students had no discernable input into learning activities or time use, although it is possible that teachers had adjusted routines to students over the course of the year. In five classrooms, varying in grade level and subject area, students were told what they should be doing, but could decide individually the rate at which to work for all or part of the class period. In one classroom, after completing assigned work, the students suggested playing 'Hangman' for the last few minutes of the period and the teacher agreed. In the two ESL classes, because of the small class size, students could request activities if they wished; this was done especially if they needed help on homework assigned in other classes. Finally, in the pre-school program, about half of the time was structured so that parents and children could choose among a variety of learning activities to do together.

Classroom rules were posted in most classrooms; thirteen teachers were asked who made the rules. Four explained that their school was using Assertive Discipline, and uniform, building-wide rules were developed by the teachers. Two teachers asked for input from their students, although one commented that many of her students were 'hard noses' and tended to make rules too stringent. The other eight teachers said that they simply tell students what the rules are. The two teachers of pre-school-kindergarten age children said their students were too young to make rules (one admitted, 'I'm a dictator'). The high school math teacher said that she used to have students collectively make classroom rules, which was the origin of her current rules; over the years she had begun simply passing the rules out to students. She commented that she might begin involving students in that process again.

Although the teachers controlled authority and decision-making tightly, they were usually very pleasant and seemed to care about their students; one would not perceive them as autocratic despots at all, but rather as firm parent-figures. While some were comfortable running authoritarian classrooms, others were not. One teacher explained:

> You let loose as you go along, but I find that in this type of building right now, I'm not as free as when I graduated. I don't feel as free to let loose as I had planned on doing when I first graduated. . . . My experience in the inner city has said, No, it does not work. (9 February 1988)

Yet it is important to wonder at what point young people begin to learn to exercise authority themselves within public institutions and particularly young people who are members of oppressed social groups.

What Teachers Expected to Gain from the Project

On the whole, these teachers were not terribly different from those described in other observation studies of classrooms (for example, Connell, 1985; Cusick, 1973; Goodlad, 1984; Grant and Sleeter, 1986c; McNeil, 1986), although their interactions with students were more consistently positive and their classroom time was used more productively than has been observed in many studies. But the observations revealed several patterns I would like to see changed. I was concerned about the districts' segmentation of students into a hierarchy of supposedly homogeneous groups, ranging from honors to special education. Both teachers and students became identified with niches in that hierarchy; it formed the primary way teachers described their students. In most classrooms students were 'batch processed' as a homogeneous group (Cusick, 1973) and were expected to learn primarily through whole-class recitation and individual seatwork. Much of the knowledge being disseminated was controlled by the textbook, especially in general education academic subject areas; much of also took the form of atomized bits of information and skills, decontextualized from real life. Classroom knowledge featured White males more than any other group, although it focused on skills more than people or social issues. But while the institution of schooling tended to reproduce a hierarchical, stratified structure in which obedience and mastery of skills were paramount, and in which White men were celebrated as most important, this was being done in a humane and orderly fashion in most of these twenty-nine classrooms. The teachers I observed were very warm and personable and most classrooms were bright and colorful. Most of the teachers were the kind of person children would want to please.

In the first interview, I asked the teachers what they wanted to gain from the staff development project. Eleven said that they had been getting more and more students who were culturally different from themselves and wanted to relate more effectively to them and their parents. The teachers expressed some frustration and perplexity with behavior of many of their students and wanted to understand why they behave as they do, what they think about, and how they learn best, in order to instruct them more effectively. For example:

> I'm dealing with Hispanic kids, I'm dealing with Black kids, . . . If I can understand their culture, their way of doing things, I can be a lot more tolerant, a lot more effective in working with them. (7 January 1988)

Two more teachers emphasized the urgency of 'doing something' for the growing numbers of 'at-risk' kids, although they were not sure what to do. For example, one said, 'We have to have something going for these kids. We may not find the answer, and it's probably a long time coming, but there are more of these kids coming up, let's do something for them' (4 December 1987).

Five teachers wanted to improve instruction for students of color at the whole-school level. In addition to wanting to learn more about their own students, they also wanted to make an impact on other teachers. For example, the Mexican-American teacher wanted the group to investigate 'the dropout rate among minorities and . . . suggestions that would make the school systems in the area aware of the need to address the problems of the minorities' (11 December 1987). A white elementary teacher wanted her school to institute a more effective parent involvement program, and said that,

> At this school I think we need more empathy toward minorities because some of the teachers look at the class and say, 'O-o-oh, I'm getting some more from this family', and they make no effort whatsoever. (December 1987)

Five teachers wanted to learn to help students relate better with each other, get along and fit in. The two ESL teachers emphasized how different their students feel, and the need to help them feel appreciated and teach others about their backgrounds. An elementary teacher was especially concerned to learn how to integrate handicapped children into her classroom:

> I feel that now I've integrated successfully the Black and the Mexican children, and that really for me personally is not a problem, but now I have these handicapped children and it's like going back ten years. (8 December 1987)

Three teachers who had participated in multicultural education workshops years ago said they wanted 'a change of pace', a 'refresher', they wanted to see if this project had any new ideas or techniques they could use. For example:

> What I hope to get out of it is, like I say, a better insight or maybe new things about the backgrounds, I know the background of Black people, I know the background of the Spanish people, you know, if there is anything that's come up that's new, I'd like that. (15 December 1987)

A music teacher wanted music resources from different cultural groups, finding herself 'constantly put in a position to recognize the pluralistic nature of my classroom when picking concert music, holiday selections, ethnic day selections, and classroom activities' (15 December 1987)

Two teachers had mixed feelings about coming and were not sure the project would offer them anything of value. One confessed that, 'I really entered it under Rona's plea, honestly, she really wanted someone to go with her, and I don't know what I expect' (15 December 1987). The other wanted to debate the extent to which teachers should be 'asked to adapt to the cultures of these multicultural students (rather) than having the students adapt to what we call our American culture' (19 November 1987). He was concerned that multicultural education programs are destroying the idea of the melting pot and wanted to find out what this type of program teaches.

These initial comments illustrate the different agendas the teachers brought with them. Eighteen came mainly to improve their ability to teach students of color — to improve their efficacy in academic instruction, as Ashton and Webb (1986) put it. Five were more interested in improving student-student relationships. One specifically wanted more multicultural music resources. The other five did not have a specific purpose for coming; they seemed satisfied with their teaching and came mainly to see if we would suggest anything they perceived as useful to add to it. For many teachers, their own agenda acted as a filter for screening out ideas they perceived as irrelevant; for others, it acted as a focal point for organizing and interpreting the experience. To the project directors, these various agendas posed a challenge; we could not assume that all participants came wanting much the same thing. The next chapters will chronicle what happened as they experienced the staff development program over a two-year period.

Note

1 Only twenty-nine teachers are described in this chapter since the thirtieth teacher who was part of the group that was studied joined during the second set of observations.

Chapter 4

Experiencing Staff Development

Multicultural education is a way of doing schooling that is fundamentally different from how it is normally done. Its advocates envision schools working with and supporting the aspirations of oppressed people, equalizing not just access but also outcomes, and building on their strengths rather than emphasizing limitations. They also envision schools engaging students as future citizens in a critique of our society's structure and helping them develop the skills, knowledge and inclination to build a more egalitarian society that prizes its diverse public.

These are lofty goals. How does one package them into a series of staff development sessions? Obviously, trade-offs must be made, such as:

- helping teachers develop a broad understanding of issues involved in multicultural education versus helping them learn to implement one or two new skills well;
- facilitating the exploration of issues teachers want to explore versus providing them with knowledge 'experts' believe they should have, even if the teachers do not view such knowledge as immediately relevant;
- sticking to the Teaching the Culturally Different approach and applying it to low-income students and students of color in the teachers' schools versus sensitizing teachers to additional forms of oppression and additional approaches to multicultural education;
- addressing issues and problems that many teachers would find threatening and offensive, and risking losing them in the process, versus planning sessions that they would want to keep attending; and
- addressing the 'least common denominator' for teachers in grades K-12 in a variety of subject areas versus zeroing in on curriculum and instruction specific to grade levels and subject areas of the majority of the group.

The planning team wrestled with these dilemmas as we considered teachers' interests and responses to the curriculum and instruction assessment.

We tabulated the topics from the list of twenty teachers had rank-ordered during the first session. Those receiving ten or more checks included: helping kids who have low basic skills (eighteen checks), parent involvement (sixteen), making curriculum multicultural (eighteen), cooperative learning in racially mixed classrooms (fifteen), ethnic learning styles (thirteen), dropout prevention (twelve), improving student-student relationships (twelve) and racism, sexism and classism in society today (ten). Topics receiving fewer than ten included Black English, Southeast Asian immigrants, bilingual education, what low-income students do when not in school, Hispanic culture, Black culture, Indians today, relating the curriculum to culturally different students, disproportionate minority student discipline, college preparation for low-income and minority students, sex equity and global education. In the small group discussions, teachers had talked most about the need for greater parent involvement, describing its lack as a big problem. They discussed wanting to know more about ethnic learning styles, cooperative learning, how to help students with low basic skills, how to make curriculum more multicultural, and how to prevent students from dropping out.

On the curriculum and instruction assessment, many of the teachers' suggestions for the hypothetical class of students focused on remediating low skills, 'correcting' grammar, and enforcing punctuality. Most of them modified lessons by inserting items here and there; few substantially rewrote or critiqued the lessons holistically. They did a very good job of adapting the lessons to diverse student skill levels; some of their ideas were quite creative. About half made at least one of the following alterations: adding multiethnic content, incorporating student life experiences and interests into curriculum, adapting instruction to students' preferred learning modalities and adapting to student preference for groupwork by using cooperative learning. Very few modified the lessons to try to make them gender-inclusive, give students decision-making power, or address multiple languages and dialects.

We considered teachers' interests and assessment responses in relationship to goals of multicultural education and literature on staff development for multicultural education. Based on the stages or components of multicultural education that authors such as Gay, Baker and Grant and Melnick described, we decided that the earlier sessions would focus primarily on awareness and knowledge acquisition and the later ones primarily on teaching skills. We also recognized teachers' need to take something from each session that they can use, and tried to make sure that the last part of each session included some skill or practical application. Further, throughout all the sessions we tried to build in activities for processing personal feelings and attitudes, such as large or small group discussion and the sharing of personal experiences.

We decided to treat a broad range of topics in an effort to help teachers develop a 'whole picture' of multicultural education, but at the same time to provide depth in some topics so that teachers would acquire some background knowledge and also some skills. This meant that many potentially relevant topics were not included at all, but there was enough breadth to encourage teachers to conceptualize issues in some complexity. It also meant that no topic or skill received ongoing attention. The districts offered staff development in skills such as cooperative learning and TESA (Teacher Expectations and Student Achievement), so we reasoned that teachers could develop such skills further if they saw a connection between them and multicultural education.

We also decided to devote more time to providing teachers with information from 'experts' than to involving them in dialog and personal exploration. The discussions and assessments indicated that most of them did not have much background knowledge in multicultural education and wanted it. We had obtained funding for honoraria and transportation for consultants, so we decided to invite individuals with local and national reputations in particular areas of expertise to provide much of the training. Readers will notice disjunctures, contradictions and overlap in content, which is probably common when different people conduct a series of sessions.

Since the local student populations that were being served least well were primarily African American, Latino and low-income White, we decided to focus most attention on these groups. We also decided to focus some attention on gender, partly because it is an equity issue the teachers did not seem to be connecting to multicultural education, and partly because most of the teachers were women and we reasoned that they could draw parallels between their experiences with sexism and other forms of discrimination. We also included a strand on 'teachers as leaders', hoping that the participating teachers might disseminate what they were learning in their own buildings.

There were limitations that we acknowledged from the beginning. The staff development was not school-based; sessions took place in the staff development center and involved teachers from eighteen different schools. It had administrative support only to the extent that the district administration approved the project and building principals allowed their teachers to use the release days; actual principal support varied widely and we had no authority to make sure that teachers were using new skills in the classroom, nor had we resources to help them do so.

The Staff Development Sessions

The schedule of sessions is shown in table 4.1. Each full-day session lasted from 8.30 a.m. to 3.00 p.m., with a lunch break of about forty-five minutes, and fifteen minute breaks in the morning and afternoon. The after-school sessions lasted from 3.30 p.m. to 6.00 p.m. Teachers evaluated each full-day session on a 1–5 scale (1 = low, 5 = high); they were asked to rate the extent to which the session provided new information, was relevant, useful and practical, and changed their attitudes in a positive direction; they were also asked to give the session an overall rating. Space was provided for written comments.

Table 4.1: Schedule of sessions the first year

Full-Day Session #1:	Introduction, Assessment of Interests
Full-Day Session #2:	Building Home-School Partnerships
After-School Session #1:	Star Power
Full-Day Session #3:	Race, Ethnicity, Social Class and Gender in Society
Full-Day Session #4:	Ethnic Learning Styles and Racism Awareness
Full-Day Session #5:	Community Resources
After-School Session #2:	Discussion
Full-Day Session #6:	Working With Curriculum and Instruction
After-School Session #3:	Teachers as Leaders
Full-Day Session #7:	Cooperative Learning
Full-Day Session #8:	Library Resources for Multicultural Education
Full-Day Session #9:	Drop-Out Prevention Programs, Motivation and Self-Esteem and Sharing

Building Home-school Partnerships

The second session opened with a talk by the African American principal of a predominantly African American, low-income elementary school; she discussed the importance of working with low-income parents and difficulties teachers must anticipate when doing so. She described the disintegration of family life and deficiencies of education in urban areas, pointing out that most urban Black families have not experienced quality education and cannot be worked with as if they had. She stressed that low-income families are busy addressing survival needs and often do not provide the kinds of support for education that teachers expect. Further, many do not trust school people. Teachers should demand structure and discipline from children since many do not get it at home, but should accompany their demands with love. Her talk carried a cultural deficiency analysis of low-income families in that she urged teachers to assume that 'parents know nothing and go from there'.

Teachers then viewed a videotape by an African American educator who discussed various forms of racial discrimination such as disproportionate rates of referral to special education and school suspension and adult unemployment. He discussed parents' rights and responsibilities in their child's education, such as rights to visit the school and to challenge interpretations of the child's behavior and responsibilities to provide a proper diet for children and discipline them.

After a break, the session continued with a panel of parents: an African American parent who had worked as a teacher's aide and was now enrolled in a pre-service teacher education program; a Mexican-American parent who worked as a professional in one of the school districts; and Susan (one of the project directors), who had a son who was half Thai and half White, and had been a single parent for several years. They described their own personal experiences with schools, emphasizing stereotyping and low-expectations they had encountered and the need for teachers to inform them immediately of problems rather than waiting. The African American parent emphasized that teachers should not worry about what occurs in her home, pointing out that she provides the emotional support her children need and expects the teachers to concern themselves with academic instruction. This provoked an outburst from some of the teachers who argued that they need to know what goes on at home because it affects the child.

After lunch, coordinators of federally funded projects in one of the districts discussed how their offices work with parents. Then a principal shared many concrete ideas she had developed over the years. She explained that she had begun as a poorly informed but idealistic middle class White woman, and had learned through trial and error many effective ways to link the home with school. She described procedures she had used, sharing materials children made to send home, projects advertising to parents what is happening in the classroom, folders teachers can send home with children for specific parent responses, and so forth.

The teachers spent the last part of the session in small groups brainstorming strategies they would try using, which were compiled onto a fairly long master list that later was sent to all of them. The main strategies they discussed were positive and informative phone calls and notes home, awards and illustrations of student progress (capitalizing on ideas shared by the last speaker), having an open door policy in which parents are always welcome to visit, holding parent conferences and issuing special invitations to parents and grandparents, and sending home projects with students that would engage their parents' help for completion. At the conclusion of the session, they were given some handouts one of the school districts had produced on 'The Year of the Family in Education', which explained what The Year of the Family was and summarized quotations from research providing evidence that 'Parent Involvement Works'. One also reported on a research study that concluded that:

> American school children are falling behind their counterparts in Japan and China. Part of the reason could be that Asian parents expect more hard work of their children and help their children more with their work.

The stereotype here that Asians work hard (and by implication other groups do not) was not critiqued. Nor was the ideology of cultural deprivation directly challenged except by the parent panelists, who were all college educated and not among those generally considered culturally deprived.

Teachers gave this session an average overall rating of 4.28, with the lowest rating (3.2 average) given to newness of information. In interviews later, some said they did not see the parent panel as representing parents of their students:

> I had a hard time relating to what they were saying. . . . I am talking about the parent that doesn't care, you know, doesn't help, spend

time with their kids, doesn't come to the school and be a part of their child's education. (9 February 1988)

OK, we had the thing on parent involvement. Who did they have? A Black and a Spanish and that just really kind of irked me because you know there's the White woman who is single who is kind of in the minority, and there's just other groups. . . . More and more fathers are coming to help teachers. (4 December 1988)

In addition, the session had not allowed teachers to express their own needs and frustrations or to talk about what they had tried. As passive recipients of information who were not invited to unload their own concerns first, some teachers tuned most of it out.

Star Power

We preceded the third session with an after-school session that would introduce the concept of oppression and illustrate how oppressive social relationships are continually recreated in the context of a diverse population. For this purpose, the simulation 'Star Power' (Shirts, 1969) was used, which provides a good basis for a radical structuralist analysis of society.

In this simulation participants are divided into three groups and play a trading game, the purpose of which is to compete in the accumulation of points. The game is rigged so that one group continues to accumulate more than the rest, but they are led to believe their success is due to their skill. Part way through the game, the top group (the Squares) is given power to make rules for the rest of the game; the Squares usually use this power to further their own advantage and the other two groups react in a variety of ways to their powerless position.

As the teachers participated in the trading game, they followed the behavior patterns groups usually follow. The Squares abused their power when told they could set rules for the rest of the game; the middle group (Circles) continued to play fairly passively; and the lower group (Triangles) engaged in a group strategy for passive resistance.

The discussion following the simulation is crucial because it helps participants move from their own particular experiences with the game to broader issues of social behavior and social structure which the simulation illustrates. On this afternoon, the discussion ran short on time and the teachers, already tired from a full day of teaching, ran short on attention. Some teachers made good general observations about abuse of power and collective strategies to resist power, but few specific links to American society. Two male teachers engaged in a heated discussion about Congress, law-making, and power; most of the other teachers by this point looked tired and interested more in the personal fireworks than the issues being discussed.

Some teachers commented afterward that the session helped them think about how power is used, but others found it not too helpful. They thought the game was 'light and fun' (9 February 1988), but also 'drawn out' (24 February 1988) and 'too slow or too long' (22 February 1988). One said she was not sure the larger social system really works like the trading game and that in the follow-up discussion, 'We sort of got off the track' when the 'two guys' got into 'whatever they were discussing' (23 February 1988).

Race, Ethnicity, Social Class and Gender in Society

The third all-day session, held two days later, began with a two-hour multi-media presentation by the Director of Planning Information and Research in one of the districts. His presentation focused on changing demographics in the United States and locally, and some implications this has for how Americans view ourselves. The presentation was packed with statistical information, and drew heavily on television advertising and popular media to illustrate intergenerational interdependence and the hopes and dreams for a better life that diverse Americans share. The statistical information and general thrust were based on the work of Harold Hodgkinson (1985).

Next, a White university professor contrasted Euro-American and African American struggles for assimilation and success in the United States. His talk specifically addressed the question: if White ethnic groups 'made it', why are Americans of color and particularly African Americans not following the same pattern? He discussed a variety of factors, including changes in the economic structure over the last 100 years, differences between the experiences of slavery and immigration, and racism.

After lunch, another White university professor addressed the 'girl-unfriendly' classroom (which someone later accidently transposed as 'un-friendly girls in the classroom', to the amusement of the group). She discussed research on attributions of success, pointing out that boys learn to attribute success to their efforts while girls learn to attribute it to luck. She then discussed teacher-student interaction patterns that reinforce these attributions.

About an hour was available for large-group discussion. The teachers talked mainly about sexism, reacting to points made by the most recent speaker. Lee, one of the White men, argued some quite conservative ideas about sex roles (for example, men and women are innately different; women with children should stay at home rather than holding a job), which provoked lively rebuttal by the women. For the last half-an-hour, teachers viewed a videotape on bilingualism which stressed the changing nature of American society, argued that command of standard English is more important today than it was during earlier waves of European immigration and argued that bilingual education helps children acquire standard English.

Teachers rated the session highly, giving it an overall rating of 4.5. Several teachers took copious notes and requested copies of overheads. They described the morning speakers as 'excellent', 'very, very good' and 'helpful', although some commented that they had heard the first presentation before. A male technical education teacher said for years he had been trying to eliminate sexist language from his materials, but had never thought about needing to continue to work on his own awareness of sexism.

All of the presentations had taken a liberal perspective toward social inequality in that they tacitly accepted the goal of free competition among individuals and focused on barriers to competition that should be addressed: language competence of immigrants, messages teachers give students and economic conditions. They also gave more attention to demographic and job market changes than to the persistent nature of racial and class oppression. There was no discussion connecting Star Power with any of the presentations because, since we had not heard the presentations before, we did not plan one; and each speaker used his/her entire allotted time leaving relatively little time for discussion. As a result, teachers were left to process the experience on their own or with colleagues in their buildings.

Ethnic Learning Styles and Racism Awareness

One week later, the fourth all-day session was held. The first three hours were devoted to the topic 'Creating a Culturally Compatible Classroom'. The facilitator, an African American university professor, introduced the topic with a presentation on achievement and learning and how culture affects information processing strategies. She then involved the teachers in a 'right brained' exercise in which they drew their ideal classroom using crayons and newsprint. After teachers shared their drawings, the facilitator discussed cognitive styles among children from racial minority groups, especially African American children, and how their styles conflict with most classrooms. She then contrasted synergetic with analytic perceptual, communication, thinking, and interaction styles (see chapter 3). She argued that schools are geared toward styles preferred by individuals of European origin; however, most students of color, as well as gifted students, prefer the opposite style. She pointed out, for example, that many African American children find a bright, colorful classroom stimulating and a blandly colored classroom dull. She discussed the need for multisensory approaches to teaching; she pointed out the importance of interpersonal relationships and social cues to many students, particularly racial minority students. As she talked, several teachers questioned the connection between culture and cognitive style and her recommendations for teaching students of color. But most described her later as 'very informative', 'helpful' and full of 'concrete ideas'. The teachers requested another session with her.

After lunch, a panel of three professional women of color (African American, Mexican American, Japanese American) discussed their own personal experiences with racism as they grew up, such as wanting to turn

White, feeling shunned by their White peers and being stereotyped by professional educators and treated accordingly. The teachers were quiet and attentive as they talked. In the short time available for discussion, a few questions were raised, but most teachers looked tired by that point. However, during the second interview, several teachers commented on the impact this panel made on them, saying things such as 'It's unbelievable that this would happen, but I guess it really does' (9 February 1988). Teachers in the same age range as the panelists (mid to late thirties) were especially affected, commenting that their own school experience was taking place at the same time, and they had no idea these things were happening. As one put it:

> I have more empathy for what they went through, you know, I grew up during that time, their age was just very similar to mine, and, you know, some of these things that were going on that took place while I was growing up, and you never saw that. I lived during that time, I, you know, where was I, what was I doing during that time? (9 February 1988)

Teachers were given a copy of a newspaper article to take with them about the burden of 'acting White' based on an interview with an African American administrator. This session received very high ratings, averaging 4.8 overall. Teachers rated it as particularly useful and practical.

Community Resources

The following week, teachers in groups of ten visited community agencies serving low-income and racial minority residents to learn more about the needs they serve. These visits took place on three different days (one group each day). Each group visited three of the following sites: the Adult Learning Center at the local technical college, a Spanish Center (serving mainly the Latino community), a community center (serving mainly African American youth), the Fair Housing Council and an alternative high school's program for pregnant students and students with children. At each site, there was a short formal presentation by a staff person, time for questions, time for teachers to tour the site, and usually time for them to talk with clients using services there. Teachers had an hour on their own for lunch and a short debriefing session at the end of the day.

Most of the teachers commented later that they had found these visits very interesting and beneficial. The White teachers generally commented that they had not been aware of services these agencies provide or their involvement with schools, particularly tutoring programs. (One teacher subsequently spent considerable time getting a student to begin attending the Spanish Center for tutoring.) Several mentioned being appalled at the number of illiterate adults in the community who were being served by the Adult Learning Center. The teachers of color said that they were familiar with the agencies, but believed it was valuable for white teachers to 'see and understand just what is out there, the problems that the minorities have' (24 February 1988).

A few teachers criticized the visits but appreciated the chance to vent their feelings with colleagues over lunch. For example, one believed he had mainly encountered people looking for excuses for problems they had created, and another mentioned someone at a community center 'harranguing the school system, we didn't need to hear' (24 February 1988). Still another was disappointed that the people in the Spanish Center talked more about their difficulties providing community service than about 'how Hispanic kids function in a community' (25 February 1988).

This session had a liberal bias in that the agencies conceptualized the problems their clients experienced as resulting mainly from lack of access to resources. Subsequent sessions implicitly accepted the same premise; focusing on instruction in the classroom, they suggested changes that should be made to improve access to instruction for inner-city students.

Discussion

About four weeks later was another after-school session. It had two purposes: for me to share findings from the first classroom observation and for the teachers to discuss their experiences thus far with multicultural teaching strategies. To facilitate discussion, elementary teachers met one day and secondary teachers another.

My presentation to both groups was the same. Using overheads, I shared data compiled from the first observation, much as it has been reported in chapter 3. The elementary group was fairly responsive as I talked, occasionally nodding or asking questions. They discussed at some length whether Christmas artifacts such as Santa Claus and decorated trees are religious symbols; several maintained that they are not, although the staff development center director, who is Jewish, at one point entered the room and firmly declared that from her perspective they are. The secondary group was more passive as I talked; the main point that provoked discussion was whether teaching strategies such as simulation can be used in most secondary subject areas, or whether they might be appropriate mainly to the elementary grades. One teacher later told me that she and the other teachers she rode with had been very confused by the numbers on my overheads and did not know what I was talking about.

Janie:	We didn't discuss much, you know, because we just all agreed that we were kind of wondering what that all showed and everything.
Interviewer:	Oh, I wish you would have asked me.
Janie:	Well, we didn't want to make it any longer than we had to, I guess. (15 September 1988)

In both groups I then distributed an instrument for analyzing textbooks (Grant and Sleeter, 1989, pp. 104–9) and one for examining various facets of the school for bias (a similar instrument is in *ibid*, pp. 155–7). I explained how to use these, and asked teachers to analyze one of their textbooks before the next all-day session and come prepared to discuss what they found. Teachers then were supposed to discuss with one or two other colleagues what multicultural teaching strategies they had tried, what they would like to try, and what problems they forsaw. However, most either leafed through the instruments I had given them or talked about other things that had recently happened in their schools.

Working with Curriculum and Instruction

The consultant on ethnic learning styles was invited back for the morning of the sixth session. She presented a great deal of information, spending less time on activities and more on formal presentation than the first time. She reinforced her basic argument that 'Anybody can learn anything at anytime, given the time and motivation', and that success for all learners is a matter of style (research used in this presentation can be found in Shade, 1989). She reviewed basic elements of culture, focusing mainly on worldview and perceptual organization. She then described and contrasted the worldview, basic values and psychobehavioral modalities of European and African Americans and then described cognitive style characteristics of Native Americans, Mexican Americans and Asian Americans. She also discussed motivation and power thinking, the importance of positive reinforcement, teacher involvement with students and use of research on information processing. Throughout, she emphasized specific changes that should be made in classrooms in order to make them culturally compatible with the cognitive styles of students of color. Lee, a White male elementary teacher, disagreed with many of her ideas, seeing them as excuses for people not trying and tried to debate them with her. At first she responded to him, but finally told him she did not have time to finish her presentation and debate with him as well.

Later that day I asked her how she thought the session was; she said she was not sure, she saw a lot of pain in teachers' faces. Evaluations immediately after the session were mixed; some found it excellent, some did not and felt she put teachers down. Lee believed that she was racist, and another White teacher thought she was 'hostile toward Whites' (15 March 1988). However, in interviews most of the teachers' comments were positive. They said the session had been 'the most helpful thing over the past couple of months' (29 May 1988), 'interesting' (13 May 1988) and 'real good' (27 May 1988). One who had found the session stressful and painful at the time remarked later:

Interviewer: She (the presenter) talked to me afterwards, she liked working with the group, but she said, . . . she saw a lot of pain on the people's faces.

Anne:	Yes, I was one. I had a real bad day, the day I talked to her. I mean, I couldn't think of anything positive that I did. I just zeroed in on what she was saying and picked out things that I had done and I could not . . . zero in on the positive things that I do with kids. It was real depressing. I was exhausted from the experience.
Interviewer:	But how did it turn out to be helpful, because it sounds like that would be really frustrating and hurtful?
Anne:	Well, I realized what she was saying was not picking at me as a person, but only trying to help me. (13 May 1988)

After lunch, Susan distributed copies of a handbook entitled *Educating for Cultural Understanding* that had been developed by a committee of teachers in the two school districts. It had numerous lesson plans and teaching ideas, coded for their applicability to various grade levels and subject areas. It also had a list of resources for teachers and a multicultural calendar which labeled each day of the year with some holiday, event, or birthday related to a non-White cultural group, women, or a foreign country. Teachers were also given two handouts: an article arguing that the shrinking middle class and shrinking White population mean that society needs low-income children and children of color to be educated well (Hodgkinson, 1988) and a newspaper article discussing 'skills of tomorrow', such as planning, analytical thinking, interpersonal skills and creativity.

Then, an African American teacher educator from a local educational lab led a session on making the curriculum multicultural. He began by describing the history of multicultural education since the 1960s. He then asked the teachers what they had found in their analysis of textbooks, which they had been asked to do at the previous after-school session. One said she had looked at an elementary math book, and was surprised at how little had changed since publishers began to make textbooks multicultural and how many people were of ambiguous racial membership. 'Is this person Hispanic, or tan from Florida, or Italian? You can't tell.' She said she counted ten pages in which all the people were White, then there was a Black child. 'You could go for days with only Whites, then — there's my picture.' She asked whether this was being taken into consideration when textbooks are adopted; another teacher replied that it is, she had been on a textbook adoption committee three days ago.

Since no one else volunteered to talk, the consultant proceeded, describing steps in 'multiculturalizing' one's existing curriculum. His steps were quite specific and his talk was directed toward the process of curriculum revision rather than what content to put into it. Then three more teachers shared what they had found analyzing their textbooks: two were quite critical, but one thought her second grade book showed all groups except Latinos well and was quite integrated. The consultant then discussed resources teachers can use to make the curriculum multicultural, passing out some newsletters and mentioning some specific resources that are accessible to teachers. He described a variety of ideas to get students involved with material, such as debates, book comparisons and projects. At this point, he was running over the time, having thought the session lasted until 3.30; when he realized it was supposed to end at 3.00, he rapidly concluded (cutting short his discussion).

Comments immediately following his talk were positive; one teacher appreciated feeling that he stroked teachers rather than putting them down. But in interviews a month or two later, few teachers commented on the substance of his discussion. The few comments were either positive or critical of his repetition of material from previous sessions. It seemed as though most of the teachers did not quite catch the point of his talk. One said,

> He didn't finish his presentation, that's still, it's left hanging, I think. . . . Several things kind of fade off into the woodwork. . . . We looked at materials and I guess materials could be something that you could put into the lunch hour or put into the last half hour, fifteen minutes or something. (6 May 1988)

Evaluations for the day as a whole were mixed. The average overall rating was 4.1, but a few teachers rated its newness, relevance, and usefulness in the 1–2 range, which was low.

Teachers as Leaders

About one month later the third after-school session was held. Its purpose was to have teachers envision schools differently and to consider their own role as leaders in school reform. The elementary teachers met one day and the secondary teachers the next. I took notes on the meeting with the secondary teachers; the facilitator said it was similar to that with the elementary teachers.

The facilitator opened the discussion by asking, 'If you could change structural features of schools, what would you change?' Several ideas were suggested, such as going on double shift, teaching job skills more effectively to those who are about to drop out and making schools smaller so that students and teachers can get to know one another. The facilitator then asked what the teachers would do if all the district's resources for a school went unspent to that school and teachers could decide how to allocate and use resources. She emphasized that teachers should 'think outside the existing box' defining how schools are structured: 'You can't put bandaids on the same old structure.' One teacher talked about the importance of bottom-up decision-making; he would create a board of directors for the school that would comprise teachers, students, the administration (which would have one vote) and community members. Several teachers suggested decisions teachers should be able to make, but the discussion did not probe or develop their ideas. Teachers then began discussing constraints to teacher decision-making. 'The courts tie our hands more and more until it stifles creativity.' 'The school board. . . . We (alternative high school) had too much power and they didn't want us to use it.' 'The union. When our principal taught a class in (city), the (teacher's union) filed a grievance.' Teachers also discussed time and the volume of work there is to do; they then had a rousing discussion about differences in time structure between elementary and secondary schools, since one elementary teacher was attending this session.

The facilitator emphasized the importance of having a vision of where one is going with school change. Two teachers then discussed how their peers had reacted when they talked with their faculty as a whole about multicultural education, one commenting on how rude some faculty members were. The facilitator passed out an article on leadership skills and asked for reactions. Several teachers emphasized the importance of collaborating and networking with each other. They also talked about how to confront co-workers constructively and about building their own confidence. Then the facilitator asked teachers to identify the skills with which they felt least comfortable; these would be the skills that need work. Later one teacher commented that this had been 'the most important session' of the program for him because it helped him crystalize many concerns and frustrations he had about schooling.

In retrospect this was the only session to address authority and power in schools directly. The teachers' discussion indicated that most of them were not used to viewing teachers as decision-makers outside their classrooms, since they did not get beyond suggesting areas in which they would like to have input and listing constraints to their authority. It would have been useful to have given them time to vent their sense of powerlessness, seriously explore avenues for learning to exert power collectively, then relate these issues to student and community power.

Cooperative Learning

Later that week the seventh all-day session was held. Since several teachers had been grumbling about various aspects of the program, we decided to provide time for them to air their feelings. For the first two hours of the morning, two discussion groups were held in different parts of the building and teachers could participate in the one they wished. One group aired frustrations or feelings about the program itself. About half of the teachers participated; what they said is discussed later in this chapter. The other group shared multicultural activities they had tried; what they were doing is discussed in the next chapter.

The facilitator for cooperative learning was a White university professor in a neighboring state. She began with a discussion of what cooperative learning is and what it tries to accomplish. She then spent the rest of the day, with a break for lunch, involving teachers in cooperative learning activities, talking after each one about its uses in the classroom. One activity was a small group problem-solving game in which clues were given to group members who had to share their clues to solve the problem. Another activity involved teachers lining up in order of their birthdays without talking; she discussed its application to sequencing tasks. Still another activity involved the whole group in a cooperative matching game which could be used as a drill activity in virtually any subject area (for example, matching addition problems with answers). She also discussed how to make competitive activities cooperative, and distributed handouts containing several cooperative learning activities designed mainly for the elementary level.

Teachers left this session very enthusiastic, rating it an average of 4.9. They gave it rave reviews later in interviews. Several commented that it had been the most helpful session of the entire program. They found the facilitator 'excellent' and 'enthusiastic'. Some teachers said they now had a better idea of what cooperative learning is and several said they appreciated the hands-on experience and specific ideas she had given them.

Library Resources for Multicultural Education

About three weeks later a session was held in the university library, exploring resources teachers could use for multicultural education. The intent was to provide time and guidance in a library for teachers to look for material that would help them 'develop a lesson plan or answer a problem related to multicultural, non-sexist education' (agenda, 11 November 1988). A White university professor facilitated this session.

He began by having teachers discuss and identify topics of most interest to them so far or that they would like to learn more about and areas in their curriculum they would like to re-work from a multicultural perspective. He then spent about two hours acquainting them with resources in the library, especially the computerized retrieval system. He gave them handouts about these sources as well as a state pamphlet on resources for 'children at risk'. Then teachers were on their own for about four hours; he helped them as needed. They met during the last hour to share what they had found.

Only two teachers specifically looked for material they could use in their own curriculum: one found information about ethnic holidays and the other found ten books she could use on Latino and Indian history. Several teachers looked for resources on cooperative learning, but they spent more time finding the right descriptors for a computer search and learning to use the retrieval system than they spent with resources on cooperative learning; those who had located materials passed them around for others who wanted the citations. Other teachers sought or stumbled upon resources on a wide variety of topics: characteristics of effective teachers, ethnographic studies of student culture, Arab Americans, learning disabilities, Black family life, divorce and drop-outs.

They gave the session an overall rating of 4.1. Later in interviews, several teachers commented on how interesting this session had been. One captured the feeling of most when she said:

Going to the library was just a real eye-opener for me. I had no idea that the card catalog is obsolete. This has nothing to do with multi-cultural, but I was really interested to see how the library is now. (17 May 1988)

Another explained that she had spent two hours at the computer getting dead-ends; the consultant had seemed frustrated because she was not finding anything, but she found the experience valuable because she had a better sense of resources at her disposal and how to access them. Six teachers later specifically commented that this session should have taken place earlier so they could have used the library for projects over the year.

Drop-out Prevention Programs, Motivation and Self-esteem and Sharing

The last session of the year was a potpouri responding to teachers' interests. The first speaker was a White teacher from a nearby urban school district; her areas of expertise were bilingual education and drop-out prevention. She described the high school drop-out prevention program in which she worked, as well as research on characteristics of effective drop-out prevention programs. She stressed that poor school attendance predicts who will drop out, and that retention does not seem to help. What does help is personalized support and tutoring in which students are taught study skills and helped with specific plans for post-graduation; she emphasized a college focus in planning.

After a break, two African American men from the Future Bound Youth Program for inner-city youth discussed strategies they were using to build motivation and self-esteem in young people. The strategies involved having young people create a positive and ambitious self-image, select heroes and role models that support that image, learn to communicate effectively, learn to resist peer pressure and gangs, learn to handle anger, get out of the ghetto whenever possible and expect to pay dues through hard work.

A potluck lunch followed. The teachers each brought a dish that represented their own ethnic backgrounds; the table was overflowing with Norwegian pancakes, German salads and hot dishes, greens, chicken, a fruit salad in a sombrero and several desserts. While people ate, Susan showed a slide tape she had made from photographs of all the teachers in their classrooms with students, set to Jackson Browne's recording 'You Are a Friend of Mine'.

After lunch, those who wished to share something they had done in their classroom during the year were invited to do so. Six teachers brought something to share. Betty, an elementary teacher, described the coat of arms project her class had done and brought examples students had made; she also shared a finger print art project. A technical education teacher had developed a 'happygram' to send home with students praising them for good work and a letter to send home letting parents know how they could support his work in the classroom; he passed out copies. Frances, an elementary teacher, described her 'Christmas Around the World' project, a walking field trip of the local city in which students investigated its history and constructed a class book based on it, her class's 'Constitutional Rap' (described in chapter 5) and a cooperative learning activity she tried unsuccessfully. Lorraine, another elementary teacher, described a unit for teaching students to use a data base on the computer, into which she had infused multicultural content. The art teacher described two art projects, one involving West African designs and another based on Native American totem poles (described in chapter 5). Finally, Beverly, a special education teacher, described a poetry-writing lesson she had done with her ED students; one student's poem and one class's poem had been published in a student magazine, which had made the students very proud.

Teachers left with several handouts and articles about the need for everyone to complete as a high a level of education as possible, drop-out prevention programs, and programs for 'children at risk'. In the confusion of good-byes and cleaning up, we forgot to distribute evaluation forms.

What Teachers Learned

In both the second and third interviews, I asked teachers what they had been learning in the staff development sessions. Most emphasized that they found them helpful and worthwhile. Several described them with unqualified enthusiasm; for example:

> It has been much more helpful than I thought it would be. . . . I didn't really go into it with a real lot of enthusiasm or even a particular interest, to be very honest. . . . But it's been a very worthwhile experience, and I think that I've grown as a person, and hopefully as a teacher because of it. (19 May 1988)

Another teacher was asked to write an article for a local newspaper about the project. Her introduction captured her sentiment:

> Disturbed. Agitated. Overwhelmed. Depressed. Impressed. Inspired. Rededicated. That's what it's like to be a multicultural fellow at the Regional Staff Development Center. I've run the whole gamut — most of my feelings unexpected when I applied for the fellowship. (Center Exchange, May 1988)

She went on to describe the depression she felt at first when hearing about the magnitude of failure in our system, but her later inspiration and rededication as she learned 'practical suggestions on how to teach'.

Becoming More Aware

The first stage of growth for teachers in multicultural education is awareness (Grant and Melnick, 1978). The words the teachers used most often to describe what they were learning reflected this. In the second interview, twelve teachers used the term 'more aware' or 'increased awareness' for example reporting that they had gained 'an increased awareness of the concerns that I already knew' (19 March 1988), 'an increased awareness of Asians' (15 March 1988), 'awareness of so much despair that's already there that I was not aware of' (28 February 1988). Most of the teachers who said they had become 'more aware' were White. However, one of the African American teachers observed:

> You tend to assume that you know everything about Black folks, you tend to assume that you know everything about the kids you teach, because being a Black man, I assumed that I knew a lot and I was very aware of everything, but the program seems to help me focus in on some things that made me much more aware of things that I didn't really consider in my teaching. (28 February 1988)

As the year progressed, teachers focused increasingly on topics of interest to them. The main areas they described having learned more about were differences among students and student learning styles, racism in society, cooperative learning, curriculum, problems in the institution of schooling and increased personal sensitivity.

Most teachers discussed having become more aware of student characteristics. Some gained tolerance for particular student behaviors, such as talking while working or touching each other. For example:

> A situation like Pedro today talking with another kid in class, or helping another kid. I might have gotten on his case for talking earlier, but this idea of the interaction, or when that kid was talking Spanish in the hall, I probably would have gone off on that before. It has made me a lot more tolerant of the fact that, you know, they need to band together. (24 February 1988)

> It kind of answers some questions as to why do I have certain students who can't seem to stay in their seats and pay attention. . . . And why I have some that are a little bit more, you know, quiet and withdrawn. It kind of answers a few of those questions. It doesn't always help me to know exactly what to do with them, but at least I have a little better understanding. (17 May 1988)

Teachers said they noticed things or empathized better with students' feelings. For example:

> I had a Vietnamese in the afternoon class and he came with a button for the Chinese New Years, a dragon and I took time and really talked about it and you could just see his self-esteem rising, I mean, I am important, and I guess in the past I may have said something to him but wouldn't have called attention to it, to the whole group. (23 February 1988)

A few teachers became more aware of the importance of students' racial and peer group membership:

> The three speakers that came and shared their experiences with us mentioned how once they started pulling away from the group, either they became very, very alone, or they had to make all new friends. And yesterday at the 'Year of the Family' event, there was a gentleman who . . . was saying just an echo of this whole idea. What can we do to help the kids who do achieve, and I guess, then we have to get the whole group achieving more, so that they move together. (3 March 1988)

Awareness of students' characteristics can enable a teacher to maintain high expectations and teach more effectively, but this is not always the case. An elementary teacher discussed becoming better able to identify 'high risk' students who subsequently fail:

> I became very aware of the future school problems, you know, and some of the children whose needs weren't being met either in the home or in the school. I could see where the high risk students were coming from and how, you know, I could identify them even back in fourth grade and see that this is where they may probably end up, you know, because they're coming from those same problems. (18 May 1988)

Most teachers talked about becoming more aware of their students' learning styles, and particularly students' preference to work with others. For example:

> I remember the first time that I heard that different kids of different cultures learned in different ways, it made me remember and think about how some of my kids would be reacting in class sometimes, you know, where they would be helping each other and in a couple of instances where kids may have just been helping each other instead of copying, I concluded that they were copying, or cheating. (28 February 1988)

Five teachers said that a speaker's ideas about color and learning style reinforced what they already do. For example:

> Now I've always used a lot of color, but that had always been my
> personal thing, even though with training in LD they always told us,
> have a dull room, no jewelry and all this other stuff. I couldn't live
> with it that way, and I've never found it being a problem in my room,
> and I do like a lot of color, so that kind of reinforced, or took away
> some of the guilt I feel. (15 March 1988)

A special education teacher found information about learning style to connect directly with her training in a multisensory teaching procedure; she concluded: 'Stuff that I really do need to stress and I was doing it a little more, but I hadn't thought it was multicultural' (6 May 1988). One teacher made an insightful observation about the link between learning style and student achievement. His principal had expressed concern about the number of failing grades students were receiving and wanted to reduce student failure by instituting an after-school study program, but believed that, 'It is our teaching techniques that should be changed or modified, (or) our contact with home and parents should be more effective' (15 February 1988).

I was surprised that few teachers discussed having become more aware of concerns of parents. The teacher who taught in the parent-child pre-school program was the main one to discuss having gained sensitivity to low-income parents. She said that one of the session facilitators:

> ... pointed out that culture is more than just the racial groups that
> we thought we had to deal with, it's also low income families, and I
> honestly hadn't thought about that. (4 May 1988)

She struggled with deciding which behaviors from parents she should accept and which she should try to change, but tried to view things from their perspective and 'stop being so critical of them' (4 May 1988).

One-third of the teachers discussed having developed an increased awareness of racism. The White teachers expressed surprise, frustration and even anger at hearing about it, as the following quotations illustrate.

> I didn't realize how many problems there are, how much we do have,
> I mean, you think you're progressing real well and you're being more
> open to the needs of the students, and then you hear these things,
> and you think, wow, what else can I do here. (23 February 1988)

> I am wrestling with the last two sessions ... where the women's issue
> was brought up, and also the issue of the Blacks. From my standpoint,
> I left those two meetings so depressed because, I started teaching in
> the '60's when we were told to instill pride in these people, treat

them as adults, I'm speaking now of Blacks, women, you know . . . I've walked away from those meetings thinking I've wasted twenty-five years now, and I got shot down again, and once again, as a teacher, it's my fault . . . I thought we were doing well. (22 February 1988)

The stereotype thing, you know, well, other cultures have made it, why are the Blacks not doing it? You get this type of question which I've heard all my life, and I've always agreed with it more or less, and never really sat down and thought about the history. (9 February 1988)

The visit to neighborhood centers and community agencies had sensitized them to discrimination and to the work of community agencies that combat it:

I guess I had my eyes opened a little bit with the lady from Fair Housing Administration, . . . I guess we're still dealing with things that I just simply thought were sort of taken care of, that was an eye-opening experience. (10 March 1988)

One White teacher who had described racism and sexism as attitudinal problems in the second interview, by the third interview had constructed the beginnings of a radical structural analysis:

(I'm) seeing basically how our system is set up, the value system our whole society is set up on. And it makes me feel like we are here because of a lot of suffering. We are here where we are today. And that's very sad. It didn't need to be that way, but a lot of people have suffered to bring us the affluence that we have. . . . I think kids need to get this perspective. They need to start getting some perspective about where they are and where they came from. (19 May 1988)

For university credit she read several pieces of literature and poetry by African American writers and developed a unit for teaching African American literature. In her final paper, she wrote:

Many cultures and governmental systems have been established on the idea that some people were meant to rule and live in luxury and some were meant to serve and live in poverty and suffering.

Her own experience as a special education teacher had bred anger at how the education system treats students assigned to her. She was angry with 'the system', but did not know what to do in response. She talked about a Mexican American student, how the system seemed set up against him, and her own sense of powerlessness to fight it:

I don't know what the answer is for him. I don't know what the answer is. But I couldn't just lie and say he's doing wonderful. I can't really treat him that much differently than I can anybody else. I can't change everything. (19 May 1988)

Five teachers said that they had become more aware of gender issues and were monitoring their own behavior in the classroom. For example:

For some reason I think I tend to call on boys more and I think I look at the girls in a different way now, you know and I don't know why, I think I've always kind of favored the boys. . . . Another thing, when I'm looking at books . . . I look at these books with a different view now and I think, Oh yeah, there are more boys. (15 March 1988)

Several teachers discussed having become more aware of curricular and instructional matters. Some said they became more aware of cooperative learning as an instructional strategy, that it requires planning and that it can build on student learning styles. A few teachers discussed having become more aware of the limitations to diversity in their curriculum. One teacher, for example, having analyzed a textbook for its treatment of different racial and gender groups, began analyzing the representation of different groups in other materials. She related an incident in which a sales representative was trying to sell her some teaching materials in which only one Black person was pictured.

Two teachers talked at length about problems in the institution of schooling, which the sessions had made them think more about. One discussed his perception of the difference between principals who manage and those who lead and the other vented her frustration with teachers who 'don't care', and their effect on students' decisions to drop out.

Kids are dropping out, yes, because of bad parents. They are also dropping out because of bad teachers who don't care. . . . The system is full, absolutely jam packed full of teachers who don't care. And, you know, I feel awful about saying that, but I have been at three different, this is my fourth school and if you can find a handful of teachers at each of those schools who are willing to work with some special ed kids! (19 May 1988)

Several teachers commented on becoming more sensitive to expressions of diversity around them, such as biased comments by other people (as well as by themselves), or materials. For example:

I'm more aware of little subtle things that I've said, and I hear others say. . . . Lee was saying, No teacher would come right out and say,

> That child is Black, I can't expect much of him. And (Frances) said, Oh, but what goes on in the lunchroom? . . . In the lunchroom, the teachers are constantly saying, Look at that family, you know, you can't expect any more of those kids. I have to remember, also, what I might say in jesting might be taken a different way by some other adult. Because I'm sure sometime or other I've said, too, Look at your name, what can I expect, I had his uncle and he was a real dingaling. (25 May 1988)

> I guess it's made me much more sensitive to not only the other cultures, but, for example, posters in my classroom have often been White Americans. I tried to use animals because I couldn't find a lot of other posters, but I'm much more conscious of it than I was. And the articles now are jumping out of the newspapers at me. (17 May 1988)

Teachers found interacting with other teachers in the staff development program particularly valuable and, for some, this was at least as valuable as the content of the sessions. They valued exchanging insights and opinions, sharing teaching ideas, sharing concerns, giving help, and sharing articles they had read. For example:

> That day that we went out to lunch I was with teachers from (name of school) and one of them is Hispanic and we talked a lot about his culture, that was interesting to me. (10 March 1988)

> What has been valuable to me has been being able to share the same problems, to see that the same problems exist not just in my building or not just in my classroom, but in the other schools. (3 March 1988)

> See, we take those little breaks, now we might throw the schedule off a little bit, but the time out there, I don't see it as *spending* time, . . . I like to *invest* that time. . . . The interaction we get in those little breaks, you know, you can pick up a lot, you know, just tidbits of things, especially when somebody relates a problem that they are having with something that was discussed in the meeting. (23 February 1988)

At the same time, when asked what should be cut in order to make more time for interaction, most could not say, reasserting that all the sessions had been good.

Resisting a Liberal Perspective Toward Inequality

Most of the sessions had a liberal orientation in that they focused on various processes in schools and the wider society that discriminate against people on the basis of culture, race and sex, and that should be changed in order to make institutions function more fairly. Over the year, about one-third of the teachers resisted this orientation, some doing so progressively more vocally. The resistance took various forms. One form was resentment toward the proportion of time they spent as receivers rather than sharers of knowledge, since they regarded some of what they were receiving as less valid than what they already knew. This was a major concern in the discussion that preceded cooperative learning. The facilitator of that discussion summarized concerns some teachers expressed:

> The group felt that, as learners, (they) have not been treated like mature, adult, experienced, intelligent professionals. . . . (F)ar too much time was spent with 'experts' talking at passive students. . . . (They) have not been provided with enough opportunity to talk to each other and to share among themselves the lessons and insights which their own experience and thinking have produced . . . (report, 29 April 1988)

They were concerned about an ideological division developing among the group. They disagreed with the liberal value premises of most of the faciltators and felt there was insufficient discussion time for them to present their own more conservative interpretations of the same topics.

> The climate of the workshops has not been conducive to open, frank, honest communication. . . . (T)hey feel that a good many thoughts and attitudes have been repressed by participating educators who are genuinely concerned and committed, but who have been afraid to disagree with the party line as portrayed by the experts. Many said that they would have preferred a more exploratory process in which many of these issues could have been examined among the Fellows themselves, rather than a process which seemed to assume the correct position on important questions. (report, 29 April 1988)

Resistance also took the form of five White teachers wanting sessions to focus on groups other than African Americans and Latinos. For example:

> To me, all of the speakers were slanted for blacks or Hispanics only, and I think that's an injustice. . . . Get Indian children, get their views as to what they feel about American playgrounds and classrooms. Get some Indian parents, Far East Indian I'm talking about, and also American Indians. (15 May 1988)

> I've had a lot on multicultural, you know, I taught in an inner city school, and we had a lot about habits of the Hispanic, habits of the Blacks, so probably that's kind of re-doing it. (24 March 1988)

I have some Arabic students that are from Jerusalem and I would like to know — Moslems, you know — I would just like to have kind of an overview.... it would be lovely to have lectures on different groups and to learn more about them and the ways they think, their religions, the kinds of foods that they eat, what difficulties they might have in the public school systems that are different from their homelands, that kind of thing. (17 May 1988)

This issue had also surfaced during the discussion in Session #7, in which some teachers,

wanted a broader conceptual scheme for 'diversity' in which issues relating to gender, social class and even life style choices would have been equally considered... including those whose 'way of life' is White, middle class and traditional.... (report, 29 April 1988)

Several teachers were troubled by challenges to the ideology of individualism. A few White teachers expressed anger at their perception that the program was teaching that culture or gender should be accepted as excuses for individual failures. They felt that they as teachers and as Whites were being blamed for other people's problems when 'some burden must be placed on the individual' (24 February 1988). For example:

I guess I finally got to the point where I thought, again, we, as the power structure, as the teachers, as the White majority, are getting blamed again.... One of the things she (Mexican-American panelist) said was, I was never invited over after school or people would have parties and I was never invited. She took it as being because she was a Hispanic.... I have not been invited to parties, but I didn't blame it on the fact that I was a Hispanic or a Black, or so on. I had to blame me, which is the worst thing in the world.... It's much easier to blame someone or some other thing, so I guess I'm refuting what they said in that area, that did bug me a lot. (22 February 1988)

From a conservative perspective, discrimination is a result of individuals treating other individuals unfairly, and one combats it by eliminating biased attitudes of individuals. An exchange between June and myself illustrates:

Interviewer: What about the White kids? Do they need to be learning any more about cultural diversity or racism?

June: (Pause, looks confused) I've never seen them overtly shut these people off — I go in with expectations, I demand.... If they (the White kids) have prejudices, probably some of them do, I tell them I won't let them manifest them, and they don't. (24 February 1988)

A month later, June questioned the relevance of multicultural education to the economics curriculum (her subject area). I suggested the possibility of teaching about discrimination through economics, but June emphatically,

> insisted that economics properly does not study people; it studies trends and statistical information, such as supply and demand curves. She said she has had her hand slapped by economists for addressing people issues. People issues are sociology, not economics. I suggested that was a philosophical conception of what economics was; she insisted I was wrong. (from field notes, 23 March 1988)

For June, discrimination was an attitudinal issue addressed by modeling and demanding accepting attitudes; it was not a social structural problem to be studied in school.

A conversation with Frances offers another example of a teacher equating discrimination with interpersonal attitudes and behaviors. She remarked that she did not see much of a problem in her building, since most of the teachers treated their students humanely and as individuals. I asked her about student achievement in her building, which she interpreted as changing the subject. She responded:

> There was one teacher who was in our building for umpteen years and has transferred to another school, she went to a suburb school, and her comment was, they are above, I mean one of our top students here went to another school and they said, she's fighting. Here she was top and there it was more competitive for her.... Basically we have more of the below level than we do of the high achievement. (9 February 1988)

I pressed her to explore why the achievement level of this school was low, whether that was a problem, and how much power the school had over students' achievement. Her responses were not very clear, but suggested that the school could do more if it had more materials and more active parent involvement and that lots of drill and repetition in the classroom seemed to produce the greatest student achievement. She did not seem to see accepting low academic expectations as discriminatory, but rather as inevitable, given the socioeconomic status of the school.

Several teachers had worked to learn to overlook race and culture, to treat students as individuals rather than acting on negative stereotypes based on their racial backgrounds. They had difficulty seeing behavior as culturally conditioned, and emphasized the importance of treating each child as an individual. They insisted, for example, that learning style 'doesn't go down to any race, I think it's basically the individual personality type thing' (9 February 1988), and insisted that teachers should, 'just take children where they are and forget their racial background' (23 February 1988).

Two male teachers resisted analyses of sexism, asserting individual choice as the best explanation for gendered patterns. For example,

Interviewer: It appears that females don't much take the technology education courses. I don't know if males take the home ec. courses (in this school). I haven't been in them at all. Do you see a gender issue there at all?

Jorge: Nope. I don't see a gender issue at all. And the reason I say that is that, let's face it, people would not take their $20,000 car to be repaired by a female mechanic. . . . I have worked with women welders in several places, and I guess that they usually don't last very long, the men are constantly laughing at what they are doing.

Interviewer: Well, is there any sex-stereotyping on the part of the men that in some way or another should be addressed?

Jorge: How can you do it? You know, these are adults on the jobs.

Interviewer: No, I mean kids who are going through —

Jorge: Oh, no. I'd like to have more girls in class, and they just don't take the class. (24 February 1988)

Resistance also took the form of teachers saying they were not learning anything they could apply. Over the year, while several said they found sessions to be practical and 'solution-oriented', others felt they were not getting many ideas they could use in their classrooms. Some viewed themselves as already doing what the program suggests.

This might sound funny, but I do most of what people are telling me. The stuff on color, brightness, I realized that a long time ago, I didn't need to be told. (24 February 1988)

(The program) just sort of emphasized things that I've already done before, Hey, that is the right type of thing to do. (7 March 1988)

If one believes one is already doing 'it', then one does not need to re-examine one's teaching. Others argued that the program emphasized broad ideas at the expense of practical application. During the discussion in Session #7, while about half of the teachers discussed things they had tried in their classrooms, some of those airing concerns believed they had not received much that was useful to them.

The program has been too theoretical. . . . Not enough time has been given to concrete, hands-on, action strategies. Many said they came to the program hoping to learn how to do some things differently and more effectively in the classroom, but that most of the time has been spent just talking or hearing about the problems. . . . (report, 29 April 1988)

By the end of the year, four teachers stated that the program had offered nothing new they could use. One was quite adamant:

> This is going to be a short interview. . . . Because of the way our classes run, because we work with first, second and third, because we're so pressed for time, you know, we really need things that are good, that will work, and that aren't a whole day experience. . . . And I know from talking among ourselves at lunch time, there are a lot of other people that are feeling the same, whether they have verbalized it or not. But it was a new year, you didn't really know where you were going or how to actually pull the speakers together or what the speakers would actually talk on. So I think we're all very understanding of that. If you do it again, I really think it would be much better if we had more concrete type things. . . . With teaching you can have all the platitudes you want, but it's when you are in that classroom and you're trying it with human beings that it makes all the difference. (22 April 1988)

Lee was the most vocal resister to ideas in the program. At each succeeding session he became increasingly outspoken, challenging ideas of presenters. Teachers tended either to side with him (some silently), or to oppose him. This is how he saw it:

> *Lee:* A lot of people are thinking and not saying, where I say many of the things that I think.
>
> *Interviewer:* How do you know what people think without —
>
> *Lee:* They've told me, and that's the important thing, 'cause I've wondered, you know, I've said to myself, like I go home shaking my head sometimes after one of my meetings there and I'll say, Gee, I don't know, why does it seem like I'm out of step with everybody there? Well, it's not that I'm out of step, but there is just a lot of people who don't voice what they're thinking. (23 February 1988)

A few teachers verified that he was saying openly what they were thinking. For example,

> He's verbalizing what many of us hold inside and I'm amazed that he's that aggressive about verbalizing it, and yet — the one day I just felt terrible, when nobody would even eat with him, and yet, he's not

saying anything that we haven't either heard or maybe thought ourselves. (15 March 1988)

Others, however, said they were becoming tired of listening to him and felt
he was trying to monopolize discussion when they were more interested in
hearing what the presenters had to say. One said,

> I'm frustrated because I don't have the guts or whatever to [inaudible]
> ... To have one person monopolize so much of the time has been
> frustrating to me. I don't know what we can do about that. . . . I hear
> very little support for what he (says), you know, . . . everybody's
> opinion seems to be I wish he'd shut up. (10 March 1988)

Probably the level of open resistance was not very strong and came from
only a few teachers, because those who chose to participate generally agreed
that children from low income and racial minority backgrounds are not being
as well served by schools as they could be and were looking for more information and strategies. Most teachers' basic perceptions about White racism, classism, and oppression versus individual mobility had not been directly
challenged.

Summary

To summarize, the staff development sessions included a wide range of topics,
but about two-thirds of them focused on strategies to improve instruction for
students of color, such as building on their learning styles, communicating
more with their parents and using cooperative learning. The sessions also
included a strong thread of racial and racism awareness, usually conceptualizing racism within a liberal framework. Social class issues received negligible
attention; sexism received a small amount, also conceptualized within a liberal
framework.

All of the teachers continued to attend sessions and most repeatedly
commented on how much they were learning. However, about one-third (all
White) expressed some difficulties with what they were hearing about race
and racism and as the year progressed, a division became apparent between
those who accepted a liberal interpretation of racism and those who adhered
to a conservative interpretation.

By the end of the year, the teachers had experienced about eighty hours
of staff development in multicultural education and seemed to be learning a
good deal. How much impact did it have on their work in the classroom? The
next chapter follows them back into the schools.

Chapter 5

Looking for Effects of
Staff Development in the Classroom

Ultimately, staff development in multicultural education should lead to changes in school and classroom processes. To what extent did it actually affect teachers' daily work in schools? That is the subject of this chapter, which synthesizes the second and third classroom observations and interviews.

Communication with Parents

In the first session, teachers had expressed a strong interest in parent involvement, which we interpreted as a desire for strategies for communicating more effectively with parents. Hence, the second session featured a panel of parents talking about their experiences with schools and hands-on strategies a former teacher had used. In interviews, I asked them to describe anything new they had tried.

About one-third of the teachers described having worked on improving home-school communication, which entailed mainly sending or phoning home positive messages, getting parents to help more with homework and looking for ways to make parents feel welcome in the building. For example:

> I do have a pretty good amount of parent involvement already, but I've made it more of a point to make sure that I do the positive phone calls and that I'm sending home the rewards and stuff. (19 February 1988)

> The kid who is doing well in the classroom, I'm really not giving them the attention that they deserve for the effort that they are putting in. So what I do now is, I have that slip [gives me one]. . . . and I just tell them verbally that this is my way of showing you that I appreciate that you are doing a real good job in the classroom, and you follow instructions and your behavior's real good. . . . Also I tell

them, this is for you to take home and have your parents sign and let them see it and see that you're doing a good job. (3 March 1988)

Two teachers wrote plans to use with open house: an ESL teacher developed strategies to bridge the language barrier between parents and the school and a special education teacher developed units for teaching parenting skills, such as dental care.

One elementary teacher, George, had already been working with his principal to develop a building-wide plan to involve parents and the staff development session had given him more ideas. Part of their plan entailed informing parents of homework assignments and asking them to sign students' homework; another part was an open gym night, which proved a success:

(Out of) twenty-two kids in my room I ended up with nineteen kids. All had to be accompanied by an adult, and I had a gym full. I had close to sixty people that night. . . . I'd see so many of the parents at an inner-city school so threatened by coming to a school because of previous bad experiences, they've come so many times and the majority of them have come because its been a poor report card or its been a behavior problem. . . . I told the kids it's not a parent-teacher conference and it's not a meeting to discuss behavior, it's a fun night. (9 June 1988)

Half-way through the year George assumed principalship of another school, where he continued to promoted parent involvement:

I stand out of the building at the beginning of the day and I talk with anybody that comes close to the building. . . . And every kid that I've had a behavior problem with, I take him home. I walk them to their house and then I talk to parents. . . . And I've already started trying to see how we can get some involvement in our PTO next year. . . . I think if they feel comfortable talking with you out here (on the sidewalk), maybe I can get them to come into the office and do some things. (9 June 1988)

George and Karen, who taught the pre-school parent-child program, sustained the most active involvement with parents over the year; their efforts were encouraged by the staff development project, but did not result from it. The ESL and special education teachers also communicated regularly with many parents, as did a few general education teachers.

At the same time, several teachers expressed frustration about parent involvement and seemed skeptical as to whether some parents could become very involved. For example:

This year's group, the parents have been very responsive, I really can't judge it because last year it was a much more diverse, I would say, multicultural type learning situation, with a lower economic type thing, and I had a very difficult time keeping them motivated enough to help the children. (29 February 1988)

It's very difficult in our school, very difficult to get parent involvement here. . . . We get wonderful attendance for Christmas concerts, anything that's non-threatening, but conferences, or come and help us, or things like that, we do have a difficult time. (15 March 1988)

Considering that parent involvement was a topic teachers had ranked as very important in the first session when they were asked to voice their own needs, relatively few had done very much more than before. Further, they mainly interpreted involvement with parents as meaning sending more, and more positive, messages from school to home, which is only one type of involvement in which schools can engage.[1]

Classroom Physical Environment

The decor in most classrooms stayed much as it had been in the first observation. The most noticeable change was in elementary classrooms, where Christmas decorations gave way to Valentine themes in February, shamrocks or spring flowers in March, then colorful April showers and May flowers. The halls of some schools were decorated with pictures of Martin Luther King, Jr. and African American themes for Black History Month in February, but this theme intruded surprisingly little on valentines inside classrooms. The other main change over the year was that teachers who hung quantities of student artwork on the walls periodically updated their displays.

The quantity and quality of decorations representing human diversity stayed much the same, although a few teachers obviously prepared displays with diversity in mind. For example, an elementary teacher put up a display entitled 'I'm Glad I'm Me' containing faces cut from magazines; she had used it in previous years, but this year she adjusted it to make it more multiracial. (I counted about equal numbers of both sexes, and about two-thirds White and one-third black faces; some pictures were small and hard to identify a racial group.) Another elementary teacher, while teaching a unit in social studies on American Indians, had a large display of about fifteen famous Native Americans (mostly male) from different tribes, and a list of Native American names for local places. Michael, the art teacher, made sure his 'Art News' bulletin board represented diverse groups. Two teachers also reported working on building-wide decorations: one put up signs in Spanish since many students and their parents spoke Spanish as their first language, and the other helped locate and put up material on Black Americans for Black History month.

Curriculum and Materials

Much of the curriculum remained similar to what was described in chapter 3: skills taught out of context of daily use. Further, about half of the teachers seemed to see making curriculum more multicultural as irrelevant. For example, a primary grade LD teacher was observed for forty-five minutes in late April. Nine students were in attendance. For the first fifteen minutes she introduced new words to the four first graders, and they practiced reading and using them. At one point a student asked, 'How come people talk different ways?'. The teacher replied, 'We're all different. Now, open your book to page 22'. She finished the lesson and sent these children back to their seats with a workbook assignment, then worked individually with another student. He read a story about a female Asian-American veterinarian. She asked him a series of comprehension questions as he finished reading each page, giving clues as needed until he would answer correctly. She then sent him back to his seat with a workbook assignment and called another student over to her. They went over a series of two-sentence passages, each followed by a comprehension question, such as 'Why did Ron get up early this morning?'. The teacher then checked other students' work, and greeted a student arriving late: 'My goodness! You missed spelling and reading today. I'll catch you up this afternoon.'

In lessons such as this, content was incidental, a backdrop for skills which in this case consisted of receiving information through print and identifying an author's literal meaning. As teachers explained in interviews, they were concerned about how to teach the required skills more effectively: the content itself was simply of much less importance.

Teachers in non-academic subject areas put more effort into making curriculum multicultural and relevant to students than did academic subject area teachers. Art, music, home economics and special education curricula were flexible and could accommodate new units, depending on teacher interest. The elementary curriculum in both districts was quite full, although some teachers found time to add lessons about family heritage or individual differences. The secondary academic content area teachers had more flexibility; how much teachers tried to make their curriculum multicultural depended mainly on interest.

Over the year about half of the teachers tried to make some of their curriculum multicultural. A few developed and taught full-blown new lessons, some of which were quite substantive. For example I watched Shari, a high school special education teacher, teach a history lesson about the development of labor unions. She described working conditions in the 1930s and obstacles workers faced in unionizing. She also described labor laws Congress passed, and some famous people involved with labor, including Frances Perkins whom Shari pointed out was the first woman Cabinet member. On another occasion, I observed her teaching a lesson about civil disobedience. She discussed terms and events of the 1960s such as freedom riders, black Muslims, non-violence and lunch counter sit-ins. She described Black leadership in the Civil Rights movement and racial riots in Watts and Detroit. Students appeared interested and their comments showed that most of this was new information to them.

Anne, a middle school home economics teacher, developed and taught an excellent unit on culture and clothing. It involved a variety of activities, such as a family history investigation, a fiber-climate matching exercise that examined the relationship between climate and clothing, a Black fashion museum and clothing vocabulary from countries around the world. Her introductory lesson about ethnicity and culture, which I observed, featured Swedish basketball cheers from her own ethnic background, which students found amusing.

Sara, a junior high special education teacher, was observed teaching a lesson about disabilities. The class read a story about a girl who lost her legs due to serious illness, got artificial legs and eventually became a physician. The discussion of the story branched out to other disabilities, such as blind people skiing. Then Sara had students write with their left hands how they would feel if they lost the use of their right hands. Students did not write much, but they reacted verbally to the assignment. On another occasion, she taught her LD students some lessons on black poets:

> I think I probably would have passed on it. For one thing, I thought poetry was a little hard for the kids. It takes so long for them to understand what it's saying. It worked out real well. I was real pleased. It was on Langston Hughes, and then it had an autobiographical section on him. But I really think I would have passed that by otherwise before. (27 May 1988)

Michael, the art teacher, showed me two art projects in which he had drawn on non-White cultural themes in order to teach art concepts:

> The first ethnic group that we used was the African culture. I laminated some pictures from my book with African designs and simply spread them out on the table and the students selected what designs they wanted to use.... The instruction was given to them that they were to use warm colors in the center and cool colors in the outer part of it, using materials of watercolors and markers so they could see the effect of what happens when you use watercolors and markers combined together.... (Then) we started doing totem poles. (I wanted) to get the kids away from just doing 2-D artwork and get them involved in 3-D artwork.... So the same process was used that was used for the African design. (13 May 1988)

He had spent time in West Africa and knew a fair amount about West African art. He included in these units information about use of color and design in West African and Northwest Indian cultures. He commented that, in the

African unit, 'Students were not that thrilled about the colors. But they were interested in knowing the meaning behind them' (1 May 1988).

An elementary teacher developed a project that drew creatively on student interest. Entitled 'The Constitutional Rap', it was a rap students wrote, produced, and videotaped about the first ten amendments to the Constitution. They also developed dance steps and made it like an M-TV video. The entire class participated, and spent time and effort polishing the production. Another elementary teacher developed and taught a social studies unit about Indian contributions (for example, names of geographic locations). I asked if she emphasized Indian contributions to Whites or to Indians, and she said mainly contributions to Whites.

Several teachers inserted new 'cultural' material into existing lessons. For example, a fifth grade teacher integrated content about famous black Americans and women into units teaching students to use a data base on a computer, but said she was having difficulty finding time to teach these units. Another fifth grade teacher taught a textbook lesson about Plains Indians, using a chapter titled 'The Last Frontier'. It described culturally different concepts of land ownership, treaties and broken treaties. Between passages which students read orally, he inserted short discussions about fishing rights disputes today, why Indians do not trust the federal government and where the nearest reservation is. On another occasion in the context of teaching health, he taught his fifth graders about some physiological differences among races, such as melanin in skin, in an effort to stop racial name-calling. A kindergarten teacher taught a lesson about individual differences in feelings, which was somewhat multiethnic but male biased. After counting in English, students counted to ten in Spanish, students were asked to interpret the feelings of a Black male in a poster, the teacher read a story about an inchworm (referred to in the book as 'he'), students sang a Hawaiian song along with a recording of a male singer, the class discussed the meaning of 'brother', then students responded to 'I'm happiest when . . .'. Another elementary teacher described a 'Christmas Around the World' unit in which students researched how Christmas is celebrated in different countries and made a classroom display about this.

Three teachers used the multicultural calendar in the handbook *Educating for Cultural Understanding*. For example, one said that, 'When a holiday comes for a student whom I know, for example a Buddhist holiday, or whatever, I'll mention that and have them talk about it a little bit if they feel free to do that' (17 May 1988). Six used lessons from that handbook or *Multicultural Teaching* (Tiedt and Tiedt, 1986). They were enthusiastic about how students had responded. For example, the home economics teacher bubbled about a lesson she taught on the family:

> The kids just ate it up. They just loved it. That one sheet in the book,
> I just drew it on a card and then I had the kids in the circles put the
> names of their family. And some said, 'Well, my mom and dad don't

live together'. But I said, 'Your mom and dad are still part of YOUR family'. So then we put mom and Larry together on one side and we put dad on the other side of the tree. But then they started, 'Can I put my mom's birthday down?' And, 'Can I put my aunts and uncles here?' 'Their favorite color is . . .' and 'Our favorite food is . . .' and 'Our things that we like to do are . . .' It was just a really neat activity. (3 March 1988)

A fifth grade teacher talked about her experience with a lesson:

We are talking a lot about their heritage and they have gone back and found all neat things that are going in their families, and now they've started bringing in recipes because we're going to make a recipe book from some recipes that have been handed down in their families. . . . It raised their whole awareness and they're really excited. . . . It's just been really involved with the whole family, that's the thing I like. (16 May 1988)

Lessons on family ethnic background can have a European bias, however, lending themselves best to Euro-American students or recent immigrants. When asked how her African American students responded to the activities, she remarked:

I only have three Black students in my room and they have not gone back further than Mississippi, and it's been, no way are they going to go back further. So that's alright, so then they have located the places in Mississippi. . . . Yeah, the one little boy said, 'We didn't come from Africa', that was the first thing he said when we started from where our ancestors came. . . . One of my little girls who is Black also has Indian blood in her background and, oh, other kids denied this and said, 'No way'. I said, 'The Black slaves escaped and went to live with the Cherokees', and so we discussed the Indians, where they lived, and then the death march when they went to Oklahoma. (16 May 1988)

For university credit, four teachers developed multicultural units to use in the future, but to my knowledge only one was ever used. The alternative high school math teacher revised and subsequently used the curriculum for a sophomore course which focused on self-exploration, career exploration and communication skills. Her revision incorporated lessons on individual differences, sex stereotyping and ethnic family background.

At the same time, several lessons contained obvious biases and some attempts to make curriculum multicultural resulted in more stereotypes and biases. The 'Christmas Around the World' unit probably taught students that virtually everyone in the world is Christian and the unit on Indian contributions to White society was biased by what White people rather than Indian people consider important. The music teacher developed a 'Children Around the World' concert that was creative but contained several stereotypes: more European countries were included than countries from any other continent, and Africa was referred to in terms of animals and Tarzan whoops. An elementary teacher taught about the four food groups; foods depicted fit a White middle class diet more than that of any other cultural or other socio-economic group, discussion of the 'meat group' did not acknowledge vegetarianism, and discussion of milk did not acknowledge that it upsets the stomachs of many African American children. The teacher of the pre-school parent-child program taught a lesson involving cutting out Easter eggs in order to teach the shape 'oval'. A parent took her aside and told her the family were Jehovah's Witnesses, so she quickly changed Easter eggs to bird eggs, and commented to me later that this lesson should be re-done to recognize religious diversity. An elementary teacher apologized for using a male-dominated story when she was being observed:

> See this sexist book? I was looking for something with a harmonica, something they can hear, then see. It had a boy playing the harmonica, and the colonel owned the whole town! I thought of taking that book and making picture cards, making Lentl a girl, having all the pictures have both sexes. But everything like that takes time. (24 March 1988)

The high school economics teacher conducted a simulation to teach about supply and demand, which championed competition and material gain. The class was divided into entrepreneurs and consumers. The entrepreneurs had money; their object was to buy land, labor and capital from the consumers, convert these into products, and sell them to maximize their profits. The consumers were to sell their labor, land or capital, then buy as many goods as possible. At the end of the period, the entrepreneur with the largest profits and the consumer who bought the most each won a candy bar.

I also watched, in several classes, the teaching of 'Daily Oral Usage', required by both districts. Teachers would write two, three or four sentences containing syntactic and punctuation errors on the board, then involve the class in identifying errors and correcting them. It was never clear to me what the 'oral' part of this work was. But I also noticed that dialect difference was never mentioned, and some of the 'errors' were common Black English patterns. For example, the sentence 'The goats done that' was 'corrected' in one classroom to read 'The goats did that'. Use of the word 'done' in Black English was not mentioned.

The day-to-day curriculum in most teachers' classrooms, as described in chapter 3, was somewhat multicultural when the year began and stayed about the same overall. About six lessons observed in each round of observations taught content about Whites in some form, such as a story in which characters were White, a social studies lesson about a President, or a film involving mainly White characters. Between one and three lessons in each round of observations taught about African Americans, mainly in the form of a story with African American characters. Latinos appeared in the content in three or fewer lessons in each round of observations, but rarely were the focus of a lesson. Native Americans received very little attention, appearing mainly in infrequent units which had historical more than contemporary orientations. Asians also received very little attention, appearing only occasionally as a character or picture in a textbook.

Greater gender balance was achieved over the year (which is interesting since the project did not focus very heavily on gender). In the first two observations more males than females appeared in the curriculum, although by the third observation about equal numbers of both sexes appeared. But very few anti-sexist or role-reversal images were noted in any of the observations. People with disabilities appeared in the curriculum of one or two classrooms in each round of observations, mainly in lessons taught by Sara. Lower class people or issues related to social class did not appear in most classroom curricula at all.

Teaching Strategies

The percentage of observed time teachers spent using different instructional strategies is shown in Table 5.1, categorized according to whether children worked alone, as part of a large group, or as part of a small group. As this table shows, over the three observations teachers slightly increased their use of small group activities, from 11 per cent of observed time in the first observation to 13 per cent in the third. At the same time, they decreased slightly their use of seatwork from 21 per cent to 19 per cent of observed teaching time, and of recitation from 19 per cent to 13 per cent of observed teaching time. These figures represent a small change and readers may wonder how significant it was. Teachers perceived that it was quite significant.

Several teachers discussed trying some group or pair work after the session on learning styles, usually consisting of students each having their own worksheet to do, but encouraged to help each other. Groupwork was new to most of teachers, so they used it sporadically and not always effectively. The following excerpt from observation notes illustrates one of the more complex group lessons; its structure did not require most students to participate to accomplish their task.

> Teacher tapes signs to board.... Game about New Deal programs. Teacher explains rules: teams, you must consult, one person goes up to board. She divides students, tells them to decide who will be spokesperson. Game starts. Teacher asks a question about the Depression, New Deal program. Keeps score. Student picks a word card off board, puts it on blank area. What they are doing is categorizing programs

Table 5.1: Teaching strategies

| | Percentage of teaching time spent on this: | | |
	OBS. # 1	OBS. #2	OBS. #3
CHILDREN WORKING ALONE:	33	28	30
Seatwork	22	20	19
Reading silently	3	2	1
Working on computer	2	1	0
Taking test	1	1	1
Other solitary work	5	4	9
CHILDREN WORKING AS PART OF LARGE GROUP, INTERACTION (IF ANY) PRIMARILY WITH TEACHER:	33	27	30
Recitation	19	15	13
Lecture	5	6	8
Demonstration	3	3	1
Whole-class discussion	3	1	7
Films	2	0	1
Oral reading by teacher	1	2	0
SMALL GROUP WORK:	11	10	13
Projects, discussion	7	2	10
Seatwork in pairs	4	5	2
Group games	0	2	1
Simulation, role play	0	1	0
WHAT ELSE WERE CLASSES DOING?			
Time used for non-instructional purposes	7	12	8
One-to-one tutoring	4	3	6
Singing or doing something psychomotor	6	4	3
Other	6	16	10

into Relief, Recovery, Reform. Students don't seem at all used to cooperative work; these are large teams (eight people each), but there is very little interaction about answers to questions. Some just sitting. They DO look interested in the score — only two look totally tuned out. (25 February 1988)

Fifteen teachers described their use of group work in the third interview, which followed the session on cooperative learning. Three were getting ready to try cooperative learning; the other twelve teachers had begun to use it. They were generally enthusiastic about it, even though they did not always experience success. The following comments were typical:

I did some of the cooperative learning. I tried that. It wasn't real successful yet. They didn't cooperate real well. I did a social studies class that I team teach and we gave them their groups and, you know, put them in their groups. And then you have the ones that didn't want to cooperate and the usual complaints about 'I can't work with him'. . . . It was a little discouraging but yet that class is an unusual class. (27 May 1988)

I had them get into small groups and analyze whether they felt that this high school was integrated, desegregated or segregated, and I had integrated groups talking about it. As I said, I was afraid that I might end up with a race riot on my hands, but it worked very well. The kids came up with some real good reasons why they felt the school is truly integrated. . . . They had to do problem solving, they had to analyze where they were coming from, what was going on and use a real life situation to relate to the history lesson. (5 May 1988)

The teachers who tried cooperative learning commented that they liked seeing their students help each other, and that the activities seemed motivating. Some of them were working systematically to develop cooperative skills; others were mechanically trying activities that had been modeled at the session on cooperative learning. For example, for university credit an elementary teacher studied cooperative learning independently. By May, she had developed skill in using it, as notes from the following observation illustrate.

Cooperative groups are formed of two or three students each to discuss the story they have read and answer the questions. Each group elects a leader to keep everyone on task, a recorder to write answers to the questions, and a reader. Teacher circulates among groups and guides students. Teacher now asks questions, the reader from the group stands and answers the question about the story, 'The Queen who Couldn't Bake Gingerbread'. Each question is answered by two groups and they compare to see if they had all the information to completely answer the questions. Teacher talks to the kids about why they used cooperative groups this morning and how it helped them each help each other and how they each need to take turns as recorder, speaker, and leader. (16 May 1988)

For university credit, two teachers developed plans for the coming year that used cooperative learning. An elementary teacher developed a plan to involve first and fifth graders in cross-age tutoring; she had used peer tutoring informally in her classroom during the year and had studied cross-age tutoring in her Master's degree coursework. An ESL teacher developed a packet of cooperative games that involved two or more students, and could be implemented easily in her small classes; the following year, she used them.

Modifying instruction to fit student learning styles does not necessarily mean using cooperative learning. The teachers tended to equate these two concepts because their students usually responded well to it. Two teachers also mentioned changing the modality of instruction somewhat, relying less on print and more on oral input in some of their classes. One supplemented the reading of stories with film, and another supplemented silent reading of the text with oral reading. But cooperative learning was the teaching strategy that caught their interest.

Teachers generally made adaptations to the whole class rather than to individuals within the class. If a reading lesson was taught cooperatively, for example, it was taught this way to the whole class. If oral input was substituted for some reading, this was done for the whole class. So far, there was fairly little flexibility for individuals and student input into decision-making.

Cooperative learning has the potential to redefine students from consumers to producers of knowledge, and from passive followers to active leaders and decision-makers (Sapon-Shevin and Schniedewind, 1991), as in the elementary class's 'Constitutional Rap' production. So far, however, it was being used largely to accomplish the same ends as recitation and seatwork: to fill in worksheets, answer workbook questions and 'fill' empty minds with pre-digested knowledge or decontextualized skills.

Teacher-Student Interaction

Throughout the year, the teachers usually interacted with their students very warmly. Field notes were filled with descriptions such as,

> Has excellent nonverbal behavior that communicates warmth, liking. Tone of interaction warm, enthusiastic. Kids sit close to teacher. She smiles, leans forward. Kids pay attention to her, focus on her most of the time. (23 February 1989)

Over the year I saw a marked and consistent change in distribution of questions and praise across racial groups. The presenter on ethnic learning styles pointed out that African American children prefer a personalized relationship with the teacher, and consider touching and close proximity to be signs of caring. She also stressed that African American males are either ignored or reprimanded and criticized in classrooms more than any other group. The presenter on the girl-unfriendly classroom included information about sex differences in how teachers call on and talk with students. Teachers appeared to have tuned into both of these messages and monitored their interactions with students accordingly for a while.

In the first observation, teachers had called on and praised boys disproportionately more than girls; in the second, following the session on the girl-unfriendly classroom they called on and praised both sexes equally. However, by the third observation, as table 5.2 shows, teachers had returned to nearly the same pattern as in the first observation.

Table 5.2:   *Teacher-student interaction: gender patterns*

AVERAGE CLASSROOM COMPOSITION:

Females: 46%
Males: 54%

WHO GETS CALLED ON:	OBS. #1 (24 classrooms) %	OBS. #2 (14 classrooms) %	OBS. #3 (16 classrooms) %
Females:	39	47	38
Males:	61	53	62
WHO GETS PRAISED:			
Females:	32	51	43
Males:	68	49	57
WHICH STUDENTS INITIATE QUESTIONS:			
Females:	35	22	19
Males:	65	78	81

However, they continued to give increased attention to African American student, especially males, as table 5.3 shows. Over the three observations, White students received an increasingly smaller proportion of the questions, dropping from 62 per cent to 50 per cent, and African American students received a growing proportion, from 27 per cent in the first observation to 36 per cent in the third. In particular, African American males gained ground; African American females were called on in proportion to their representation in classrooms. In addition, African American students' share of the praise increased markedly, from 23 per cent to 43 per cent; males made more gains than females.

As the year progressed, teachers gave slightly less praise per question they asked, the ratio of questions rising from four questions to five-and-a-half per utterance of praise. The ratio of student-initiated to teacher-initiated questions also dropped, from 1:4 in the first observation to 1:11 in the third. Girls were learning to be more silent than boys, and White students, White boys in particular, were increasingly dominating student-initiated questions. It could be that the White boys sensed they were not being called on as much as previously, and even though students in general were learning *not* to ask questions, White boys continued to ask questions in order to get attention.

In interviews, eight teachers commented that they were paying more attention to their interaction with students and particularly making sure they interacted positively with everyone. For example, one mentioned noticing that her African American students seemed to like physical contact, so she put her hand more frequently on a student's shoulder when talking individually with him or her. Another said that he was making a point to move around the room and make contact with everyone.

Table 5.3: *Teacher-student interaction: race patterns*

	OBS. #1 %	OBS. #2 %	OBS. #3 %
AVERAGE CLASSROOM COMPOSITION:			
White	65	62	59
African American	23	23	26
Latino	11	14	15
Asian	1	1	0
WHO GETS CALLED ON:			
White	62	61	50
African American	27	26	36
Latino	11	12	14
Asian	0	1	—
WHO GETS PRAISED:			
White	49	51	45
African American	23	35	43
Latino	28	9	12
Asian	0	5	—
WHICH STUDENTS INITIATE QUESTIONS:			
White	56	72	76
African American	25	17	24
Latino	17	11	0
Asian	2	0	—

Authority and Decision-making

Over the year, I tried to assess how much decision-making power students had, and the extent to which teachers involved them in making more decisions about classroom processes. In twelve classrooms, from kindergarten through high school, students had very little decision-making power in all three observations. Some teachers allowed them to decide where to sit or the pace at which to complete seatwork; teachers also occasionally had open-ended discussions in which students could help steer the direction of the discussion, or allowed students to decide what to do when they had completed required work. But teachers made the decisions about class content, learning activities, materials, and most time use and expected students to obey.

In sixteen classrooms, students occasionally had input into content, materials, or learning activities. For example, some teachers regularly encouraged students to express their own thoughts in class discussions; some encouraged students to select stories they wanted to read; some encouraged students to decide how to process an assignment in a cooperative group; and some specialists asked students to decide when they needed to use class time to receive help with assignments from other classes. But the difference between these sixteen classrooms and the twelve above was very small; in all twenty-eight, students had relatively little authority over their own classroom experience.

Two classrooms were quite different. The pre-school class was run much like an open classroom; the room was full of educational activities, the teacher demonstrated and pointed out new activities each session, and children with their parents decided what to do for a substantial part of the period. In the art class, Michael selected the main concepts students should learn, the basic structure of art projects and the classroom rules; students selected themes of art projects, materials, time use and table partners.

When students were invited to make decisions, it was virtually always at the individual level. Classrooms were not involved in making collective decisions democratically, although some classrooms elected class officers. Further, the amount of student decision-making did not change over the year, except that cooperative learning sometimes provided a new context in which students could decide group processes. Democracy and decision-making had not been a topic in the staff development sessions, so one would not necessarily expect a change. But it is important to note the extent to which students were learning to follow orders, obey and stop asking questions rather than work collectively to control some of the conditions of their own lives.

Spreading the Word

To find out how much ripple effect there was from teachers' participation in the project, we asked them to what extent they had talked with other teachers or administrators about it. They reported mainly discussing information with colleagues and/or giving short reports to their principals. Discussions with colleagues emanated mainly from curiosity about why they had been away the day before; short reports to principals had the main purpose of keeping the principal informed of their actions.

About half of the teachers said that they had informal discussions with colleagues at lunch or during their prep period. These conversations were not usually planned (one teacher referred to this as 'spreading the pixie dust here and there' (17 May 1988). For example, some shared articles or the book *Multicultural Teaching* (Tiedt and Tiedt, 1986). Several said that they had mainly shared information about cooperative learning, since their colleagues expressed interest in it.

> The only thing that I've really told a lot of people about was the session on cooperative games. . . . A lot of people seem to be either taking classes or studied it a little bit. (17 May 1988)

Two said that colleagues had approached them to find out whether the program would be worth participating in next year. They reported sharing pieces of interesting information, such as cultural difference in eye contact, demographic changes, or teacher interaction patterns with girls. Some discussed events that happened, such as the debate between the two men during Star Power. Most of these discussions did not appear to have the purpose of challenging or broadening their peers' perceptions, however; for example, one mentioned that, 'We've all been through the same things (prior multicultural education in-service sessions), and so it's probably old hat to them, but we'll talk about it for a while until somebody starts on something else' (15 March 1988).

A few teachers talked with another teacher(s) who was interested in something in particular they had learned. For example, a high school teacher talked about demographic changes with an interested English teacher; an elementary teacher talked with other teachers at her grade level about cooperative learning. A technical education teacher gave lists of materials to the reading specialist and the librarian to order: 'There was nothing on co-operative learning, there was nothing on whole group instruction, there was nothing on multicultural education in the professional library' (20 May 1988).

Janice, a fifth grade teacher, had begun doing some serious planning with a colleague. This was different from what other teachers were doing because she and and her colleague Jill developed a year-long project that would transform both of their teaching. Janice taught fifth grade 'at-risk' students and Jill taught severe LD/ED students. Janice planned to relocate her room so it would be next to Jill's, separated by a folding wall. They were writing a proposal to team teach using cooperative learning. Janice had studied and used cross-age tutoring before, so she was comfortable with students working together. She and Jill spent a weekend looking through materials, deciding how they would structure their work.

Some teachers indicated feeling guilty for having not talked with many people, but also discussed reasons for this. Proximity and in some cases isolation was a big reason; for example, one teacher mentioned, 'I don't have much contact with very many people in the building' (16 May 1988). Time was also a major factor:

> I'm totally consumed while I am here every day. Totally. I take off a half an hour for lunch, and I usually just run home or I run out and do an errand, you know. I'm just absorbed the full time I'm here. (19 May 1988)

While several teachers passed out copies of materials they had received, some did not have time to make copies and did not want to circulate their only copy. One teacher said she did not feel ready to present information and probably quite a few felt the same way. Two teachers did not see much point in sharing ideas with most of their colleagues whom they perceived as uninterested in minority students.

Six teachers gave short reports at staff meetings, two by themselves and the others in pairs. For example, a first grade teacher gave a 'short spiel' on the project, commenting that there had been a lot of questions, especially about community services that are available (29 February 1988). Anne and Michael (middle school home economics and art) had been called on to talk for three or four minutes at staff meetings about the project, but were both frustrated by the lack of time. Michael commented that, 'both Anne and I can talk for days and days on this', and that they were discussing how to package a more indepth presentation for their co-workers (3 March 1988). Three said they had been scheduled to talk to the faculty, but for various reasons their presentations had been canceled.

Not every teacher wanted to make a formal address to the staff. One of the shyer teachers commented that,

> I'm not good at speaking in front of groups, I mean our principal has asked me a couple of times, would you like to share that at our staff meeting, and I was like — uh, uh. I wish there was some way that we could share it without myself being a spokesman. (29 February 1988)

Another teacher approached sharing information with colleagues by putting articles received in the project on the bulletin board in the faculty lounge. One he had just put up had disappeared, so he assumed someone was reading it.

Several teachers had talked with their principals. George was already working with his principal on a parent involvement plan for the school, and said the project had given him some good ideas to work into that plan. Four teachers said they had given short overviews to the principal and had talked with him/her more than with other teachers; they anticipated being asked to do something with the whole staff later on. A fifth typed up her notes from each session and gave the principal a copy, along with copies of any handouts; she said the principal found it interesting, but did not agree with everything teachers had been told. Another teacher said her principal was very interested in the learning styles material because he had attended a workshop on that and knew something about it; he wondered if she would later in-service the staff in learning styles.

Two teachers said they had mentioned things they had learned to the principal, but that she was very busy with other things. Another two had talked with their principals, but were not sure they were interested in multicultural education ideas. For example, Bart mentioned to his principal (who was concerned about the large number of students receiving failing grades) that cooperative learning seems to help Black and Latino students learn better, but the principal said teachers perceived students as copying each other and many would not be receptive to that idea; the principal himself did not seem very enthusiastic about the idea either. The teachers in one building found their principal unapproachable and had not mentioned anything to him.

At this point, what teachers were taking back to their buildings involved mainly tidbits of information, information about the project itself and summaries of topics that had been discussed. For the most part, it did not involve critically examining processes in the school that could be changed, or engaging colleagues in dialog aimed toward changing their perspectives substantially. Most of the teachers in the project were themselves learning new information that they had not yet assimilated; they were excited about it, but most did not have a clear vision of what needed changing in schools. Some of those who did have some important insights about school change, such as Bart, encountered disinterest when expressing their concerns and were not sure where to go with that.

Most of the teachers had a colleague in the building who was also participating in the staff development project. We wondered if this made a difference for them, so we asked.

Six teachers were the only participants in their buildings; their feelings about that varied. Two said it did not matter much since they were already active in some aspect of multicultural education in their buildings and had already built a network of colleagues with whom to talk. Two teachers said that it did not matter, 'as long as I'm getting something out of the program' (20 May 1990), as one put it; but one added that if more teachers participated the school administration would pay more attention to issues they brought back. Two would have liked a colleague, and one had tried unsuccessfully to recruit one. Four of these teachers mentioned other teachers in the staff development project outside their buildings with whom they talked and shared thoughts and feelings.

Two buildings, on the other hand, sent three teachers each. In each of these buildings, two of the teachers talked quite a bit with each other but much less with the third teacher, mostly because of their schedules and class-room proximity. For example, Karla, Cora, and Janice came from one element-ary school:

> *Karla:* Cora and I do (talk) because we're both on the primary end
> (of the building), so we talk over things more than we do
> with Janice. Yes, I do (talk) to Cora but not to Janice, and
> that's just because of our schedules. (7 March 1988)

It appeared, based on listening to all those who had participated with a colleague, that teachers continued to discuss the project using existing patterns of interaction with colleagues, which depended mainly on scheduling and location within the building. Teachers who ate lunch together, taught similar grade levels or subject matter, had overlapping preparation time, or carpooled together continued conversations that had been started in the project. Teachers who did not otherwise see each other usually did not continue these conver-sations nor make a point to seek each other out. For example:

I talk to Shiela a lot (both taught ESL and shared a room part of the day). June, over at (name of high school) is in the room across from me, we — if we see each other and have the time, time is really the big factor. (22 February 1988)

I have contact with maybe mostly third through fifth grade teachers, and I will talk at noon or whatever with that group, but I don't have a lot of contact with the lower end, primary, and the other person who is the Fellow is the kindergarten teacher, and they eat completely separate from everybody else on the staff. They eat like 11.00 or whatever time they're done, so the exposure's not what I think it should be to be helpful. (23 February 1988)

The structure of a teacher's day does not provide much time for reflection, professional growth, or involvement in projects that would involve school reform. Further, the structure of teachers' work promotes 'individual entrepreneurialism' more than it promotes 'cohesive faculty action' (Little, 1990, p. 195). The time teachers have to talk with each other is defined mainly by lunch and preparation time, location in the building, grade level, or department. Teachers can make use of time and promixity to the extent it is available, but most are simply too busy to carve out additional times to work together.

What did the teachers discuss when they did manage to get together with colleagues who were participating in the project? This depended mainly on their own personal feelings about it. They tended to seek out others who shared their biases, and used these interactions to process experiences in a way that was congruent with their feelings and prior beliefs. They described this processing in similar ways, even though their biases differed. For example:

It carries the discussions that get started here over to the school, we do discuss things, we've talked about things a lot more, you know, what did you think about such and such that happened, or what are your opinions of it. (19 February 1988)

Stuff sits there in your brain sometimes, and talking with someone clarifies it, or you get busy and it gets you thinking again. We're right across the hall, we don't have to seek each other out. . . . But (Peg) and I both have high school age kids, and we have somewhat the same experiential background, so we can share things. (24 February 1988)

In most cases, discussions allowed teachers to vent feelings or opinions. In a few, the teachers also worked together on something related to the project; the most active pair was Anne and Michael, who discussed strategies to involve their whole middle school staff.

Most teachers perceived value in having colleagues with whom to process their feelings and ideas after the sessions. These discussions, however, tended to help teachers integrate what they had heard with what they already believed.

If they believed schools do not serve many children well, their discussions elaborated on this belief. If they believed schools are doing the best they can and that too many people are looking for excuses for not trying, or that they are already doing multicultural education, their discussions reaffirmed this belief. Three pairs fell into this latter category; their discussions helped them minimize potential challenges to their thinking. One said:

> The day of the panel with the three women, she (colleague) said she was depressed, she was devastated to realize we weren't making progress. At lunch we talked about how a lot of us had those same experiences they had talked about, we could all give a tearful story. Their story wasn't as sad as we had originally thought. (24 February 1988)

What this suggests is that teachers perceive interaction with each other as valuable, but spontaneous interaction does not necessarily move teachers in the direction desired by program planners. Spontaneous interaction depends on networks that are already in place, which depend on factors related to scheduling, location of classrooms, residential proximity and subsequent carpooling, interpersonal liking and so forth. Further, spontaneous interaction takes directions that help teachers resolve questions or discomfort. They may resolve those questions by deciding to work together to try something new; they may also resolve them by deciding that what they thought they heard was not really valid or new.

Only a Beginning

Given the relative length of the staff development project and the fact that the teachers had volunteered to participate, one would hope to see systematic changes in their work at school. Observable changes, however, were spotty. The most dramatic change in their teaching was their increased attention to African American males. Less dramatic was their increased use of cooperative learning, although at this point they were talking about it much more than they were actually using it. Aside from these two changes, there were no overall, systematic changes in their teaching. Some tried to communicate more often with parents, especially those who were already contacting parents with some success. Some teachers put up new posters that depicted people of color. A few wrote and taught new lessons, a few tried out human relations lessons in materials they received and several added a little bit of content about people of color and white women to their curriculum. These efforts changed or added to what individual teachers did, but they did not constitute systematic changes on the part of the group as a whole.

Funding was obtained to continue the project for another year. A second group of thirty teachers participated in sessions that were much the same as those described in chapters 4 and 5, and the teachers in this study were invited to participate in a second year. Most of them chose to do so. Chapter 6 examines what happened.

Note

1 Joyce Epstein and Susan Dauber (1991) described six types of parent involvement practices: (i) schools assist families in parenting and other skills for building home conditions that support schools; (ii) schools send information to families; (iii) schools recruit and train parents to assist teachers in the school; (iv) teachers involve parents in guided learning activities at home; (v) schools share formal decision-making with parents; and (vi) schools engage in collaborative relationships with community organizations.

Chapter 6

A Second Year of Staff Development

As I entered Janice's fifth grade classroom the following May, Janice, Jill, Jill's three aides and about thirty students were pushing back desks to clear the floor. Janice quieted students and reviewed rules for working cooperatively. A reading specialist entered the room; she was teaching this combined class of 'at risk' regular education and severe LD students to make hot air balloons out of tissue paper. This was the culminating project for their science unit on air and developed the school's theme for the year 'Up, Up and Away'.

After a few directions, students moved into their groups and laid out large colorful strips of tissue paper on the floor. All of the groups contained both special education and regular education students. Each group had chosen their own color scheme; some were a random assortment of bright colors, some had a systematic pattern and one was brown and black 'camoflage'. Students placed a pattern over the tissue paper; some students held the pattern, some traced it and some began to cut. They worked carefully and most of their interaction was about the task. One boy sat to the side near me for a few minutes and complained that there was nothing for him to do. His group ignored that complaint and after making it he joined the group and held paper while another student cut.

As each group finished cutting, a teacher or an aide showed them how to glue sections together. This task required some students to hold the paper while others matched sides and one applied glue. As one of the groups finished, three students (an African American boy, a Latino boy, and a White girl, two of whom two were in special education) invited me to see a project the class had made earlier in the year. They took me to the library and proudly showed me a display of insect kites, naming each insect.

A few days later the balloons were taken outside and filled with hot air; most of the school turned out to watch these beautiful balloons being launched. For the first time, the special education students had completed a project that was the envy of the rest of the school. Furthermore, they had completed it working as peers with a class of regular education students.

Janice and Jill had transformed the structure of much of their teaching. They had learned how to merge their regular and special education classes

136

for some subjects (mainly science), using cooperative learning as the main vehicle. They did not simply add lessons or activities onto what they were already doing, but fundamentally transformed part of the day. Their students were actively involved in constructing knowledge rather than passively receiving it; adults guided and helped; professionals worked together rather than alone; and no one was 'dumb' or 'slow' in this context. Their two classrooms were merged physically by pushing back the folding wall, and furniture was rearranged to suit different activities. The students were excited but also task-oriented when I saw them; they helped each other and were proud of their accomplishments. Janice and Jill created the most dramatic changes of any of the teachers participating in the project; but several other teachers also continued to grow and create during the second year of the staff development project.

The Second Year of Staff Development Sessions

The foundation extended the project grant an additional year. We involved a new group of thirty teachers in a series of sessions similar to those described in chapter 4, and invited the original thirty teachers to continue for a second year. I did not study the new group (except Janice's colleague, Jill), but I continued to follow those of the original group who chose to participate a second year.

Eighteen of the original thirty teachers elected to continue the second year. Twelve declined for a variety of reasons; some had changed jobs and were no longer in the classroom, one was finishing a Master's degree and said she simply did not have time and a few were not interested. The greatest attrition was regular education elementary teachers: twelve had initially joined and only four remained. Half of the original thirty had been specialists or teachers of elective 'non-academic' subject areas; now about two-thirds were. The disproportionate exodus of teachers from academic content areas in general education suggests that they viewed multicultural education as less useful than those more on the margins of the education system.

Regardless of whether they continued to participate in staff development sessions, I wanted to follow up with observations and interviews to see to what extent they continued to grow. Twenty-five agreed to at least one observation and/or interview and most agreed to two.

Summer Activities

During the summer, several teachers elected to pursue independent study projects for university credit. Teachers had been asking for guidance in working with their colleagues, so five decided to synthesize what they had learned into a resource packet that could provide the basis for in-service sessions. They met several times to design it, divide the work and compile it; Susan or I

137

joined them for most of their meetings. The packet they developed eventually took the form of a script with illustrated overhead transparencies or slides (both were available) and fact sheets to accompany each major topic in the script. The script first reviewed demographic changes; four fact sheets provided statistics on demographic changes, drop outs and changes in the social and economic structure. The script then explained why teachers should cultivate 'multicultural attitudes'; a fact sheet defined terms such as ethnic group, melting pot, stereotype and institutional racism. The script made recommendations for 'multiculturalizing our schools': using 'updated, unprejudiced instructional materials', adapting to students' learning styles, using cooperative learning, increasing parental involvement and 'building a support network' that would link resources in the school and community. Fact sheets provided ideas for parent involvement, strategies for sex equity (from one of the school districts), information on teaching-learning styles, activities for making the curriculum multicultural (adding facts about famous people and conducting personal or family investigations), and cooperative learning games. A bibliography listed a wide variety of multicultural teaching guides and books written about areas such as multicultural education, 'children at risk', and learning styles. The packet was subsequently reproduced and distributed to all participating teachers.

Two additional teachers completed independent study projects. One was working in a summer program for talented African American and Latino students and completed case studies of families with whom she was working. Another developed a packet of cooperative games and activities for teachers at her grade level, although many of the activities involved individual competition rather than cooperation, and I wondered how much effort she had put into it.

In August, a dinner was held at a local restaurant for all thirty teachers; most attended. It was intended mainly to recapture the spirit of the project and focus teachers' attention on what they had gained from it as they began their year. Dinner was followed by an inspirational talk by a nationally-known Mexican American history professor, who discussed tensions between pluralism and unity, and reasons why Americans need to pay attention to cultural diversity. Afterward teachers received certificates for their participation and a copy of the book *Making Choices for Multicultural Education* (Sleeter and Grant, 1988).

Action Research and School-based Change

We had become concerned that many teachers were viewing multicultural education as add-on activities disconnected from an impact on students. Therefore, we decided to focus the second year on action research. We wanted participants to identify a problem or issue in their own school, design an intervention based on what they had learned the year before, implement it and assess its effectiveness. This first session would involve teachers in dialog with their principals about problems in their schools and help them begin planning how to address one or two problems. Four more release days had been funded for each teacher; we intended to have them use that time for working on a project, and we would provide guidance or organized sessions as needed.

Most teachers arrived with their principals. The project staff discussed the focus of the second year and asked teachers to review what they had learned the year before. Then members of each school discussed problems in their building; the few teachers without principals there joined other small groups. Most of the principals left at noon.

After lunch, teachers shared potential projects they had discussed. The most focused project came from the alternative high school, in which the teacher and her principal wanted to increase passing grades and school attendance by training the staff in cooperative learning. To do this, the teacher said she would need to study cooperative learning more, develop a plan for teaching it to her colleagues, and begin monitoring students' grades. Most of the other teachers described tasks to accomplish, but did not link them with specific outcomes. Some described a limited number of tasks; two presented laundry lists of tasks that one or two teachers could not possibly accomplish. Some of the tasks included improving the decor of the building, sharing information and materials with other teachers, instituting a program for parent involvement, making recess more orderly, and instituting a specific program in which the principal was interested. One teacher said his principal wanted to improve students' grades and self-esteem by instituting an after-school study program; he was not convinced this was the best way to do that but agreed to study its impact.

The directors of assessment for each school district discussed data teachers could easily access, such as data on school attendance, suspension rates and tests; they also discussed assessing opinions and attitudes using focus groups. They offered to meet with teachers individually as needed to help them. Teachers then met in small groups to discuss how they would like to use the remaining four sessions. While a few were interested in pursuing a focused project, most felt they did not yet know enough. They expressed the greatest interest in organized sessions on the following: working with multicultural education in specific content areas, cooperative learning, parent involvement, staff development, and building self-esteem. We decided to offer six organized sessions; all teachers were to attend the last one, but they could elect how to spend three release days, choosing among organized sessions or using the time to work on their projects.

Working with Your Staff

In January ten teachers attended a session Susan led on staff development. Several had expressed interest in spreading what they were learning to their colleagues and were considering doing so mainly by giving short workshops or putting articles in mailboxes. Susan wanted to help them conceptualize staff development as a planned, long-term process of growth.

She began with an activity in which teachers were to find someone in the room who matched several phrases, such as 'admits to correcting papers during staff meetings'. This activity led to spontaneous discussion about several issues: merit pay, bilingual education and needs assessment. Susan showed how to structure the matching activity around specific issues one wants discussed. She then differentiated between trying to teach teachers by doing something to them, versus involving them in learning for themselves.

At this point, Lee (yes, we were surprised he was still with us!) and Esrold (African American man) began a heated debate about racism. Lee wanted to debate whether policies such as desegregation are good and wondered how long Whites will have to continue to pay for 'things we don't have any control over now'. Esrold countered, arguing that racism creates Black/White distinctions rather than being created by them and that we cannot simply sit back and allow children not to receive quality education. Susan tried to redirect the discussion by asking what teachers would do if this happened in a staff meeting, but the debate continued, with Beverly (African American woman) adding that women also need protection from discrimination. Finally, the music teacher asserted that there are at least two perspectives on every issue, arguing that we all fear losing something based on our own experience and need to listen to what other people fear losing.

This ended the debate and Susan continued with stages of concern teachers experience when given new information, and how adults react at different stages. She discussed characteristics of adult learning and research on career stages among teachers. The main idea she stressed was that any given staff of teachers vary widely and staff development projects must accommodate those differences. She then passed out readings on models of staff development, such as clinical supervision, peer coaching and individually guided professional development. Most of the rest of the day was spent discussing uses of these models, then how to use effectively the packet of in-service material teachers had developed over the summer.

Making the Curriculum Multicultural

About six weeks later, I facilitated a session on making the curriculum multicultural. Six teachers elected to participate, representing a wide range of grade levels and subject areas. They were told in a memo to bring with them 'A lesson or unit you will be teaching in the future, . . . Any previous assessments you have done of your classrooms . . . (and) Any additional materials you think will help in multiculturalizing your lesson plan'. Much of the day was to be work time; I reasoned that their needs would be so different we could not develop curriculum together that they could all use.

I began by giving an overview of approaches to making curriculum multi-cultural and provided a packet of lesson plans illustrating each approach (from Grant and Sleeter, 1989). I also brought several books they could use as resources. My presentation was interspersed with considerable exchange of ideas which related to cooperative learning more than multicultural curriculum. We then discussed what teachers planned to work on. A high school math teacher wanted to work on cooperative learning, two elementary teachers had specific topics for which they wanted to locate resource information, the home economics teacher wanted to teach her students the importance of work, a special education teacher wanted to address teen pregnancy and an ESL teacher wanted to determine the main components of American culture that immigrants should learn and was intrigued by the book *Cultural Literacy* (Hirsch, 1987). I helped teachers focus their ideas, then sent them to the university library to work.

We reassembled for the last hour to debrief. An elementary teacher had sought information about Korea and Russia for a Children of the World project in which her school was engaged; she had found considerable background information but nothing she could use with children. The math teacher had found a very useful book on cooperative learning and had spent most of the day reading it. The ESL teacher had done a lot of 'wheel-spinning' looking for information on cultural literacy and had realized her topic was too broad. She explained, 'There's a debate in books about who determines what culture to teach, but not what American culture is.' Somehow this led to a discussion of what products are manufactured outside the US, and whether people in Third-World countries are being exploited by being paid low wages.

After allowing for discussion, I redirected teachers back to what they had done. Shari, a special education teacher, had located and read material on adolescent sexual activity and found it very depressing: 'Lower class adolescent males are simply not interested in family planning. That is their last priority.' The home economics teacher showed some articles she had located on Black family life, and she and Shari discussed reasons why adolescents often choose to become pregnant. The discussion then shifted to the school districts' experiences with sex education curricula. An elementary teacher had 'pulled together some ideas for Women's History Month'; for example, she had developed a list of tasks that women no longer have to do, such as baking bread. Finally, Anne, the home economics teacher, discussed some material she had found about work motivation; she also showed an article about housework as unpaid labor.

Three of the teachers said they had found the day productive and useful. Three had not; they had expected to listen to a speaker for most of the day and had not brought enough of their own material to work on. As one put it later, 'I was thinking that this year was going to be more where I was on the receptive end. I wasn't ready to put out' (30 May 1989). I asked the teachers why I was seeing more interest in cooperative learning than in making the curriculum multicultural. They replied that cooperative learning is more concrete and specific; teachers are free to teach how they want but not what they want (some had tried previously to change curriculum and had gotten their 'hands slapped'); and the curriculum contains too much to cover as it is and there is not room to add more.

The discussion had unearthed issues that warranted more attention than I gave. The ESL teacher's disinterest in debates about who defines what American culture is, women's work as unpaid labor, exploitation of Third World labor and lower class adolescents' perceptions of the opportunity structure all merited investigation. Further all of these issues could be developed into curriculum for students. But the day had ended. I left feeling frustrated.

Cooperative Learning

Two weeks later a session on cooperative learning was held. Thirteen teachers participated; they wanted more basic information about how to use it in their classrooms. The first hour was facilitated by a local principal who had studied cooperative learning extensively. He demonstrated two simple cooperative learning activities, and in the process discussed practicalities of making it work. A discussion ensued about competition versus cooperation: one male teacher maintained that students need to learn to compete in the business world, but other teachers argued that they need to learn to cooperate first. Teachers also shared experiences with cooperative learning. Following a break, another local principal, who was a former special education teacher, discussed her use of cooperative learning and how important it is to mainstreaming. The teachers discussed their feelings about mainstreaming, such as the difficulty special education and regular education teachers have finding time to meet and the length of time needed to have a student tested for special education.

After lunch, eight teachers shared cooperative learning projects or activities they had developed and used. For example, the music teacher had developed a cooperative game to teach about the life of a composer. The home economics teacher had developed a unit on nutrition in which students work in groups to plan menus for a hypothetical family whose members have different needs and food preferences. The math teacher shared her use of jigsaw cooperative learning for teaching problem solving, which she said 'helped tremendously', students were working together and enjoying it, and taking responsibility for getting their peers to work.

In the context of sharing their work, various issues emerged for discussion. One of the technical education teachers mentioned having only one girl in the class; two women asked what he would do next year to change that. He replied, 'I have no idea', and went on to say that he uses four different rooms, so students can hide and do things other than work. He was teased heartily about this. Later as a special education teacher talked, a discussion ensued about mainstreaming: some regular education teachers commented that students were often unprepared for the regular classroom and were sometimes mainstreamed at inappropriate times during the day; the special education teachers shared their frustrations when resources and support services are not available or regular education teachers refuse to work with them. One teacher commented that some parents had been concerned about others getting credit for work their own child had done, which sparked a discussion of grading and how to indicate who did now much of the work while at the same time rewarding the group as a whole.

In subsequent interviews several teachers commented on how helpful this session had been, although two said it repeated much of what they already knew. Teachers also commented on how helpful they found sessions that gave them specific practical strategies; for example:

That, I think is the most useful, when you've got someone showing you things or telling you things about what worked for them, and doing some hands-on things, you get more out of that. (4 May 1989)

Building Self-esteem

Three weeks later eight teachers attended a session on self-esteem; it was facilitated by a project consultant. Most of the teachers who attended were specialists teaching students who were unsuccessful in the regular education program and were concerned about their students' self-esteem.

The session began with a videotape of *The Oprah Winfrey Show* in which people described their favorite teachers. One teacher later said that the tape 'brought tears to my eyes' (4 May 1989). The rest of the session developed activities teachers can use to help students feel good about themselves. For example, teachers brainstormed different ways to acknowledge what students do well and discussed activities that spotlight interesting things about each child, such as origins of their names. One teacher later described an adaptation she used of one of these ideas:

I have . . . a big flower, and it has petals for each student, and it has their name and then it has all these words that describe that student. . . . Now they have about a dozen words per student, and I put up big words that they don't know, you know, they have to find out what they are, like affectionate or intelligent. . . . And the whole flower is supposed to be the whole group. (17 May 1989)

The facilitator discussed peer coaching and its use in helping teachers improve their own performance in a non-threatening manner. He emphasized the importance of stressing good areas of a person's performance in addition to areas that need more work. When teachers observe each other, they want to hear what they are doing right; students are the same. Nevertheless, one teacher commented that, 'The minute you start evaluating in any way, even to help improve, it becomes frightening'. The facilitator wanted teachers to come to grips with fear that surrounds evaluation, both their own and students' fear of failure, so they would concentrate on giving positive strokes for things people do well.

Most of the teachers who attended this session found it very useful. One, however, thought it over-simplified the issue of self-esteem, commenting that, 'You can't just give somebody a sticker and put stars up' (10 May 1989).

Parent Involvement

The second group of thirty teachers who were participating in much the same series of sessions had a workshop on parent involvement that was facilitated by an African American man who worked with Title I/Chapter I parents. It was opened to the teachers in this study. Nine wished to participate, making the total group size thirty-nine.

He began with a formal speech about changes in society and the importance of parent involvement. Then he discussed different roles parents can play in education, principles of effective family-school partnerships and barriers to parent involvement. For example, he talked about the importance of two-way communication, turf battles between parents and teachers and processes in families that actively support children's education. His talk was filled with facts and figures; it was also energetic and inspiring. Then he invited the group to discuss their own schools and their own efforts to work with parents; at this point, he listened while teachers expressed their viewpoints.

After lunch, he described models of parent involvement, such as the PTA, volunteer programs, Headstart and the Comer model in New Haven. He gave many handouts about parent involvement, and discussed the concept of megaskills (Rich, 1988). He also discussed his own work with parents in Title I/Chapter I schools. He had intended to have participants set goals for parent involvement in their own buildings but ran out of time. Teachers' reactions to the session were mixed. Some were disappointed that he spent most of the time talking while teachers listened, but others found his ideas useful. One was 'just thrilled' with the session and got 'so many good ideas from him' that she could bring back to her building.

Preparing for Change

The final session involved both groups of teachers: the seventeen who were continuing from the first year (Lee dropped out in mid-spring) and the second group of thirty. We wished to use the session to help teachers see themselves as part of a collective school change network rather than as individual change agents.

The morning opened with a talk by a project officer from the foundation.

He discussed the importance of multicultural education and school change from his vantage point and his excitement with what the teachers had been experiencing. Next was a talk by the African American man who had consulted the previous year on making the curriculum multicultural. His talk entitled 'How Deep in the Mud?' opened with an anecdote about a construction engineer who had been hired to erect a stadium on a muddy plain; others had viewed the task impossible, but he approached it wanting to know what obstacles he would confront so that he could plan successfully for erecting the stadium. The speaker used the anecdote to illustrate the importance of teachers understanding the problems and obstacles facing urban education in order to plan how to address them. He likened teachers who do not want to teach in urban schools to doctors who do not want to enter hospitals because they are full of sick people. His talk was witty but very clearly challenged teachers to roll up their sleeves and work rather than giving up on children or their parents.

Following a break, a panel of three educators discussed blocks to change at the classroom, school and school district levels. A high school teacher who had conducted research on change issues presented her findings on individuals' responses to change. The director of the staff development center discussed how the culture of a school can hinder change efforts. A district administrator outlined how to work with central office to eliminate some of the bureaucratic blocks to reform projects.

After lunch, teachers were grouped by level of schooling to discuss changes they thought should take place at their level and how they could organize for change. Most of the discussions, however, revolved around specific problems in their buildings or things individual teachers tried doing in their classrooms. The day closed with a discussion of how the teachers could organize to form a support system and to lobby for changes in education. They agreed to form a Multicultural Network through the staff development center and would begin organizing it over the summer.[1] Then they were awarded certificates for their participation.

Teachers felt the session had been very inspiring and the emphasis on collective action appropriate. As one put it:

> I tend, when it comes to government making changes, I tend (to get involved) only when I get really, really angry — then it's too late. . . . I guess I spend most of my time in the classroom with the kids, and what they were saying is, 'That's not good enough.' . . . I really valued that. (30 May 1989)

What Teachers Were Learning

I interviewed twenty-two of the original thirty teachers in the fall and seventeen in the spring. When asked to describe the biggest impact of the staff development project on themselves, most of the teachers discussed its impact on their classroom teaching, which is described in the next section of this chapter. Those who talked most about what they had learned apart from classroom strategies said the least about how they were applying what they had learned in the classroom and reiterated much of what they had said the previous year.

Half of the teachers said that the project had made them much more aware of various things; they mentioned most often other people's attitudes and prejudices and their own attitudes:

> I think the biggest impact was in the classroom, and it did change my attitudes toward different cultures and children and different ethnic backgrounds, and how I related to them when they came to school. . . . I feel it's changed me, and of course it's going to reflect in my entire life, you know. (6 December 1988)

> I had never thought of being prejudiced on certain issues, and then when I — the more I became aware of them, the more I realized yeah, there are some things in which I am. (9 December 1988)

Some elaborated on how their attention was now drawn to problems or needs around them that they had not thought much about before. For example, a White teacher discussed her feelings about the word 'color' and different terms that are used for racial minority groups. Having not thought much about terminology before, she had now decided not to use the term 'minority'; further, she had noticed that administrative forms requesting children to identify their racial background do not usually provide for biracial children.

Several teachers discussed growth in their awareness of student characteristics. For some, this awareness translated into a stronger sense of power to teach effectively and a broadened repertoire of teaching strategies. For example, a technical education teacher described his attempt to make a computer program sensitive to learning style differences among his students. An elementary teacher discussed his own modality preferences and his increased use of visuals for students with visual strengths. An ESL teacher said that this awareness of differences helped her get past the paralysis she felt when confronted with the magnitude of social and educational problems:

> So I guess it's just the feeling that at least we can make a dent in the problem by the methods that we're using in teaching and like changing the style a little bit and trying to adapt to the students rather than expecting them to make the swing and adapt to the way that we're teaching. (18 May 1989)

However, other teachers incorporated their increased awareness of differences into a cultural deficiency perspective that was still intact. For example, an elementary teacher said:

The (community) center, it makes you think, well, if they're working with people that are turned off already, and they have this inspiration, they have to keep going to help these people — it gives you that incentive. . . . Just in general, all these Blacks, like they're coming to school late everyday. Well, nobody takes care of these children, you know, they have to get up and everything like that. Well, you have to start changing that attitude toward children and making it, 'Oh, thanks for coming to school today I'm glad you got here'. . . . Instead of getting on their case, 'Oh, you're late again.' (7 December 1988)

This description defines African American people as problems and does not refer to anything specifically learned in the project except the importance of being positive toward children. Another teacher said:

I look at so many of the children that I'm working with now and I just think, what is it? If nothing can motivate them now, what is going to motivate them when they get to high school age or, you know, what is going to make them want to do things in the classroom or make them want to work for something? Because it seems like it's not important and they don't get that motivation from home. (9 December 1988)

Some discussions voicing frustration with families had a similar cultural deficiency thrust. One teacher, for example, described her efforts to involve parents, and the lack of response she got:

Sometimes I think we do all these things with the parent, you know, for the parents, and it just doesn't seem like there's any — they just don't want to become involved. And it's like, you constantly are doing, doing and doing. (8 December 1988)

As in earlier interviews, Lee expressed disagreement with what the project was about; this time he talked at length about his own perspectives on a variety of racial and issues. He argued that people do not discriminate against prospective neighbors anymore on the basis of race but rather how they will maintain their property. He challenged the idea of discrimination against women, pointing out that American men 'idolize' women and put them on pedestals. He repeated his frustration with the speaker on learning styles, arguing that teachers should not change how they teach based on the race of their students, but rather respond to the dynamics of their particular classes. He also challenged her ideas on group work, even though he often had students work together in his own classroom. And he emphasized his belief that anyone who wants to learn or succeed can do so by trying hard and should not use race as an excuse, which was why he did not support programs such as affirmative action. The project had frustrated him because it was one-sided, when it should have fostered dialog and compromise.

I wondered why teachers with strong cultural deficiency perspectives had continued to participate a second year. It seemed they found new information they were acquiring interesting and did not realize that the way they were interpreting it was contrary to the cultural difference perspective most of the sessions had taken. It was disconcerting to realize the extent to which information from the previous year had been filtered and become enmeshed with other ideas, perceptions and experiences. Teachers talked more freely about race than they had a year ago, but a tone of cultural deprivation pervaded many of their comments. It appears that basic beliefs several teachers held before had remained intact: that society is fair and open to all, some do not succeed because of overwhelming family and neighborhood problems and need special help, and African American children often present teachers with problems.

What Teachers Were Doing in the Classroom

Most of the teachers who continued through the second year discussed specific things they had been doing in their classrooms rather than what they were learning in general. I observed nineteen teachers in the fall and seventeen in the spring. As I had done the previous year, I began by asking teachers to describe their students, wondering to what extent their descriptions would have changed.

The Students

Most began by comparing this year's class with last year's on a dimension that had become either better or worse. Some teachers compared classes on the basis of academics; for example: 'The performance of the students in the classroom I think is better than last year' (12 November 1988). Some compared them on classroom behavior; for example: 'They are lot easier to handle than the group I had last year' (30 November 1988); 'The work habits are just unbelievably different. They weren't always the easiest kids to work with last year, but they could get their work done' (1 December 1988). Several teachers commented on changes in their class size, and a few described changes in the racial composition. Teachers then elaborated on characteristics of their students that seemed most salient to them.

As was the case the previous year, the most common way they described their students was in relationship to grade level norms and remedial programs, using categories such as average kids, slow kids, 'basic' kids, bright kids, honors kids, repeaters (students who had been retained), LD kids, and 'at-risk' kids. For example:

Well, it's a basic level class, and certainly we have some at-risk students in there. We have, this class I think has about five LD students in it. (30 November 1988)

One special education teacher described some of her students resisting the imposition of a label on them.

There's a couple of those eighth graders in there that still (say), 'I'm not LD.' You know, I mean, David, who is in LD classes all day long almost, 'I'm not LD.' Well, what are you David? 'Well, I'm just in these classes.' (15 November 1988)

She saw it as important to help these students to accept and become comfortable with the designation 'LD'.

Like the previous year, most descriptions of students' academic characteristics did not elaborate on strengths. Two teachers linked academic problems with cultural diversity by first mentioning the racial diversity or socioeconomic status of their students, then immediately describing their academic problems. For example:

Well, we have quite a mixture (of students). We have two Vietnamese children. I have a mulatto. I haven't counted the Blacks. I have a few Spanish, a couple Spanish. And the majority of them do come from a low socioeconomic class. But then I do have a couple of them, about four, from the higher middle class, you know. So it is quite a motley crew of kids, and you've got your middle straight down. There's twenty-seven and they aren't the brightest group that I've had. . . . It's basically an average, low average class. (9 December 1988)

But they emphasized that they expect all students to learn and expressed concern about not leaving any behind.

As in the first interview, teachers also described students in terms of classroom behavior, group dynamics and developmental level. Classroom behavior received almost as much attention as academic characteristics. Some descriptions highlighted positive student behavior, some negative. For example:

They're eager, enthusiastic, lovable, that sort of thing. They want to learn, they seem to enjoy being with other children. (18 November 1988)

This group is particularly a more difficult group. They are notorious about not getting along together and not getting work completed. . . . So I've been trying to adjust my teaching by having some work that is just straight done in the classroom, and some of it so that they don't have quite as much to have to take home to finish, you know, shorter math assignments, or maybe alternating a math page with a worksheet that goes home. (1 December 1988)

Two teachers linked behavior problems with cultural diversity. One, who conducted much instruction through whole-class recitation, was quite strict about students being quiet and raising their hands for permission to speak.

> They are very much culturally diverse. That population is getting more and more, I think the percentage (of minority students) at the school here is over 40 per cent. And I'm seeing the same kind of thing reflected in the classroom. And I've noticed this group has a lot more of the characteristics that we've talked about as far as learning styles, and, you know, different behaviors and things to look for. . . . The shouting out of answers. You know, the answering, like they're the only one, and not following the rules. But just kind of blurting things out. (1 December 1988)

The other applied a concept from special education, 'attention deficit', to describe one of her African American students, when it would have been at least as appropriate to examine her teaching strategies or expectations for behavior.

On the other hand, one teacher described students' diversity and how students perceived it as a strength:

> I feel that this school has one of the best support systems for minority children. In the . . . last class I was just in, we have Black, White, Hispanic, Native American and we have two kids in there with handicaps. One boy is deaf in one ear and one has a malformed hand that has been operated on about seven times to separate the fingers and things like that. And all the kids are very supportive. You know, they never flinch at holding a hand. They never flinch at supporting one another when the chips are really down. (2 March 1989)

Finally a few teachers mentioned students' home and family lives. The few whose jobs had given them entree into students' family lives — mainly the ESL teachers who often helped with language in family matters — talked descriptively and supportively of families. Two others specifically described students' home lives as problems, for example:

> Some of them (students) don't even see their parents at home sometimes. Some work; some go out to the bar as soon as they get home; they come home at 2:00 in the morning. . . . I've explained to parents, too that the kids put the same value on their education as you place on it. . . . They get something different at home — 'Ah, education's not that important. I never got an education'. . . . Now, I think I did all I could do this year in terms of getting my parents involved because what more can you do except call them, encourage them, write to them, send articles home. (28 May 1989)

In summary, teachers used very much the same organizing framework to describe their students as they had the year before. They described students' academic characteristics mainly in relationship to grade level norms and special programs. They described students' behavior mainly in relationship to the extent to which it facilitates or hinders 'batch processing' (Cusick, 1973) groups of students through a standardized curriculum. Special education and ESL teachers, having smaller classes and lacking a rigid or prescribed curriculum to follow, tended to talk more personally about their students than regular classroom teachers. But teachers talked more readily about students' race than they had previously. Having participated in the project for a year and having gotten to know me, they probably felt more comfortable at least mentioning it and believed it would be of particular interest to me. Some mentioned race descriptively, but some directly connected it with problems.

Communication with Parents

Four teachers described systematic, on-going efforts to involve and communicate with parents more effectively. As a principal, George had been walking through the neighborhood, personally walking children home who had been referred for disciplinary action and talking with their parents at home, recruiting parents to help in the school, and developing student recognition programs that drew parents into the building. He said his turn-out for PTA meetings was much higher than it had been in that school before; he was now trying to figure out how to keep parents coming.

Sara, a junior high special education teacher and Dee, a junior high English teacher, were on a school committee for developing a parent involvement program. The Committee was initiated after a summer middle school conference which had focused on parent involvement; about twelve teachers were on the Committee, including another teacher who was participating in the staff development project. They held three seminars for parents on topics such as self-esteem and teen stress; a total of about 120 parents had come, from a building of over 500 students. Sara was disappointed that few minority parents or parents of low-achieving students had attended:

> I don't think you can say that they don't care, because I know that that's not the case. I think there's a lot of reasons, they're intimidated, they feel they don't have any clothes to wear. We offer babysitting, we offer to pick people up; we've offered all kinds of things like that, but you know, there's a lot of variables, and plus, so many of the parents work. (4 May 1989)

The Committee's other thrust had been to bring parents into the building to help in classrooms. A mother had taken charge of recruiting parents; she now had about twenty whom she matched with teacher requests for parent help. Sara had found the staff develoment session on parent involvement to give her some new ideas; for example, she commented that she would try to target the churches next year.

Janice had started sending home with her students daily folders of work that were to come back signed by a parent. She explained that Jill had started her doing this; out of fifteen she sent home, about thirteen came back signed each day, which was much better than she had expected. She felt the support she was getting from parents was 'great', and these folders had helped her develop much more contact with parents than she might otherwise have had.

These were long-term systematic efforts to develop better linkages with parents and both George and Janice were experiencing good results. I wondered how many other teachers would also experience better communication with and support from parents if they persisted trying to communicate with them.[2]

Classroom Physical Environment

Most of the classrooms looked very much the same as the year before, although several teachers replaced old posters with new ones and updated student work. Rooms that previously had been lively and stimulating were still lively; drab rooms were still drab.

Seasonal themes again defined how many teachers decorated their classrooms. Twelve teachers were observed during November; five had put up Thanksgiving displays. Two consisted only of Pilgrims with animals, but three included stereotypic commercially-produced cut-outs of Indians. Another teacher also had an Indian display, unconnected to Thanksgiving, which consisted of workbook pages depicting American Indians at the time Columbus landed. As we have seen, the curriculum offered little to counterbalance this relatively small but stereotypic seasonal presentation. One teacher commented on her growing discomfort with how Whites portray Indians around Thanksgiving:

> I heard an Indian woman speak at a church conference over the summer, . . . I asked her how she felt perhaps we were handling or mishandling the Thanksgiving season. And she said, 'Well, I'm glad you asked. I'll tell you. My little grandson came home from kindergarten and said, "Grandma, are we Indian?" And I told him, "Yeah, we are Indian." I mean, they are full-blooded Indian. And the little boy said, "But Grandma, my teacher said Indians wear feathers, and we don't wear feathers."' . . . I didn't do a thing with my very young children this year about Pilgrims and things, other than to mention that Thanksgiving is a time when people are happy to have their

food and families come together to share. I am so uncomfortable with what we are teaching that, well right now, I just choose not to try to teach it. (30 November 1988)

Six teachers were observed in December; Christmas displays similar to last year's had been put up in two classrooms. The spring observation revealed Black History posters still up in two classrooms, and a Women's History Week poster up in one.

Room decorations portrayed racial, ethnic and social class diversity much the same as the previous year. Whites outnumbered other racial groups, with African Americans second. No people with disabilities appeared. Males outnumbered females by about two to one in the fall and the sexes were about even in the spring. (This was true both years; the shift in the sex ratio may be due to Women's History Week, which occurs in March.) In two classrooms during the fall student-made projects portrayed the sexes stereotypically, with White females as glamour figures and African American and White males as athletes.

Some teachers, however, had made an effort to make their classroom displays more racially diverse than previously, and again they drew my attention to new additions. For example, a technical education teacher had put up an assortment of posters; those with people in them were unrelated to his subject area, but livened and humanized his room. He pointed them out to me, saying he had acquired them over the summer:

One, two, three, four posters with Blacks on. And a Hispanic poster, and back in the corner I have a multicultural poster, but right now with the dark light it's hard to see that.... And an Indian over on the board, American Indian. (8 December 1988)

Over the two years, while a few teachers had added multicultural posters and calendars, systematic, patterned changes were not noticeable. Those who were uninterested in room decor remained so; those who displayed mainly student work continued to do so, as did those who displayed mainly academic material (for example, spelling words) or non-academic posters. Probably the main reason teachers did not work more systematically to make their room environments multicultural is that students did not respond to things they added, which usually consisted of posters that were unrelated to what they were teaching. Some students may look at a new poster when it first appears, but after that ignore it.

Seating patterns changed noticeably in response to greater use of cooperative learning. More desks were pushed together to form pairs or small groups. Straight rows, as such, appeared in progressively fewer classrooms. In most classrooms student seating was mixed by race and sex in all five observations. As teachers began pairing or grouping students for cooperative learning, most deliberately mixed students. Students of color were usually paired with White students, and some teachers deliberately mixed students by sex; one commented:

> It was interesting to see their reactions when I assigned them and they found out who their partners were. . . . Because in so many of the classes I had to mix boys and girls. And I wanted to do that. . . . But at this age they don't always like that. (30 November 1988)

Curriculum and Materials

When I asked teachers to talk about the lesson I observed, they described their curriculum in much the same way as they had during the first interview. Several regular education teachers said it was shaped by the textbook, the required curriculum and the availability of materials. For example, Janice explained that she could spend only a limited amount of time on major co-operative projects with Jill's class: 'My problem is that I must keep these kids on the fifth grade curriculum, so we work like a tiger until that time comes (for cooperative learning projects)' (1 November 1988). Special education and ESL teachers' curriculum was also shaped by requirements of the regular classroom in that their job was to try to catch students up to grade level and help them complete regular classwork successfully. For example, an ESL teacher explained:

> Part of what we do is help students with other classwork. Now, what I have planned and what actually develops might be very different. . . . If this boy brings history to me, that he's having trouble with, I usually do that first and then my lesson for today will be tomorrow. (17 November 1988)

As in the first interview, some teachers also described areas in which their curriculum was shaped by what kids need to know to function in society and especially in a changing job market; for example, a special education teacher was thinking increasingly about what her LD students might do after high school and was teaching skills such as filling out job applications. Personal interest on the part of either the teacher or the students helped shape curricula of specialists and teachers of electives much more than that of regular education teachers.

As teachers taught and talked, I was struck by how they treated areas of knowledge as concrete objects. I had begun to record statements such as, 'Three minutes until language' and 'Later we will have music'. These kinds of statements reflected the reified and decontextualized way knowledge was presented in most classrooms. Language, for example, rather than being a tool we use all the time to express our thoughts and feelings, became a body of drills to 'do' at a certain time during the day.

Overall, the curriculum was no more multicultural than it had been the year before, although in a few teachers' classrooms it was. At least half of the lessons were not about people, focusing on content such as language skills, math skills, how to operate a machine, or how to draw plants. In the fall, out of twenty lessons that were observed Whites appeared in four: as scientists, teenagers and family members, a family during the Revolutionary War, and various story characters. African Americans appeared in two: as a police officer and a teenage boy. Latinos appeared as a Spanish matador in a story and as characters in a book a student was reading. Native Americans appeared as Eskimos in a social studies videotape. Asian Americans did not appear at all, nor did people with disabilities. Males appeared in far greater numbers than females; scientists were portrayed as male in three classrooms and as female in none. Student-selected materials tended to embody sex stereotypes; for example, several boys in Michael's art class chose as art themes football players, guns and cars, while girls tended to choose inanimate objects and one chose a human figure with a heart shape. Only one lower class person appeared, who was homeless. A question about wealth distribution appeared in a history textbook an ESL student was working from; the ESL teacher helped him locate an answer, which he copied onto a worksheet without discussion: 'Another goal [of the Progressive Movement] was to destroy privilege. They also tried to give equal opportunity to all people.'

Because teachers in special education and non-academic subject areas seemed to have the most latitude with curriculum design, I expected to see them doing the most to make the curriculum multicultural. That is exactly what I found.

For example, in November I watched Sara teach a lesson to her LD students about labels and stereotypes, using two short stories. The first was about an adolescent boy and girl who lived with her divorced mother. The second was about an adolescent African American boy who happened to be in the wrong place at the wrong time and was wrongly accused of causing trouble; he also wore tennis shoes his friends said had the wrong label. Sara then had students write about how labels can be good or bad, stressing that there was no right or wrong answer. She later explained a system she had developed:

Every month I have a theme. And the first month it was 'Identity and Diversity'. I took it from a lot of the stuff that we grabbed through the program. . . . I had a couple of good plays that we read, . . . the one we did this last month, it was on prejudice, on a Black family moving in. Because then in October I moved into 'Stereotypes and Prejudice'. . . . I only do that either part of a lesson a couple of times a week, or sometimes I'll take a whole day. . . . I figure if I'm reading something, I might as well have it be related to [a theme]. . . . I found a lot of interesting things. Or things I remember doing before that I didn't treat the way I think I'd treat them now. Even

the article on the labels, I don't think I would have treated it the way
I did. (15 November 1988)

Later that month her class did 'just a little bit on Native Americans', mainly
reading a play about a Native American boy in historic times. After that, she
had a long unit on African Americans. Students read selections about several famous African Americans such as Martin Luther King, Jr. and Harriet
Tubman. Sara commented that the Black students were more vocal in discussions during this unit. She then taught a unit on Latinos, but was short of
material. She was eager to get to a unit on disabilities, since issues related to
prejudice against students in special education came up frequently. She had
collected some good activities and stories, although had not yet located a
story about learning disabilities. Two other special education teachers had
developed similar calendar-based systems for making their curricula multicultural; Sara had used hers most regularly.

   I watched Shari show a film to her ED students about a White elderly
homeless woman and a White teenage girl who grew from ridiculing this 'bag
lady' as well as her own grandmother, to having empathy for both older
women. She led a discussion afterward about personal differences and the
need to treat others with respect; she then had students write about their own
feelings about elderly people. She explained to me after the lesson that,

   I'm trying to get them to talk about it. They're different. That older
   lady was different. There are a lot of different kids in special ed,
   respect the fact that they are different because we are all different in
   our own way. You know, because they can be extremely cruel to somebody that they perceive as less, that they can get away with being
   cruel to. (8 December 1988)

She also was including content about Americans of color wherever she could.
For example, she had a Latino student reading *Five Families* by Oscar Lewis;
previously he had 'done as little as he could', but found the book very interesting and was reading it quite quickly. Shari said:

   I would have never thought of coming up with a Hispanic tinge to an
   English class, just for (him), you know. . . . There is a whole spectrum
   of culture that I would like to be able to show this kid and have this
   kid be aware of. . . . His family is bilingual. They are not real supportive of him, and I want him to become aware of his cultural heritage.
   (8 December 1988)

She was also hoping his academic skills would sharpen enough that he could
get into college; this reading material seemed to be helping.

   Anne, the home economics teacher, was in a different school teaching
different grade levels this year, and was very busy just keeping up. But food

and clothing lend themselves to cultural diversity; in most of her cooking labs she incorporated 'some kind of ethnic food', and shared some of her own family food traditions and encouraged students to do the same. She was currently teaching a unit on grains, and chuckled:

> I can't hardly wait to see what they are going to say about the cornbread, you know, when we make cornbread. Because they always, it seems like it's a cultural thing. . . . And my seventh hour class, there's this one dude, he always wants to make 'neck bones'. And I had to have that explained to me. . . . I guess that's something that I better learn how to do.

Interviewer: Greens, are you doing vegetables?

Anne: Greens I have no problems with. (29 November 1988)

She had her sewing class make a large quilt and taught them about the history of quilting; she 'found this wonderful film that shows women of all backgrounds and all cultures that were doing this [quilting]' (29 November 1988)

Michael, the art teacher, developed an interesting art project around student interest. He had observed students doodling on their folders, so he had them design a composition of doodling and graffiti. Several boys' compositions featured rock group logos; girls' featured names of friends. Most were visually eye-catching, students having been helped to consider balance and color. This was one of the most extensive uses I saw of students' popular culture in instruction.

Most attempts to make curriculum multicultural either added isolated facts and people into the existing curriculum or were built around human relations themes. One of the worst examples of the additive approach was a fifty-minute fifth grade history lesson based on the textbook. It began with a review of material students had read about the Industrial Revolution. The teacher asked about a potpourri of facts, several of which involved different ethnic groups. For example, she said that immigrants were treated unfairly due to stereotypes, defined the term 'stereotype' and asked for examples of ethnic stereotypes; students suggested two Polish stereotypes. She asked why immigrants came to America, why people did not like the Irish, how the Chinese contributed to California, why transportation and banks are important to industrialization, and how one becomes a citizen. She skipped to the next unit (Westward Expansion) and reminded students Indians were already there, then asked about the settlers, US acquisition of Alaska and Hawaii and how barbed wire changed life in the Southwest. Students then read and answered questions over two chapters about the Plains Indians and the making and breaking of treaties.

Teachers sometimes developed human relations lessons oriented around self-esteem and stereotyping. For example, Janice and Jill concluded a cooperative learning lesson on characteristics of fruit by giving students cups of mixed fruit salad to eat, and pointing out that 'Different things can work well together'. The alternative high school teacher taught a life skills class, into which she had incorporated many multicultural lessons obtained in the staff development project: 'It's an excellent thing for kids to be happy, to be proud of who they are, and to show them that no matter what their background is, there is something they can be proud of' (17 November 1988) Lessons explored feelings, interests and family traditions; the unit culminated with a food fair.

Frances' elementary school was involved in a year-long project called 'Children of the World'. Each classroom was assigned a country to research over the year; in May there was a big festival in which each classroom represented their country. Countries were selected based on the ethnic backgrounds of children in the school the previous year. Frances' class had Korea, but she explained that the Korean family whose child had attended her school had moved; two of her students this year were Vietnamese, but no classroom was doing Vietnam. She was having some difficulty locating materials on Korea. Later her room also acquired Russia. I watched her class work enthusiastically on a variety of projects, such as papier mache construction of the Kremlin, decorated Ukrainian eggs, a welcome sign in Russian, and colorful fans and headdresses. Afterward, I asked her what children were learning; most was a child's view of other countries. They were surprised by differences between American and Russian schools and interested to learn about Samantha Smith's visit to Russia. Students compared what they had seen of the Olympics in Seoul on TV with information about rural Korea; they ate some Korean food; and they were surprised to realize that 'So many of the things that they're wearing and that they play with are all manufactured in Korea' (4 May 1989). Frances explained that the classroom doing South Africa, the only African country, had expanded to include the whole of Africa.

> I asked why Africa was all lumped together, and Europe wasn't, and Frances wasn't sure. I think that this is a good example of White Americans being so conscious of ethnic diversity that comes from very different European countries, that it's real hard to apply the same level of consciousness to the ethnic diversity in other areas of the world. (Field notes, 4 May 1989)

Some of the multicultural lessons I observed were built on a conservative perspective of American society, emphasizing individual mobility through hard work. For example, a fifth grade class read a story in a textbook about Maria Tallchief (Clymer *et al.*, 1985). It began by describing the ballet dancer's Indian background, and her separation from it:

> As a child, Betty Marie liked to watch the dancing of the Osage tribe. But she saw these Indian ceremonies just on special occasions.

The Osages had given up many of their old customs to live the way most other Americans do. (p. 310)

It went on to describe her entry into ballet dancing, the work she put into it and her success. It mentioned that she refused to give up her last name because she was proud of her Indian heritage, but treated her Indian background as fairly inconsequential. The story emphasized the desirability of cultural assimilation: it is fine to keep some vestiges of one's family background, but real success will come with giving up the 'old customs'. Its message was not discussed; the teacher had students work on vocabulary words instead. Sara's students read a dramatization of the movie *Stand and Deliver*. It, and the discussion that followed, emphasized that students can learn if they really want to and work hard. It did not discuss why predominantly minority schools are often academically poor, why students were stereotyped as 'unable', and what barriers Escalante faced in helping his students succeed. Instead, it put the burden for academic success solely on the students.

In summary, much of the curriculum remained skills-based and decontextualized from daily life. The greatest change in curriculum took place where teachers had the most flexibility: special education and electives. Teachers who infused content about oppressed groups into the curriculum did so based on the conception of society and diversity that they already had. While a few were quite knowledgable about content they added, several added stereotypes and trivia, some focused on family background and individual differences and some tied diversity to the notion of pulling oneself up by one's bootstraps. Rarely did the curriculum suggest that America might have unresolved social justice issues that ought to be studied.

Teaching Strategies

For most teachers, learning styles meant cooperative learning and this was the area in which they put the most effort. About half gradually used cooperative learning increasingly. By spring, the proportion of observed time in which children engaged in cooperative learning and other groupwork had jumped from 12–13 per cent to 30 per cent. Table 6.1 shows the percentage of observed time sixteen teachers who completed the two years of staff development spent using different organizational patterns for instruction over the five observations: children working alone, one-on-one tutoring, large groupwork, small groupwork and other activities (such as games, cleaning up, socializing). As this table shows, while they increased their use of cooperative learning they decreased their use of individual seatwork and large-group instruction.

The frequency with which teachers used cooperative learning varied: some used it occasionally for a special project, some used it sporadically for short assignments, some used it weekly in a specific subject area, and a few

Table 6.1: Organizational patterns for teaching strategies — percentage of observed teaching time in sixteen classrooms

Observations:	1	2	3	4	5
Minutes:	**749**	**659**	**673**	**844**	**729**
Children working:	%	%	%	%	%
Alone:	26	27	30	15	14
One-on-one with teacher	7	6	3	13	4
Large group	43	38	39	41	34
Small group	13	12	13	12	30
Other	12	17	15	18	18

used it several times per week. Jill and Janice were the most frequent users. Jill explained:

> That cooperative learning has gone from just an isolated cooperative learning (lesson) in science to everything they (students) do, they do cooperative learning almost all the time, and aren't even aware of the steps anymore. (5 May 1989)

They changed their teaching dramatically, using cooperative learning for portions of the day to merge their general education and special education classes. (Their classrooms were separated by a folding wall which they gradually pushed back.) They had begun by using limited pair work, but because of student interest they developed whole-class projects involving both classes. Their first full-blown cooperative learning lesson was held when I was observing in November. They first explained roles of group members, assigned groups and reviewed rules for working together. They introduced the lesson (characteristics of fruit), then gave each group a worksheet and fruit to examine. Students worked in their groups for about twenty-five minutes. Most of them interacted well and stayed on task the entire time; there was some excitement as students discovered things such as the different layers in a banana peel and the different colors one can see on the skin of an apple. A whole-class discussion of what students had discovered concluded the lesson. Afterward, they told me other teachers would 'get real uptight' about what they were doing because it appeared disorderly. But they could see changes in their students since the beginning of the year:

> They are finally taking the risks to talk, and that's been a first, because up until this year they have been shunned as a group. They have been the kids that no one would talk to in line. They were the 'mentals'.... I have kids in my room who are doing things that I never thought they would be able to do before. [Both teachers give examples of social and academic achievements of specific children.] We're hearing feedback; I'm beginning to hear more and more said in the planning room about kids, you know. 'Boy, they're not as bad

as last year when I had them, you know. This kid isn't that bad.' And I really think it has something to do with giving them a little bit more. (1 November 1988)

When I walked into their combined classroom in May, Janice was reviewing directions for working with the tissue paper. Students then got into groups on the floor of the classroom and hall outside, and began to work. By this time they functioned comfortably and productively in cooperative groups.

While other teachers did not transform their teaching to such a degree, several made fairly extensive use of cooperative learning. For example, the high school math teacher incorporated it into her individualized math program. Once per week, small groups solved word problems; her main goal was to have students analyze the problem and estimate an answer that makes sense. She developed a jigsaw system, in which students learned strategies in one group first, then regrouped and taught each other the strategies they had learned. She also set up a point system for tests, combining individual scores with group average scores. She said most students liked it, although she was not sure whether their problem-solving skills had improved.

A fifth grade teacher, who had been hesitant about using something as 'disorderly' as cooperative learning began to use it fairly regularly. When I observed in May, she had students spend about twenty minutes completing a textbook assignment in groups of four. Students were assigned different roles: writer, reader, praiser and encourager. They were to use quiet voices, stay in their group, use praise, and turn in one paper per group. She played soft music while they worked, and walked around monitoring and helping. Groups who completed the work on time and used the best cooperative group skills earned bonus points.

Teachers described several benefits of cooperative learning; for example:

I liked the fact that it kind of relieves a lot of pressure on the teacher, you know, if it's organized correctly, the kids kind of take over.... And the kids have been more excited, too; I've gotten more work out of them. (25 May 1989)

So many instances where the kids were working together, where a child could teach another child something that I could not get that point across, and they would do it like instantaneously, and it just amazed me. (26 May 1989)

Frances (4th grade) and Janice (5th grade) had both teamed their classes with a special education class, and commented enthusiastically on changes they had seen in the students. For example:

I've seen a lot of — and she has too — a lot of difference in her children when they come in.... (My students) are saying, 'Wow, he knows that' you know, 'and he's younger than me, and he's in a special class', but gosh, they're seeing them in a different setting rather than out on the playground beating them up. (4 May 1989)

Teachers also discussed a few problems they were having with cooperative learning. Two found their efforts hampered by frequent student absenteeism. One was not sure the extent to which she should let students struggle when they had difficulties figuring things out; she tended to step in and help but thought she was doing that too much. Another was unsure how to evaluate students, commenting that, 'It's like I still have to go back to a regular test, it seems, to see how much they've picked up' (4 May 1989).

About half of the teachers increased their use of cooperative learning, and half continued to use the same patterns of instruction that they had used previously for various reasons. Some simply preferred whole-class instruction. For example, a primary grade teacher who preferred whole-class instruction, especially recitation and individual seatwork, explained:

I do a lot of whole room teaching because when I am teaching the children workbook pages or whatever, I don't ever just make them do something without ever being introduced to it first. I use the overhead. That's my right hand, you know. . . . I use the board all the time, to model, to show them how it has to be done. To think it out; let's think this out together. (7 December 1985)

Two more primary grade teachers who used individual seatwork and whole-class instruction extensively also often encouraged students to help each other in pairs. The ESL teachers usually had only one or two students at a time, whom they tutored individually; however, they used cooperative learning when the opportunity was available. A few teachers who tried cooperative learning once or twice felt they needed more help with it. The technical education and home economics teachers had already been using some pair or small-group work and continued to do so.

A few teachers commented briefly on attempts to teach to students' preferred learning modalities. For example, an ESL teacher said that her students liked being able to manipulate items and seemed to learn more when she gave them hands-on work. A fifth grade teacher paid attention to how his students processed information and tried to gear his presentations to that:

One example, we talk about going from the big picture to the details. And from the details to the big picture. Some kids like for me to get up and explain what this thing is all about. Some don't like that. . . . They like to do one little part. And a good example of that has been the maps, mapping in social studies. (17 January 1989)

A special education teacher used 'a lot of current movies in teaching 'cause the kids are visual' (8 December 1988).

The main observable classroom impact of the staff development project was the increased use of cooperative learning. Teachers found the sessions on cooperative learning helpful; they also got help from colleagues who used it, and a few consulted published material on cooperative learning for help. It was used by teachers at grade levels ranging from primary through high school, in both special and general education, and in various subject areas. Teachers said cooperative learning appealed to them because it could be broken down into a series of definable, practical steps they could learn to implement. Those who used it most reported student interest as their main motivation; those who used it least felt they taught more effectively with other teaching strategies.

I had reservations about how cooperative learning was being used in many classrooms. Learning style refers to learning preferences of individuals in addition to preferences common to the class as a whole. Most teachers did not work much with differences *within* the class: for example, the whole class either did cooperative learning or did not do it. Further, while in some classes students were encouraged to think analytically and generate new ideas in cooperative groups, in others cooperative learning served as a management tool for processing textbook and workbook assignments. General education elementary teachers particularly seemed bound to the textbook, and their main task seemed to be marching the class through it as efficiently as possible.

Teacher-Student Interaction

As in the previous year, the tone of teacher-student interaction was usually friendly and supportive. Teachers usually maintained eye contact with students, smiled and joked while remaining in control of the class, put an arm occasionally around a student's shoulder and so forth.

As teachers used more and more cooperative learning, and as the size of the group dwindled, I was able to record teacher-student interaction patterns in the context of whole class instruction in fewer and fewer classrooms: seven in the fall and only three in the spring. As shown in tables 6.2 and 6.3, during the fall teachers called on students in very close proportion to their racial and gender representation in the classroom. As in previous observations, teachers praised African American and Latino students proportionally more than White students and boys more than girls. Apparently this year they still tried to make sure their students of color were not being ignored, but not as hard as they had at the end of the previous year. Praise was given no more prolifically than it had been the first year; the ratio of teacher questions to praise was four:one.

It appears that those who preferred to use whole-class instruction were attempting to distribute questions equitably. Three teachers said they were monitoring who they called on, one commenting that my observations

Table 6.2:   *Teacher-student interaction: gender patterns*

AVERAGE CLASSROOM COMPOSITION:

	%
Females:	45
Males:	55

WHO GETS CALLED ON:

Females:	45
Males:	55

WHO GETS PRAISED:

Females:	38
Males:	63

Table 6.3:   *Teacher-student interaction: race patterns*

AVERAGE CLASSROOM COMPOSITION:

	%
White	65
African American	20
Latino	15

WHO GETS CALLED ON:

White	68
African American	15
Latino	18

WHO GETS PRAISED:

White	47
African American	29
Latino	24

reminded her to do so: 'I sometimes wonder — you sit and observe. You mark down who you call on. You know, I really think, am I doing this right?' (29 November 1988)

Authority and Decision-making

Decision-making patterns in classrooms did not change much during the two years. Of the sixteen teachers I observed in the spring, eleven involved students in very little decision-making. A few let students decide where to sit and occasionally how fast to work. In the context of whole class instruction teachers occasionally encouraged students to share ideas and opinions and ask questions, but teachers decided the main topics that would be discussed.

Cooperative learning activities provided more occasions for student decision-making: students could initiate more questions and spontaneous comments than they could in whole-class instruction, and some teachers had students decide who would occupy which role (for example, recorder, leader, praiser); but teachers continued to decide on the content and activities.

Three classrooms allowed for a little bit more student input into decisions than the eleven above. The teacher retained control over most decisions, but turned over selected areas of decision-making to students, such as inviting students to lead a lesson, request an activity, or help design a project. For example, the home economics teacher explained that in a foods class she appointed production managers and had them assign work roles to other students. She also had students analyze their production rate and figure out how to raise it when the class was producing pies for a sale.

As before, Michael's art class and Karen's pre-school program involved students consistently in considerable decision-making. Both teachers structured the main activities that were to be done but built into them considerable latitude. Students could decide what to work on, when, with whom, where and much of the substance they worked on. It is interesting that pre-school children were given so much decision-making authority; teachers may perceive older children as having more ability to make wise choices, but I saw pre-school children making more choices than elementary or junior high students.

Patterns of power and authority in the classroom had never been directly discussed in the staff development project and teachers did not connect this with multicultural education. As in most American classrooms, they taught their students to be good followers and obeyers; it did not occur to most of them to help their students learn to take charge over institutions in which they participate. Teachers who are involved in multicultural education do not necessarily connect it with power relations. If multicultural education advocates want teachers to make this connection, they need to make it explicit.

Spreading the Word

We had intended to involve teachers in action-research projects in their buildings this year, as a way of helping them connect multicultural education with changes in schooling that impact on students. Most of them were not ready to do such a project, and did not follow through on ideas they had discussed in the first staff development session in the fall. However, some did complete projects.

The alternative high school math teacher had planned to help her colleagues learn to use cooperative learning. During the year she coordinated two in-service sessions for her building. She presented material in the first one on learning styles and cooperative learning, which she felt was 'real successful'. She invited a guest speaker to facilitate the second one on cross-cultural communication styles.[3]

Beverly, an African American special education teacher had decided to improve the climate among her teaching staff. She administered and analyzed a survey on career stages to find out 'if we have a large number of teachers who are still very enthusiastic about teaching and implementing new programs or if we have a lot of people who are basically dead weight and just want out' (10 May 1989). She felt this would be important to assess in order to determine the most effective ways to work with her staff and had found the session on working with staff to be very helpful. She identified a large core of teachers who would be receptive to trying new ideas, and suggested having them work with new teachers and burned-out veterans to lend support and encouragement. She also had come to appreciate the impact isolation has on teachers, and was helping institute social activities to improve teacher-teacher relationships.

> I feel very strongly that most of our people here have a lot of strength, but because they only know *their* strengths and no one else knows it, then the low self-esteem that comes along with the monotony of what you view as a thankless job is just compounded by the fact that you get no recognition either for the job or the person that you really are. (10 May 1989)

She also helped institute a conflict mediation program in her school and a nursing home adoption project to provide an opportunity for students to interact with grandparent figures. The staff development project cannot claim responsibility for either of these two programs; this teacher had a track record of involving herself in a variety of programs designed to improve the climate for students and teachers in her school.

A technical education teacher had spent the year evaluating his school's after-school study program and was the only teacher to use three release days to work on his action research project rather than to attend organized sessions. He examined students' grades over two quarters and administered a questionnaire to students and staff who had participated in the program. The main thing he learned was that many students do not assess very realistically how well they are doing in their classes and whether they need help. He also discussed issues involved in adding an after-school program and expecting teachers to participate in extra duty. He wrote up a detailed report and submitted it to his principal.

Karen, the pre-school teacher, had analyzed some elementary social studies textbooks used in her district. She found the materials 'bleak':

> Indians were helpers. And I think on that page it showed a little picture of an Indian showing how they could put fish in with the corn to make it grow better. And, I guess, living here in (state) and having had the more recent spearfishing controversy, one wonders just what

a little child does face when you look through their eyes. (23 May 1989)

She found little mention of Black people and nothing about their persecution. She speculated, 'I wonder about the kids who are White, I mean, it just sets us up as supremists' (23 May 1989). She also wrote up a report that she submitted to the district curriculum administrator in charge of social studies and requested to serve on a curriculum committee the following year.

Five teachers had planned to give presentations to their staffs but for various reasons did not do so. For example, Sara and Dee had planned to investigate demographics in the school: 'the kids on the different teams, in the different clubs, . . . referrals and suspensions' (15 November 1988). However, they were so busy working on their school's parent involvement program that they did not have time to do this. The pre-school teacher had wanted to do a presentation on textbooks, but her school changed principals, so this did not happen this year.

Michael, the art teacher, set up a multicultural section in the library which included a folder of articles, mostly about children at risk, and a few other resources he had acquired. (Of fifteen articles, eight had the term 'at risk' in the title.) He said he had loaned some of the materials to teachers who had requested information, particularly about immigrant students. The music teacher showed me materials she had acquired and shared with other teachers; they included a human relations curriculum guide (Ethnic Cultural Heritage Program, 1977), a set of Martin Luther King materials, and excerpts from *Multicultural Teaching* (Tiedt and Tiedt, 1986).

Sara described an activity she had worked on in a graduate course. Students in small groups were to develop a semester unit on 'some aspect that we thought was missing in the curriculum, so my group did ours on multicultural education awareness' (4 May 1989). Their unit included student activities on prejudice and stereotyping, various racial groups, the handicapped and aged people. It drew heavily on resources she had gotten in the staff development project; she said it was quite well received.

Summary

The main purpose of this study was to explore the extent to which a staff development project in multicultural education affects what happens in schools. By the end of the second year, some patterns had become clear.

First, almost half of the original group dropped out after one year. Four were no longer in classroom teaching positions; the rest apparently did not find continued staff development in this area to be worth their time. Those who left were all White and most were general education elementary teachers; why they did not regard continuing as worthwhile is examined in chapter 7.

Second, most of the teachers added information and teaching strategies they acquired in the staff development project to what they already knew and did, selecting that which fit comfortably. Few experienced a transformation in thought or practice, with exceptions such as Janice's and Jill's merging of special and general education and a special education teacher's development of a radical structuralist insight into the organization of school and society. If teachers' initial perspective about low income people and/or people of color was a deficiency perspective, they added more data to it rather than questioning it. If their mode of relating to students' homes and neighborhoods was to send messages home, they added more such messages. For example, an elementary teacher who stuck with the project both years discussed in May her lack of clarity about what multicultural education is. I pressed her to explain what she was trying to accomplish through it, but replied:

> I guess I'm still looking for more of way to go. . . . I've used Indians, and I've done some things, you know, but more on the cooperative learning, and I guess I'm still kind of, is this what I'm supposed to be doing? . . . It seems so broad, . . . I think I'm working on more of a broad level than I am on a goal-centered level. (4 May 1989)

She viewed multicultural education at this point as a series of activities to do, rather than as an orientation to teaching. She was engaged in adding pieces to what she was already doing; she felt that she had not added enough pieces, but was not sure what was missing.

Third, the most consistent and dramatic change was in teachers' increased use of cooperative learning. Teachers generally liked the way their students helped each other and stayed on-task during cooperative learning activities. Some used it as a way to process textbook assignments and worksheets and in that sense did not substantially change what they had been doing; others used it to stimulate divergent thinking and problem-solving.

Fourth, the teachers who tried to use what they were learning most frequently taught in special education or electives (art, music, home economics). The music and home economics teachers had considerable latitude to create their own curriculum and saw their subject areas as fitting well with multicultural education. The special education teachers also had considerable freedom to create curriculum; some saw their main work as fitting their students back into the regular classroom, but others saw it partially as developing social awareness and personal interests, which they could work on from a multicultural perspective.

Finally, the impact of the project on the schools as a whole was minimal. The alternative high school probably experienced the greatest impact because the math teacher saw to it that staff development in cooperative learning was provided there. Some of the teachers' colleagues acquired articles or lesson plans, and two or three buildings acquired displays in the halls that participating teachers made. Otherwise, the project did not appear to have made an impact on the schools of participating teachers.

Notes

1   A Multicultural Education Network was subsequently formed. During its first year several meetings were held but the group floundered. The Network did not have a clear mission or focus; the agenda usually had several different items, and different teachers attended each meeting (about eight teachers per meeting), several of whom had not attended this staff development project. Some teachers found meetings to become 'gripe sessions' in which teachers complained about students and parents. The following year, the Network focused meetings on studying Native Americans. Three meetings with speakers were held; a fourth was cancelled because too few teachers signed up for it. However, those who attended found meetings beneficial. At the time of this writing, I do not know whether the Network will continue.

2   Some teachers, such as the pre-school teacher, the ESL teachers, and some special education teachers, had been communicating actively with parents of their students since before the staff development project began. Here I am reporting new efforts teachers described rather than on-going efforts in which some teachers were already engaged.

3   In subsequent years cooperative learning continued to be featured in a long-range improvement plan her school developed.

Chapter 7

Preserving the American Dream

The American dream holds that any individual can achieve his/her desires through hard work. Americans generally believe that United States society is sufficiently open that anyone can succeed to whatever extent he/she desires and that schools provide the next generation with the intellectual tools and discipline for pursuing their dreams. As I discussed in chapter 1, structural functionalism undergirds these beliefs. It upholds individuality and competition among individuals and explains inequality as the natural result of competition among individuals who differ in natural endowment and willingness to work. To many conservatives, ascribed group membership (sex, race, social class) is genetically linked with natural endowment: society needs different kinds of people filling different kinds of roles, and nature has provided this differentiation. To other conservatives and to liberals, ascribed group membership should be irrelevant to life chances, and matter only if individuals choose to make it matter for personal reasons. Ascribed group membership may be connected, however, to debilitating cultures of poverty and other forms of disadvantage that individuals need to transcend to get ahead. In New Denmark and Gelegenheit, these beliefs had come to dominate interpretations of European ethnic ancestry and, by extension, racial group membership.

Radical structuralism focuses on competition among groups rather than between individuals. It holds that groups are socially created (for example, race is a social rather than a biological construct and lines differentiating racial groups are reconstructed over time), and group competition for material and political resources shapes the terrain within which individuals act. Radical structuralists view inequality across groups as unjust and believe the American dream should be reconceptualized from individual gain to social justice across groups.

Radical structuralism has always engaged only a small minority of the American citizenry, and its appeal has waxed and waned. Most debates about social and educational policy have been between liberalism and conservatism, although radical structuralist insights had informed much of the social activism of the 1960s and early 1970s, particularly that led by Americans of color and feminists. Multicultural education grew out of that ferment and has concerned itself with group struggle and social justice. In the 1980s, conservatism was reasserted quite strongly; liberals found themselves on the defensive and radical structuralist critiques virtually disappeared from the popular media.

In this chapter, we will examine why most teachers participating in the staff development project felt they had learned much, but why changes in their classrooms were generally quite limited. First, their conceptions of multicultural education will be described. Then I will analyze three contexts in which those conceptions were constructed: their work at school, their personal life experience in the wider society and the staff development project.

How Teachers saw Multicultural Education

Toward the end of the first year of the staff development project, twenty-six of the teachers were asked to discuss their goals for teaching and how they saw multicultural education contributing to those goals. Their discussions illuminate their perspectives on the American dream and their active engagement in selecting, rejecting and interpreting ideas related to multicultural education.

Conservatism: Multicultural Education as Irrelevant

Seven teachers saw multicultural education as irrelevant to their work. They described their main goals as promoting academic achievement and individual development; two stated that their main goal was to get students to perform at grade level. Those who also discussed individual development defined it within the parameters of grade level achievement. For example:

Darcy:	I'm a person who is a very strong believer in working children at their own developmental ability pace and . . . I'm not a person that can always go along with the reading chart they give us because children just develop mentally and not all are ready at the same time for the same thing. . . . I think they should be able to grow in the amount of time they need to grow, without a feeling of pressure. . . .
Interviewer:	When they leave you, what are the main things that you want them to know or be able to do? . . .
Darcy:	Well, I really want them to be able to function, to be ready for second grade, to be able to do written expression, to be able to put things down on paper. . . . To be able to do the math. (1 June 1988)

Teachers also spoke of wanting their students to think, solve problems and feel confident in their ability to achieve.

> I try to accomplish the goal of having every child leave my class with a spirit of self-confidence, knowing that they can believe in themselves and do whatever they set out to do if they have enough determination and self confidence. (18 May 1988)

For the most part, these teachers felt optimistic about society, believing that everyone who works hard can achieve their goals. Those at the primary level believed that if they made learning fun and gave students plenty of reinforcement, they would achieve. Those who taught older students admitted perplexity about some of them; they attributed failure to families that simply did not encourage and support achievement and learning. One commented:

> Where are they coming from?. . . . What's going on in their brains, you know? Because sometimes I realize how irrelevant it is to stand up here and talk, and I have a very close family, . . . (my husband and I) have been very strong disciplinarians and we encourage the work ethic. . . . I realize how foolish and presumptuous (it is) to think all these kids are coming from the same thing. . . . Just to have a totally helter skelter house where there is nothing regular and the people who are your parent figures come and go and — you don't know, you know what I mean, just what is going on in their brains and where they are coming from. (16 May 1988)

All seven of these teachers were White and two were male. They did not perceive multicultural education as useful to them mainly because of its stress on ascribed group membership, particularly race. Most of them adhered to a 'color-blind' philosophy, believing that acknowledging color or other ascribed characteristics would either reinforce limiting stereotypes or excuse people from performing. They emphasized paying attention to individual needs, not group membership.

> What's the big hangup, I really don't see this color until we start talking about it, you know. I see children as having differences, maybe they can't write their numbers or they can't do this or they can't do that, I don't see the color until we start talking multicultural. Then, oh yes, oh yes, that's right, he's this and she's that. (16 May 1988)

The only usefulness multicultural education had to them was its insights into culturally-different students that might help teachers reach students with whom they were having difficulty.

To me it has meant not only learning more about the Hispanic families, the Black families, the Puerto Rican families, but also what
incites getting those students happy, how they interact with their
parents, what their parents are like when they interact with schools.
(10 February 1988)

These seven teachers held a conservative perspective about social inequality and, because multicultural education challenged that perspective,
most of them saw no value in continuing to participate in the staff development project a second year. Two of the conservative explanations for inequality discussed in chapter 1 were embedded in their comments. The
culturalist explanation holds that 'disadvantaged' groups develop cultural
characteristics that hold them back. To a limited extent multicultural education
offered strategies teachers might employ to compensate for such characteristics, but they believed educators should try to prevail over home influences,
not support them. The market explanation holds that gatekeepers discriminate
unfairly on the basis of prejudice; these teachers tried actively to be colorblind
so they would *not* be among them. Probably all seven rejected the sociobiological explanation for racial inequality and in so doing regarded themselves
as relatively progressive. As long as they saw their own expectations as
appropriately high and their own treatment of children as caring and unbiased, they did not see themselves as potential roadblocks their students
would face in pursuit of their dreams and thus saw no need to change what
they were doing.

Liberalism: Multicultural Education as Human Relations

Six teachers saw multicultural education as human relations. They described
two main goals for teaching, usually in the same breath: promoting academic
achievement, and helping students get along with and appreciate each other.
For example:

Academically and behavioral. Academics: I want them to be as near
grade level as possible, which for some kids isn't a problem but for
a lot of kids is a very big problem, so it's as near grade level as
possible. . . . With behavior, it's important for me that they learn to
work together, so that's some of the reason I'm doing the cooperative
learning, and that they learn how to play together. (6 May 1988)

These teachers saw multicultural education as relevant to the extent that it
gave them strategies to address both achievement and interpersonal relations
in the classroom. They were quite interested in cooperative learning, seeing
it as addressing both goals.

They also infused a little multicultural content into lessons to help students understand each other better to the extent time would permit without compromising academic achievement. This infusion took the form of adding little things 'when it comes up'. For example:

> I try to include things from other cultures and we also accept what goes on in other cultures, try to make it important. One day in May it was some kind of Mexican holiday or something, one of them pointed out to me. Well, then we stopped and discussed that. *If anything comes up along the way*, we maybe do not make a big lesson out of it, but mention it and give some credit to it. (25 May 1988)

In addition, some perceived lessons on individual differences as helping to foster good relationships among students; one teacher especially enjoyed doing art lessons about individual differences.

These six teachers were all White women. But, unlike the seven who saw multicultural education as irrelevant, they were comfortable thinking in terms of race and color, and attached positive feelings to racial diversity. They also recognized a connection between race, sex, student self-image and student-student relationships. Therefore, they sought strategies they could insert into their daily work that would address these human relations concerns.

These teachers seemed less willing than those above to embrace market and culturalist explanations for inequality in that their discussions of students' home cultures focused on positive as often as negative characteristics and they did not describe themselves as colorblind. In addition, they occasionally criticized conservative national policies such as military build-up, and conservative political leaders such as President Reagan. However, they adhered to a belief in individualism and did not seem to see the social system in general as closed to those who try hard.

Their orientation toward children seemed to be very humanistic: personal fulfillment, inner peace and harmony seemed to be of greater value than material gain. For example, one described multicultural education as an 'atmosphere . . . of openness and acceptance' (23 February 1988); another was active in a peace organization in her personal life. These teachers believed in inherent inner goodness and worth in people and sought ways to eliminate tension, hatred, prejudice, and other impediments to interpersonal well-being.

Conservatism to Left-liberalism: Multicultural Education and the Struggles of Out-groups

Eight teachers were interested mainly in developing self-esteem among their students and preparing them to survive in a somewhat hostile society. They saw multicultural education as fostering empathy for the personal struggles of out-group members. Seven taught in special programs such as English as a Second Language, special education and alternative education. With the exception of the art teacher (who was African American), all of their students were 'behind' in one or more areas and were struggling in school. The teachers' goals for their students focused on their struggles for success:

> My main goal would be to teach the students English, but you can't do that unless you're also creating a comfortable classroom environment and making them feel good about themselves, that they're capable of learning, because it's so difficult to come in and not know English, and be in a position where you're really different. (17 May 1988)

> I would like them to raise their self-esteem. . . . I want them all to find at least one area where they can have success. (16 May 1988)

These eight teachers saw multicultural education as helping and supporting the individual and particularly those who had encountered many difficulties in life. They discussed sensitivity to individual needs and feelings, and optimism about the worth of individuals whom others have put down or rejected. They emphasized the value of flexibility and providing success for students. For example:

> It's just giving you a greater sensitivity to their problems and to the — and of course it's not just these kids that are suffering or having a tough time, kids in general, especially middle school, but you know they all need those same things and they need to realize that everybody else needs to belong and to have some self-esteem. (17 May 1988)

Their theoretical perspectives about social inequality ranged from conservatism to left-liberalism (between liberalism and radical structuralism) (West, 1987) and most of them described multicultural education as human relations in their emphasis on self-esteem. At the conservative end of the spectrum, an elementary special education teacher saw lower class students' homes as the main source of their difficulties, commenting that, 'I don't know how much love goes on in most of the families, or how much attention they get at home' (23 May 1988). The ESL teachers saw their students' difficulties as stemming from the fact that they were having to learn a new culture. Several liberal teachers saw their students as encountering negative experiences in many areas of their lives, including school, for reasons that included inflexible attitudes and institutions.

At the left-liberal end of the spectrum, a special education teacher saw the whole of society as stacked against her students and people of color in general:

> Our society is basically built on not being able to handle differences.
> And that's why these kids can't get through school. That's why we
> have these little red-necked teachers who will not see anything but
> their own little box. (19 May 1988)

She offered the best radical structuralist critique of social institutions of any
other teachers (see chapter 4), which she developed through her experience
as a special education teacher. The African American art teacher also periodically expressed anger about racist practices in the school system.[1]

A friend from a Latin American country remarked to me once that the
US is so large and spread out it is possible to go all the way through life
without coming into close contact with victims of oppression, which she
suggested is why Americans tend to deny the existence of oppression. These
eight teachers had daily contact with victims of a sort of oppression: children
who were unable to compete successfully in the institution of school. Most
teachers have available only a limited range of explanations for student failure:
the sociobiology explanation (which special education tends to support),
the culturalist explanation (which the at-risk ideology supports), the market
explanation (for example, 'other teachers are prejudiced') and some sort of
institutional critique of the school. These teachers tended to adopt culturalist
and market explanations. But some also questioned schools as institutions;
for example, Marilyn discussed her frustration with 'the system', and Janice
and Jill broke down an institutional barrier separating them and their students.
Because of their experiences with students who tried but were still failing,
these teachers were more ready than those above to engage in a radical
structural analysis of inequality. But since radical structuralism is not part of
the dominant discourse in the US and was particularly absent from popular
media during the 1980s, their insights rarely strayed from liberalism.

Other Perspectives

Five teachers discussed multicultural education in ways that were more complex and harder to categorize than those of the other teachers. These were
some of the teachers who had shown the most interest in multicultural education; their own insights had come in jumps and starts and, because they
were in the process of active growth, their discussions were less systematic
than those of other teachers. At times some of them espoused conservative
perspectives and at one time or another all five took liberal perspectives.

For example, an African American male teacher's main goals were to
teach students what is morally right and to help them become strong enough
to overcome life's inevitable barriers.

> My attitude is right now that in America we are raising a generation
> of wimps and followers. That's generally the way I feel. Because if

we were not, . . . the drug problem would not be as prevalent as it is. Kids are not strong enough to resist their peers or resist other people who talk them into it. (13 May 1988)

Multicultural education meant not sheltering students from tough realities they would face. It also meant believing in the capabilities of children from low-income and minority backgrounds, and helping them develop the moral strength to succeed and do the right thing. His discussions mixed together culturalist explanations of poverty with institutional explanations of racism.

A white female teacher was actively involved in learning about social issues; she was interested in Indian rights, conservation and recycling, gender issues, hunger and availability of social services to poor people. Multicultural education provided her with a vehicle for learning more about these kinds of issues and networking with like-minded people. It also provided her with insights into her own school, although she was not sure what she should be doing differently in her own program. But as she criticized the schools in which she worked based on what she was learning, the resistance she encountered propelled her thinking toward radical structuralism.

Multicultural Education and the American Dream

Most of the teachers' conceptions of multicultural education fit squarely within most Americans' views of the American dream. Their discussions emphasized individuality and success within the existing social system. They differed from each other mainly in the extent to which they saw race, culture and gender as helpful factors to consider in preparing children to compete successfully and their estimate of the kinds of support and help their students needed. Their debates were mainly between conservatism and liberalism. Because of their continued adherence to the main assumptions of the Lockean ideology and structural functionalism, most of the teachers were genuinely 'keepers of the American dream' in their efforts to pass on to their students the intellectual tools and personal desire to compete for the 'brass ring' in the wider society.

Many of the teachers' conceptions of multicultural education also fit well within the conservative 'children-at-risk' discourse, in that they focused on characteristics of students that hinder their success (culturalist explanations of inequality) rather than institutional structures that block attempts to advance. Some teachers explicitly equated multicultural education with children at risk. For example:

I took a course back last fall, I believe, which was . . . basically understanding at-risk kids and not really multicultural, but, you know, they would be included in both of those scenarios. They are at risk, many of them, because of either their background, the level of acceptance they receive from school, or just basic lack of understanding. (23 November 1987)

Most of the teachers did not link multicultural education with a collective social movement aimed at redistributing resources across groups. Multicultural education became for them a tool for addressing problems they saw in their classrooms: tensions among groups of students, boredom and failure. Of course these problems ought to be addressed, but they also ought to be scrutinized for their social origins, such as the loss of industrial jobs and the growth of lower paying service jobs in the local economy. Based on an ethnographic study of White working class high school students in a community much like Gelegenheit and New Denmark, Lois Weis (1990), for example, argued that White working class boys who see their own chances for stable work at decent wages eroding, develop antagonism toward groups competing for scarce jobs: racial minority groups and women. Teaching them not to stereotype others and to feel better about others or themselves does not change their own future prospects, nor does it help them examine how and why the export of manufacturing jobs has put them on a course of downward social mobility and what they might do about it.

There is real danger in a body of thought and practice becoming disconnected from the social movement in which it originated. It not only loses its power for social criticism and social action, it also becomes subject to reinterpretation by people with very different visions of society. Teachers who have participated in multicultural education staff development projects may become viewed as spokespeople for multicultural education, further removing the field from real social movements. To those who have been involved in multicultural education for a long time, this results in practices in schools that are called 'multicultural education', but that make its long-time advocates cringe.

In the next sections I will discuss how the structure of teacher work tends to constrain potential change, and how teachers' own personal life experiences limit their conception of multicultural education, and what they do with the autonomy they have.[2] I will then consider the extent to which the limited impact of the project can be attributed to the staff development project itself:

Teachers' Work

Teachers' efficacy attitudes are not simply mistaken ideas awaiting correction, and are not likely to be changed by preaching a gospel of positive thinking during in-service training sessions. Teachers' attitudes regarding their ability to teach and their students' abilities to learn are but a part of the multifaceted compromises teachers make with the social and organization structure of school life. (Ashton and Webb, 1986, p. 161)

Many researchers have discussed how the institution of schooling shapes teacher work and teachers' perceptions of their work, suggesting that we cannot change what teachers do without changing schools as institutions (for example, Denscombe, 1980; Fullan, 1990b) as well as helping teachers reflect critically on their own prior socialization in schools (Britzman, 1986). This literature is very instructive about why schools tend to remain the same despite efforts to change them through staff development. Advocates of multicultural education tend to reduce analysis of why it gets implemented weakly to racist teacher attitudes, often overlooking the structural context within which teachers work (Troyna, 1985). I asked the teachers to discuss constraints and facilitators to their work with multicultural education, which led to an analysis of conditions of teaching.

The Structure of Classroom Work

The work of most teachers is highly controlled. Several factors routinize what teachers do, including the nature of their students, staff-student ratio, how time is structured, and the system of accountability (Connell, 1985; Denscombe, 1980). Historically teachers' work has become increasingly controlled as teachers have become increasingly women; controls take various forms which Apple (1988) categorized as 'technicization and intensification' (p. 42): managing prepackaged curricular systems containing goals, materials, worksheets and tests; and managing an increased volume of that with decreased time for creative work. The teachers' discussions of their work in the classroom and their attempts to develop new lessons and teaching strategies often alluded to these kinds of controls.

Time was by far the main constraint teachers talked about. They said that there is never enough time to do what they would like or felt they should do, let alone time to spend designing something new.

> You know, you've got to do your job and you're thinking about that while you're in the session and you're discussing these things, you think, I could do this, I could do that. But you simply have to come back to reality and think, I don't have time to do all this. You know, it takes time to develop things to share, you can share tidbits, but to really get down and try a different type of program or to rearrange your program. (23 February 1988)

Teachers felt they lacked time to reorganize their teaching or create new lessons. But they also felt they lacked adequate time to do well many of the things that were part of their jobs, such as help individual students, provide enrichment activities, or contact parents. The time constraint did *not* mean that teachers could do nothing new; some clearly had created new lessons. But in the absence of much time for planning, teachers tended to add tidbits to what they were already doing, even those who recognized a need to restructure their curriculum or instruction. Further, the experience of being out of the classroom so many days during the year for staff development strained their time. Several teachers spent considerable time preparing for substitutes, some said their students lost ground when substitutes were there, and one said her students had begun asking her if she didn't like them because she was gone so much. It appears that the work of the teachers was structured such that they were *not supposed to do things much differently* than they were already doing them.

Class size was a constraint teachers in the general education program discussed. For example, one interview opened as follows:

> *Interviewer:* What were your main objectives [for this lesson]?
>
> *Janice:* Right now I'm so rattled I can hardly think of what my main objectives were. I have a large class, as you know, I now have thirty-four students that range in ability. . . . Some kids are reading [the fifth grade texts] and some, it's beyond some of the students' reading ability. (4 December 1987)

Most of the general education classes had twenty-five to thirty students. The assumption here is that students are sufficiently homogeneous that they can all be treated much the same, but the teachers, especially at the elementary level, pointed out at times very vehemently that this is not the case.

> We each have thirty-two kids in our first grade . . . twenty-five is a lot, twenty-two would be ideal, and that's in math, but who are you going to get to understand that? Whose going to understand that, especially in first grade and kindergarten, there shouldn't be that many in those grades. (15 December 1987)

Large class size coupled with student diversity poses dilemmas for teachers:

> This pressure to provide diverse learning experiences for children with diverse needs thus stands in dramatic contrast to the pressure to provide adequate instruction for upwards of twenty-five children at a time. A certain degree of sameness is inevitable if instruction is to be provided efficiently. (Fraatz, 1987, p. 26)

Teachers were to cover the same material with all students, and this material was codified into required textbooks for each subject area and grade level. The districts had mandated using grade-level textbooks for all elementary students, and the day was so filled marching students through the curriculum that teachers did not perceive themselves as having enough time to work directly with children who were not already performing at grade level.

You have so much you have to cover, you know, and sometimes you do the kind of things that involve a small group or that are very time consuming, and there is a lot of pressure to be on such a unit in reading or such and such a unit in math. (23 February 1988)

The pressures of getting this done and getting that done, getting this done and getting that done — and you try to do it with as much creativity as you can, but the pressure is always there, so the creativity sometimes gets lost somewhere. . . . There are certain books that, you know, that you have to finish. . . . We have to stick to time skids to make sure we are done with this, and you do have to make sure they are ready for the next grade. (1 June 1988)

When I had asked teachers to describe their students, they described them mainly in terms of achievement level (chapters 3 and 6). Having too many students with different needs, too much content to cover and too little time converged; their main strategy for accommodating student differences was to identify and remove lagging children to specialists. Students' interests, personalities, life experiences and so forth were far less important than their ability to function in a prescribed way within tight time contraints.

Members of the school administration have tried to explain to me that the content itself is not that important, the grade level skills are what counts.[3] However, it appears to me that the content is sacred: it is not to be touched. Material can be inserted if there is time, but prescribed content is not to be skipped in favor of alternative content. Locating multicultural resources did not seem to be as big a problem as finding the time to use them. Several teachers said they had 'no problem' locating multicultural resources, although two New Denmark teachers were having difficulty locating resources that used to be in the Multicultural Resource Library.

Most of the specialists said they had much more flexibility than regular classroom teachers, although this depended on their perception of how closely they were to adhere to requirements of general education classrooms. For example, while one special education teacher told me that, 'We don't really have a set curriculum. I'm a little freer to do what I want to do' (27 May 1988), another felt quite bound to follow the basic skills books. But the teachers who experimented the most with multicultural curriculum tended to be specialists and teachers of elective, non-academic subject areas.

The print form of the curriculum limited teachers' use of alternative modalities for instruction. While teachers could supplement print to a limited extent with other modalities, print was still institutionalized as the main vehicle for teaching content. Shari, for example, liked to teach content through films, but encountered resistance from the school bureaucracy: 'A fairly bureaucratic attitude in the school district is that if a kid is watching a movie, he's not learning anything' (8 December 1988). I am not suggesting here that reading and writing should not be taught well, but film, video and audio can also teach content, particularly to students who learn well through those modalities. Further, given the explosion of these media in the broader society, a strong case can be made for encouraging their use in classroom instruction.

The teachers probably used cooperative learning enthusiastically because it livened their use of textbooks. In fact, it could be adapted to a range of content areas, materials, assignments and class sizes. It interested students, and it provided a way to work with heterogeneous skill levels; it helped teachers do better what they were already doing. Because of the current popularity of cooperative learning, workshops, books and trained colleagues were available to help the teachers use it more effectively; several teachers mentioned having obtained help from elsewhere in their use of cooperative learning, once having been introduced to it.

Disjuncture Between Schools and Homes

When students do not do well in school and particularly students from low-income or racial minority backgrounds, educators often attribute failure to their home backgrounds. But blaming parents deflects attention away from how the institution of schooling serves some communities better than others (Delgado-Gaitan, 1990; Fine, 1991).

The teachers in this study responded to students' characteristics differently, although they rarely complained at length about students. Some described their diverse skill levels and learning styles as a problem in that all students would not be able to do the same thing. Others were bothered much less by this, addressing diverse skill levels through peer tutoring and paired work. Some teachers said they liked the fact that their students were culturally diverse: 'That's why I really enjoy teaching at (name of school).' Several teachers said they modified what they were doing in the classroom in response to student reactions and tended to reuse lessons that had been well received.

But many teachers regarded students' parents as a problem and hindrance to students' progress. Only about one-fourth described parent support as strong. For example, the two ESL teachers, who had considerable contact with parents, described parents as a helpful resource. An elementary teacher who had much contact with Black and Latino parents in a summer program also saw the parents as a strength and a resource:

> Their mother speaks Spanish and the kid knows two languages already. Somehow I can't understand how that is seen as a handicap, I mean, it should almost be considered gifted.... When we have conferences at their neighborhood center, I've had 100 per cent participation now for the last three years, so they do come out. Obviously they're interested. (9 February 1988)

About two thirds of the teachers described many parents as unsupportive, which limited what they believed they could do. At least half of the comments teachers made about parents over the two years located students' problems in the home and expressed frustration with parents.

> That final element of parent support hasn't been there, so I haven't been able to do as much as I can and get all the work done, too. Because we have a curriculum to teach, so I can't spend too much time, you know, doing these [other] activities [for parents]. (13 May 1988)

They talked about parents not coming to school, not contacting them about things, and not taking care of their children. A few commented that, 'Education doesn't seem like of any importance to them' (29 February 1988). Some teachers said that the Black and Latino parents were more supportive than the White parents, but others saw the reverse: 'As our student population has gone up in minorities, the parent involvement has gone down' (10 May 1988). Underlying many of these comments was the belief that many Black, Latino, and low-income White parents do not value education and do not know how to care for children properly.

I had been puzzled why so few teachers reported trying new strategies for working with parents. Their comments about the parents suggest that most of them were ambivalent about the extent to which they believed they could actually involve parents productively. Hulsebosch (1990) argued that, as parents themselves, teachers evaluate their students' parenting, then decide whether they think trying to involve them would be worthwhile. Teachers in her study who actively involved parents viewed them as a resource; teachers who did not, viewed the parents as deficient in parenting skills, leaving teachers to compensate for what the parents should be doing. Why try involving parents if one believes they cannot even function effectively in a parenting role? (Some of the parent involvement activities teachers discussed were aimed at improving parenting skills rather than improving home-school communication.)

Most of the teachers seemed not to associate strengths with the African American, Latino and low-income White communities from which students came. If they thought about the local community, it tended to be in pathological terms, as their comments about the parents illustrated. It appears that most of the teachers hoped they could prevail over the parents, pulling the children away from their home cultures into mainstream society. For example, a high school teacher commented that few students of color were in college preparatory classes, having either dropped out or been weeded out by then; she drew my attention to an African American student who was now doing well at Stanford and wondered what the student had that could be duplicated in other students. The desire of educators to pull students away from their community culture places students of color in the unacceptable position of having to choose between allegiance to their racial community versus school (Fordham, 1988). The question should not be how to duplicate successful students' separation from their community, but rather how to structure the school experience so students do not have to choose between the community and the school. Implicitly, in seeing the problems but not the strengths of students' parents, home lives and neighborhoods, teachers were setting up a choice of allegiance that the students ultimately might have to make.

The highly structured nature of classroom work, however, limited the extent to which teachers got to know or saw as relevant the strengths of homes and communities with which they were unfamiliar.

> Educators ... see only the skills children can use in existing class-room routines. As far as they are concerned, alternative skills and competencies might as well not exist. ... Children's vocabularies, their grammar, their level of 'maturity', their 'independence', their work habits, their play habits, their social skills — all of these are judged against the backdrop of the ways the schools structure learning. (Fraatz, 1987, p. 163)

Further, decontextualized learning activities inhibit parent involvement at home, since they do not draw on what parents know (Delgado-Gaitan, 1990).

Schools are constructed apart from low-income and minority communities. Textbooks are not written by people who know such communities intimately, increasingly teachers do not live there, routines often conflict with those children learn at home and so forth. As a result, students often flounder and their parents, who have had little or no voice in how schooling takes place, bear the brunt of the blame. Thus an institutional problem becomes interpreted as the failing of communities that already occupy a low rank on the social ladder.

Teacher Isolation within a Bureaucratic Hierarchy

Teachers, especially those in urban schools, work in isolation from one another under a bureaucratic hierarchy which demands accountability from them but usually shares fairly little power with them. Teacher isolation hinders collaborative problem-solving, mutual support and the formation of collective analyses of common problems. It supports treating teachers as interchangeable parts and facilitates bureaucratic control over them (Ashton and Webb, 1986; Denscombe, 1980). Both New Denmark and Gelegenheit operated strongly as top-down administrative systems, in which teachers were under the direct supervision of both their building principal and an array of curriculum coordinators, who in turn reported to the assistant superintendent for instruction. The teachers discussed the administration and school bureaucracy and their own feelings about control issues.

Most of them commented on the building principal. About half had principals they felt were mildly to strongly supportive of what they were trying to do with multicultural education, although their principals' understanding of it varied widely. One of the strongest supporters was working quite closely with the teacher to develop the school's parent involvement plan. Other supportive principals got bogged down in their own work, but the teachers at least felt that the principal would listen to them if asked.

Almost half of the teachers described unsupportive principals, but they reacted to lack of support differently. Some had learned simply to ignore the principal when they wanted to try something new.

> We have rather quite a traditional principal again. For a while he was coming in everybody's room every day. He's kind of [stopped]. I guess there's too much work to do ... So far there's nothing I've been told I can't do. (9 February 1988)

Others described lack of support as a problem. Some teachers felt they were not supported in more areas than just multicultural education; one, for example, was not sure from year to year if a program in which she was involved would still exist. A few teachers found their principal to be highly irritating and either avoided the principal or expended considerable energy just insulating themselves from the daily irritation of working with him or her.

The most striking feature of teachers' discussions of the principal is that, with one exception, the teacher was not working collaboratively with him or her on a school change strategy for which participation in the staff development project was a resource. Principals seemed to feel the project would benefit the individual teachers involved and might even bring some new ideas into the building, but they did not view it as an important resource for improving their schools.

The teachers expressed ambivalence about their isolation from colleagues, as a special education teacher commented:

> One of the things that makes it easiest for me to do what I do is that people basically kind of leave me alone.... That's one of the nice things about being in special ed, but it can also be very lonely because you don't have much support. (19 February 1988)

Teachers liked autonomy, especially from colleagues they saw as unsupportive. Several teachers pointed out that some of their colleagues were not dedicated to children (or at least to the children in their school), saw teaching as simply a job, and would block any proposal for change if it meant extra work. They saw most other teachers as dedicated to children. Project participants who defined multicultural education as irrelevant did not find colleagues' lack of interest in it to be a problem.

However, those who wanted to institute changes in their schools felt that most of their colleagues, regardless of how much they liked children, were fairly happy with the status quo and would resist changes. Isolation gave teachers some autonomy within their own classrooms, but teachers appreciated having another colleague who shared their perspective about needed changes in the school. For example, Janice found Jill to be an excellent colleague for collaboration, but she did not find most of the rest of the staff to be helpful. Working in isolation most of the day, teachers were sometimes unsure about their ideas, especially new ideas. For example, a teacher commented that a technique he had tried, then almost abandoned, was re-affirmed during one of the staff development sessions:

> For a while I was getting ready to scrap it at one point, but when I saw that at the meeting, it helped. That goes back to being isolated. . . . I associate with the teachers and we do talk, but I'm in this building. I come here, I go home, and do other things and come back in this building. I don't get a chance to visit college classes. I don't get a chance to visit other classrooms. . . . If I hadn't been at the meeting with [name], I probably would have ended up scrapping it. (16 May 1989)

Isolation allowed teachers to function like entrepreneurs within their own classrooms, but it left them without support for examining and trying new ideas.

It also left them feeling as though they faced the bureaucratic hierarchy alone. About half of the teachers discussed how the district bureaucracy constrained what they could do. These discussions usually emerged as a teacher expressed frustration with having tried to do something, or with having something imposed on him or her; sometimes particular individuals were the target of their frustrations, sometimes the school board, sometimes the bureaucracy in general. They discussed, for example, how new principals sometimes replace a school's agenda with their own, the extensive testing program, lack of control over the curriculum and lack of support for alternative education. A sense of frustration and powerlessness emerged from these discussions; I sensed that many who had been teaching for several years had learned to turn inward to their own classrooms and do as they were told without resisting.

I asked sixteen teachers in the last interview how much power they believed the sixty teachers who had participated in the project over the two years had to change the schools. I wanted to find out how they conceptualized school change and teachers' role in that process. For the most part, their responses suggested that they had never thought about this. Two simply said they had no idea.

Half of them discussed change as meaning talking with other teachers in an effort to change their attitudes. They perceived the individual teacher as the unit of change and persuasion and enlightenment as the main change strategies. For example:

I think that just by talking with other teachers, you make an impact. It's amazing, you know, how people can change. You may not be able to change them. I always feel better when I've had my say, and hopefully someday things will change. (8 May 1989)

They were not very optimistic, however, about their power to change the attitudes of many teachers.

The people that we want to reach and that we would like to change are not going to change. . . . I know from statements that have been made to me by teachers here, a lot of them feel that it is a waste of time. You know, a lot of our teachers are simply not going to change because they would have to get new material. (28 April 1989)

Two teachers described attitude change as requiring a sales strategy, one commenting that sixty teachers is quite a 'sales force'. Two also expressed concern that they as teachers do not have time in their workday to concentrate on changing their colleagues' attitudes, and would need release time in order to do so.

A few teachers focused their comments on changing their own classrooms, believing that if they could make an impact on their students, broader changes would eventually occur. One developed this theme, calculating the number of students a teacher could reach:

I can improve myself personally, which is the impact — the classroom this year, 30, 35 [students] in that school. Maybe a close colleague will try it, so you may be able to impact in one year's time, if you see between two classrooms, about seventy kids. . . . You wait next year, and get your 'nother 35. . . . So there's opportunity for tremendous impact, but I think a lot of it does depend on the individual person. (10 May 1989)

She speculated that if she got the students excited and reached enough of them, they would spread the word and eventually other teachers would sit up and take notice.

Only two teachers discussed organizing to press collectively for changes.

If we have a network, then I think we can have an impact. If we stay too isolated, I don't. . . . That's another thing the [project participants] can do, insist that they get on . . . committees. (Talks about a textbook adoption committee she will join.) (23 May 1989)

I think the only way there can be any impact is if they identify goals and — a couple of goals that everybody is going to work on, everybody is going to lobby for. . . . What is the most urgent need in this

> school district. Everybody petition, hassle, coerce, cajole their building
> principal into recognizing these needs and trying to do something
> about it. (25 April 1989)

While neither of these teachers developed her ideas about collective action
and pressure politics any further, both did recognize a need for institutional
changes and collective work to bring about such changes.

To summarize, many structural conditions of teaching did not support
teachers doing things differently: too little time, a crowded curriculum, large
class sizes for some teachers, structural disjuncture between home and school
and isolation low in the power structure. These factors standardized the work
of general education teachers the most; specialists had more flexibility. Further,
teachers felt powerless to confront 'the system'. They were accustomed to
thinking in terms of other teachers, parents, or principals as individuals, which
rendered them manageable. They were not accustomed to viewing themselves as a collective.[4] The history of teaching contains a strand of collective
activism (Carlson, 1987; Apple, 1988). This did not appear to be a history of
which the teachers were aware and felt a part. The staff development project
developed a sense of collegiality and closeness among them, which they valued.
But their own perspectives about individuality directed them toward individuals as the unit of change, a perspective reinforced by isolation and the
demands of their work.

Staff development projects such as the one studied here could help
teachers deconstruct power relations in the system and develop collective
action strategies. In turn, this may sensitize them to multicultural education's
roots in collective social action. However, most teachers' life experiences
supported a belief in the openness of America's social system and the wisdom
of concentrating on working one's way up the ladder as an individual.

Personal Life Experience

> People realize how limited they are by their experiences, but they
> don't really actually realize the ramification of those experiences be-
> cause if they did, then you know when to bite your tongue. (10 May
> 1989)

This statement was made by one of the African American teachers,
highlighting the extent to which personal experiences shape us. In spite of the
structure of their work, teachers do have some autonomy in their classrooms.
They decide what to do with that autonomy based on how they frame problems
and issues. How people frame issues related to diversity and inequality results
largely from their own positions within the structure of racial, gender and
class relations. Various theorists have examined teachers as upwardly mobile
members of the working class (for example, Ashton and Webb, 1986; Lortie,

1975), as women (for example, Grumet, 1988; Spencer, 1986; Weiler, 1988), and as working class women (for example, Apple, 1988; Connell, 1985), focusing on how they construct their understanding of reality from these social class and gender locations. Teacher race has been examined mainly by comparing how White teachers and teachers of color interact with and teach children of color (for example, Irvine, 1988). Teacher race is seen as an issue mainly when teachers display overt prejudice toward children of color, fail to understand them, or expect less of them than they do of White children.

Twenty-six of the teachers were White, and it would be tempting to attribute their understanding of, and work with, multicultural education to their own ignorance of racial issues. I will argue, however, that although most of them had been insulated from perspectives and experiences of oppressed racial groups, they had constructed a fairly well-developed conception of the social order based on their experiences as White women and upwardly-mobile members of the working class.

Teachers as White

Teachers bring to their work a worldview that is constructed within unequal racial relationships. However, they usually do not recognize it as a particular worldview and the literature usually does not interrogate location in the racial order as informing it. Weiler (1988), based on a study of White teachers, observed that,

> (A)s Whites they are in a position of dominance and thus do not identify themselves by race, since White privilege is so much a defined part of US society that Whites are not even conscious of their relationship to power and privilege. In US society, White is the norm; people of color are defined as deviating from that norm and therefore their race becomes an issue. (pp. 76–7)

White Americans and Americans of color grow up in different locations in the racial structure. According to Wellman (1977),

> Given the racial and class organization of American society, there is only so much people can 'see.' The positions they occupy in these structures limit the range of their thinking. The situation places barriers on their imaginations and restricts the possibilities of their vision. (p. 235)

Banks (1988) described the position in which Whites live as 'ethnic encapsulation' (pp. 194–5); Stalvey (1988) termed it an 'insulated cocoon' (p. 6). It is lived out in racially homogeneous neighborhoods, families, social groups and churches, and in consumption of media that are dominated by Whites.

Most Whites do not venture very far outside this privileged cocoon; they may incorporate into it a few people of color, but most Whites spend little or no extended time on non-White 'turf'.

The worldviews of Whites tend to support White privilege, but in ways that Whites interpret as natural or as fair. A contradiction Whites face is how to interpret racial inequality in a way that defends White interests in publically acceptable terms, and that do not embrace sociobiological explanations for inequality. Whites 'resolve the contradiction by minimizing racism. They neutralize it' (Wellman, 1977, p. 219) and 'are resistant to conversations that might threaten our power' (Fine, 1991, p. 155). Working class Whites are particularly apt to deny racism while adopting strategies of racial exclusion in order to protect their share of the 'American apple pie' (Boxill, 1989).

All but one of the White teachers in this study had grown up in White neighborhoods, most within 100 miles of where they were teaching. Their frame of reference about how society works was rooted heavily in the experiences of White people. Most of these White teachers liked teaching children of color; for example, one explained that she had been very apprehensive about her first job, which was in a low-income multiracial school, but she liked it; she then went to an all-White, upper middle class school and 'hated it . . . because the kids were so snobby' (20 November 1987). She was glad when an opening appeared in her present school.

But the White teachers did not bring much exposure to the life experiences and worldviews of Americans of color. Eighteen had virtually no life experience with Americans of color aside from having taught in racially mixed or predominantly Black classrooms, and in some cases having participated in formal instruction about racial diversity. They acquired first-hand experience with Americans of color mainly by having children of color in class. The other eight White teachers had somewhat more substantive life experience with racial diversity, but it was not extensive. Some had traveled; for example, one had served two years in the Peace Corps in Thailand and had traveled in the Middle East and Europe; another had been an exchange student in Mexico City one summer. Other teachers had engaged in learning activities within the US; for example, Shari had become quite interested in American Indians and had traveled to Arizona to study them.

Life experience with Americans of color can help Whites realize how much they do not understand about race relations and sensitize them to injustices, perspectives and experiences of other groups. For example, one White teacher described her first teaching experience in a university town:

> I . . . taught in the highest minority school I've ever been in, it was 95 per cent Black. And to my surprise, that's when my commitment began. I didn't like the fact that the university community didn't know there was a Black school there. And they didn't. And I knew there was something wrong. (10 March 1988)

However, such experiences can also blind Whites to what they do not under-stand, helping them get past the the discomfort people feel in the company of members of other racial groups without opening them to alternative perspectives. A few of the White teachers commented that they were raised 'to be open to anybody' and 'without any prejudice', yet their discussions revealed a limited understanding of racism.

Several teachers talked about their own European ethnic backgrounds. For example, one teacher valued her Swedish heritage and could understand why other people might value their cultural roots. But another, who was a daughter of Italian immigrants, commented:

> One of my pet peeves, that I know if you want to work, you can work. . . . I know what my father did when he was in need, . . . and we didn't have the free lunches and we didn't have the clothes that other kids wore. (15 December 1987)

Several White teachers discussed their own family backgrounds or that of their spouses to make the same point: White immigrants had worked their way up without expecting handouts and government support.

Over half of the White teachers had taken a course or a workshop in multicultural education. Four had taken a required course as part of their pre-service education, three from Black professors. They said the course had raised their awareness, but one commented that the professor had been 'really big into Black culture' (20 November 1987) and another described the course as a 'hostile experience' (24 March 1988). Eight of the White teachers had participated in workshops when New Denmark Unified School District was desegregated. Some commented that the workshops had reinforced their colorblind perspective.

> The thing that really stuck with me (from) the workshop, 'cause I was a real new teacher then, is basically I didn't feel that there was the prejudice that I had been led to believe, especially in the ele-mentary teachers. I know I've heard many people say, I don't like it when you say you're colorblind, because you shouldn't be colorblind, but I really believe that elementary teachers feel that kids are kids, and I think that really stood out in those meetings, you know, 'cause people would say, well, what's your minority breakdown, and teachers would really have a rough time saying, you know. It was like asking how many of your kids are wearing glasses. And so really, I'm not denying that there's prejudice but I just don't think it's as strong in the school system as people really assume. (15 December 1987)

A few other teachers had attended other courses or workshops on topics related to multiculturalism, such as Southeast Asia and multicultural music.

While some found such courses interesting and signed up voluntarily for more, most were uncomfortable when confronted with racial anger.

How did their location in the racial order affect the White teachers' understanding of race? Perhaps five of the twenty-six felt quite ignorant and actively sought more information. The rest were not sure race is really that important. Several White teachers tried to minimize race by negating it: 'I don't see color', 'It's economics, not race', or 'Individual differences don't relate to race'. Some tried to show interest in race by criticizing the project's emphasis on racial minority groups close to home — African Americans and Latinos — rather than those farther away — American Indians, Arabs or Japanese. Several White teachers saw racism as a matter of attitudes and as correctable. And some reduced race to family traditions.

But the White teachers still had an unresolved dilemma: how to accept all children regardless of race while explaining their difficulties in school without seeming racist. Several tried to ignore racial culturalist explanations they were familiar with (such as notions of the pathology of Black families) and attributed what they saw to the 'culture of poverty'. Even still, as described in chapter 6, culturalist explanations for children's classroom behavior and achievement crept into several descriptions of children. A few White teachers had begun to criticize racist institutions, but most were not accustomed to examining institutional discrimination.

The teachers of color, on the other hand, were well aware that racism existed and intimately familiar with strengths and resources of people like themselves. All four had moved North from Southern states, where they had grown up in segregated neighborhoods and attended segregated schools. All four had experienced racial discrimination while growing up.

> I remember my third grade teacher telling us that we were animals because we didn't know how to eat with a knife and a fork like White children, because . . . we ate with tortillas. . . . I wanted to take German in high school and they . . . would not let me take German, I had to take as a foreign language, I had to take Spanish. Jesus Christ, it doesn't make sense, I could read, write and speak Spanish because we did it at home! (11 December 1987)

All four had been angry but had learned to keep going.

> There are roadblocks, there are obstacles, there are some people who will throw obstacles in front of you or try to keep you from achieving, OK, you don't have to hate them to get back at them, you just have to do what you need to do, . . . go on and achieve what you want to achieve. (6 January 1988)

Their parents' education levels varied from not having completed elementary school to having earned a college degree; but their parents had stressed the importance of education and the teachers of color understood that most families of color value education. They identified with the minority community and tried to serve it through their work.

The main difference between the White teachers and the teachers of color is that the latter flatly rejected conservative explanations of racial inequality. Although they recognized racism as it is expressed through personal attitudes, they did not reduce it to attitudes. Neither did they accept culturalist explanations for racial inequality, although two articulated culturalist explanations for social class inequality. None of the teachers of color offered a radical structuralist interpretation of race relations, but they had many of the insights that would support that perspective. Further, they had been involved in social protests during the civil rights movement, understood that many of the battles being fought then were still not won, and could see a relationship between multicultural education and social movements for racial equality.

While Kluegel and Smith (1986) found most Americans to believe that opportunity for economic advancement is widely available and that existing inequalities are due mainly to unequal efforts and talents, they also found that,

> The largest and most consistent group disparities in expressed doubt about the workings of the American stratification order are those between Blacks and Whites . . . (N)either the disparity by status nor by sex is so large or so consistent across beliefs as that by race. . . . Blacks are the group of Americans that come closest to being 'class conscious' in the Marxian sense. (p. 289)

White Americans generally are not victims of racial discrimination and do not experience institutional rules and processes that members of oppressed groups experience as barriers. Further, Whites usually do not experience the strength and resilience of racial minority communities and families. Spending their lives on White-dominanted turf, most Whites develop an experience base conditioned by their privileged status and that experience base allows Whites to deny or minimize racism.

Women in a Gendered Profession

Two White women teachers discussed their interest in feminism, which might suggest that a feminist analysis of society would cause them to question the ideology of individualism and equal opportunity. Since most of the teachers were women, it is worth wondering how their experiences with sex discrimination sensitized them to other forms of discrimination. Contrary to what may seem obvious, the data suggest that women's *unexamined* experience with sexism limits their understanding of social stratification by encouraging them to believe they already understand sex discrimination and then to draw parallels between sexism, as they perceive it and race and class discrimination.

In the first session, very few teachers indicated an interest in studying gender equity. Their relative lack of interest seems to have stemmed from a perception that they already understood it. The Attitude Assessment that was administered the first year provides some insight into this. It was analyzed by categorizing items by race, language, social class, gender and disability. The average scores (1 = low, 5 = high) on the preassessment for items on race, language and social class were 3.54, 3.32, and 3.70 respectively; on the post-assessment they had risen to 4.05, 3.83 and 3.96 respectively. The average scores for items on gender and disability on the pre-assessment were 4.44 and 4.17 respectively and on the post-assessment, 4.49 and 4.45 respectively. These scores suggest that the teachers brought with them a greater degree of sensitivity to issues of gender and disability (many were special education teachers) than to issues of race, language and social class.

But their understanding of sex discrimination was probably a liberal understanding, locating sex discrimination mainly in biased attitudes of individuals who limit the opportunities of other individuals by treating them stereotypically. The speaker on gender equity reinforced this view by discussing how patterns in teacher-student interaction encourage boys and discourage girls. The most lively exchanges among the teachers occurred when men made stereotypic statements about what females should or should not do and the women took them to task. The teachers who interpreted multicultural education as human relations were, with one exception, all women.[5] The main solution to sexism from a liberal perspective is to try to eliminate sex stereotyping and sexist practices in social institutions, so that all may strive for their dreams as individuals, without regard to sex (Jaggar, 1983).

From a radical structuralist perspective, liberal measures to address discrimination would end neither sexism, racism, nor class oppression.[6] However, the very having of a theory of sexism can suggest to its holders that they understand one form of discrimination they can then apply to other forms of discrimination. Thus, to the extent that women are consciously aware of sex stereotypes, including those that have been placed on them, they feel quite cognizant of sex discrimination and in need of no further analysis of it.

The lives of the women teachers, however, had been structured within gendered parameters. Historically teaching has been one of the few socially acceptable routes many women have had into public life and paid work. Grumet (1988) argued that women enter teaching in an effort to move out of the domestic sphere and develop their own potentials and identities as individuals. As teachers, women experience the contradiction between being controlled by a male bureaucracy that has hired them to bring children under control, while they themselves are seeking growth, achievement, and productivity. 'Teaching had become the shelter of the educated woman. It was a refuge both familiar and alien, a boardinghouse where she didn't make the rules and didn't even have her own key' (p. 44).

All of the women in this study were married and most had children of their own. Fifteen were asked about their mothers' work. The mothers of six had been full-time homemakers (one had taught before she was married, but then quit work), the mothers of seven had been homemakers and had also held clerical jobs and the mothers of two had been farmers. Becoming teachers, all of them had ventured into the realm of full-time work in the public sphere that their mothers had not inhabited. In that sense, they had rejected gendered limitations on their lives that their mothers had accepted, although the paid work they chose is similar to mothering.

However, the women teachers with children all described a pattern of balancing and usually deferring their careers to the demands of childbearing and mothering. In this sense their lives had reproduced traditional gendered patterns. Some were consciously aware that they had initially chosen a different career.

> I was a chemist when I first got out of college, I have a degree in chemistry, and then I stayed home seven years with my children while they were pre-schoolers, and when I came back to work then I went back into education. (23 November 1987)

> My dad was a pharmacist, . . . and my mother had been a teacher, but she taught for maybe three years and then they were married and it was not acceptable for a pharmacist's wife to work, so she was at home. . . . I really wanted to go into pharmacy, but my mother told me that I should leave that for my brother, that it would be a good idea for me to go into nursing and teaching. Being an obedient child, I did. My brother tried to go to school and he did not like anything that had to do with pharmacy, not the math or chemistry that I enjoyed, and so he never did go into pharmacy. (1 December 1987)

In many cases, their career patterns were checkered by moves due to husbands' work, and stops and starts due to childbirth. The following story was typical.

> I went through the public school system, and then I got out of high school and I went to work and then got married. My husband went to school and so I started taking classes and then we had a youngster, so he finished school and went to work, and then I started taking classes and then got my degree, and was hired fourteen years ago. . . . I didn't start teaching until my youngest daughter was in fifth grade. (4 December 1987)

But at the same time, most of the teachers showed an active interest in continuing to learn, grow and create, within the bounds of their gendered lives. For example, Shari developed an interest in Indian art that she pursued with determination:

My poor ex-husband had to crawl out of and into every settlement that the Indians inhabited, whatever the height of Indians had ever been, and he had to go hiking in there because Shari was interested in it.

But her teaching career had been interrupted periodically by family demands. The first interruption occurred several years after she had begun to teach, when she began to have children.

I stopped teaching for a while, and when I wanted to get back into the field was when there were no jobs for teaching anywhere. There was just nothing, so I got a job as a teacher's aide at (school for in-carcerated adolescents), in the reading room. Terrified. First day on the job, all of the teachers leave and I'm stuck with twenty-five — and I'm going, Oh, My God, what am I doing here? Found out that I liked doing it. . . . I took kids to the movies, I took kids to the art institute . . . on field trips, they were just great. . . . Well, in the interim, my husband got transferred to Seattle, and so we moved out there, and I went out there with my teaching credentials, and they said, Gee, that's really nice, what else can you do?

Shari worked as a substitute for a while, then found a new job:

I was an Education Director for a private psychiatric hospital for about a year. It was fascinating. I did not want to come back, and I just did not want to leave. . . . I was recruited for the job here when I was still in Seattle, and my husband kept saying, we want to go back, we want to go back, you really want to work for a school district. No, I don't, I don't want to do this, but I'll do it. (7 January 1988)

The teachers seemed to accept their gendered family responsibilities and career choice and within a context that was shaped and limited by their gender, several had sought opportunities for growth and achievement. As Weiler (1988) has discussed, we see in the career choices and patterns of women teachers 'a logic of existing social structures and ideology' that sub-ordinates women's lives to men's careers (p. 89). We see a tension between acceptance of their own devaluation and attempts to control them, and their exerting control and creativity within the space that is theirs. A critical ex-amination of their own lives could form the basis for a radical structural analysis of gender oppression, but this becomes personally very threatening.

The male teachers, on the other hand, had not been victims of sex dis-crimination and seemed to see it as less of an isssue than the women did. Lee, for example, argued in favor of lining students by sex and placing women on a pedestal, even over the protests of women teachers. Jorge, who was sensitive to racism in the assignment of students to vocational classes, did not view all-male classes as an issue requiring examination. Michael's art students often used gendered themes for art projects (for example, boys drawing cars and football players, girls drawing female models and hearts), which he seemed to accept as 'normal'. When conservative perspectives about gender were articulated, it was up to the women to challenge them.

Working Your Way Up

Both conservatism and liberalism value individualism and hard work; the image of pulling oneself up by one's own bootstraps is taught to American citizens from their early years. Ashton and Webb (1986) linked the life experiences of teachers with the ideology of individual progress:

> The oft-stated observation that teachers are carriers of middle-class values is undoubtedly true. The life experiences of most teachers demonstrate their allegiance to the ethic of vertical mobility, self-improvement, hard work, deferred gratification, self-discipline and personal achievement. These individualistic values rest on the assumption that the social system . . . works well, is essentially fair, and moves society slowly but inevitably toward progress. (pp. 29–30)

Several teachers talked about life experiences that had taught them that one can work one's way up the ladder through persistence and hard work. Twenty-three discussed their parents' occupations. Four of their fathers had held jobs that normally require college education: pharmacist, engineer, manager of a company and minister. Two fathers had owned their own small businesses. The fathers of the other seventeen had worked as laborers of various sorts, such as factory worker, railroad laborer, welder, farmer and fireman.

The great majority of the teachers had raised their own social class standing by earning a college degree and becoming teachers. Further, at least twelve had completed a Master's degree when the study began, and three more were in the process of doing so. Education had served them as an effective vehicle of upward mobility and personal 'betterment'. Their volunteering to participate in this project was part of a broader pattern of bettering themselves through education. For example, Lee had grown up on the South side of Chicago. His family was very poor and he had joined the Navy at age 17 'for a place to sleep and a place to eat' (25 January 1989). Of nine siblings, he was the only one to work his way out of poverty; he was driven by 'the inner feeling of wanting to be successful' and climbed the hurdles life put in his way (25 January 1989). He did not know why so many other people do not have that same drive; it had worked for him so presumably it could work for other people.

Most of the teachers' origins had been working class, but none of them articulated class consciousness. The lower or working class was a rung on the ladder that should be transcended rather than a collective who share common concerns that should be addressed using collective action.

Many people perceive their own social standing as higher than that of their parents.

> While the most common pattern is stability of class position from one generation to the next, upward mobility has also been common and outweighs downward mobility by roughly two to one. . . . Even those who have not been mobile have benefited, on the whole, from the aggregate improvement in living standards that has taken place since World War II. (Kluegel and Smith, 1986, p. 24)

While most social mobility has been due to an expansion of middle class jobs and widespread improvement of the living standard of Americans in general, people tend to attribute their own improved status to their own individual efforts. Further, teachers whose parents or grandparents had been European immigrants understood their family's rise in social standing as the result of initiative and hard work rather than economic expansion with White people having preference for better jobs and residence.

Social Activism

Participation in social movements sensitizes people to social justice issues and protest politics. Tracing the life histories of feminist teachers, Weiler (1988) found them to have lived through, and to some extent participated in, protests of the Civil Rights movement and to have examined oppression they had experienced in their own lives using insights from that movement. Participation in protest politics tends to persist through one's adulthood. Fendrich and Turner (1989) compared adults in 1986 who in 1971 had been student activists, government leaders and uninvolved; the former activists were still the most active in protest politics, while the other two groups had become more involved in conventional institutional politics.

The White teachers in this study for the most part had not participated in social activism; the teachers of color had. Only one White teacher described such an experience and its influence on what she perceived as important to do in the classroom:

> I've got a lot of friends that have been very involved in the women's movement and equal rights movement and peace movement. . . . I

get a lot of support from my friends, they say, 'That's really neat that you're doing that, that you're taking the time to talk to those kids.' One of my kids one day kept asking me about nuclear war, and all the time he's asking me about nuclear war he's drawing these little swastikas and it was just giving me the creeps. . . . You don't want to sit in the teacher's lounge and say, 'Well, we never got to math today, we ended up talking about swastikas in the back of the room.' You don't want to say that, so I think friends have helped a lot. (19 February 1988)

Having not participated in an active social protest movement themselves, most of the White teachers had not applied a radical analysis to *any* social issue or engaged in collective work directed toward institutional change.

Summary

Regardless of how much, or little, experience with racial or cultural diversity teachers have had, they enter the classroom with a considerably rich body of knowledge about social stratification, social mobility and human differences based on their experience as women, often upwardly mobile members of the working class and Whites. Their experience is usually interpreted within a structural functionalist perspective, reaffirming either conservatism or liberalism. The analogies they draw between racism and what they know about sexism, class mobility and the White ethnic experience tend to minimize or neutralize racism and multicultural education's implications for teaching. However, from the teachers' perspectives, they are accounting for racial discrimination, not ignoring it.

Their personal life experiences do not provide most teachers with a basis for linking multicultural education with a social movement. As they construct what it means for themselves, most apply it to classroom problems they frame within the assumptions that the process of schooling is ideologically neutral, the individual is the central unit of society and effort is generally rewarded without regard to ascribed group membership in society's institutions.

The Staff Development Project

Given the conditions of teaching and the life experiences of teachers, how much mileage can one get out of a staff development project such as the one examined in this study? Occasionally others involved in staff development have pointed out to me what they believe should have been done differently in order to make the project a 'success'. I believe that it could have been improved, but only to a limited extent.

Improvements Teachers Suggested

The teachers pointed out some problems that can be addressed. First, the use of multiple consultants resulted in repetition which occupied time that could have been spent differently, and disjointed connections between some sessions. For example, the Star Power simulation was never explicitly linked with any subsequent sessions. Repetition and disjointedness can be smoothed out.

Second, the teachers often said that there was too little time for discussion, although they had difficulty suggesting what they would drop in order to make more time for discussion. But I agree that there was too much input of new information and too little time for teachers to process it, which often left them to think through ideas either on their own or in the company of colleagues over lunch, neither of which helped them make many new connections. More planned discussion time would have helped; some educators also have teachers write journals to help them reflect.

Third, some teachers said the staff development project gave them too few concrete applications, which is an inevitable problem in a group of teachers from a wide range of subject areas and grade levels.[7] A staff development project can limit who participates, for example, to only elementary teachers of academic subject areas. Then discussions of school practice can be more specifically targeted to what these teachers actually do. What would be lost, however, would be insightful exchanges among teachers who occupy different positions in the school structure and rarely talk with each other about common issues as it is.

Characteristics of Effective Staff Development

In chapter 2, staff development models were discussed in relationship to three purposes for staff development: stimulation of professional growth, improvement of teacher use of a particular skill and implementation of a broad social policy (Fox, 1981). This project was based mainly on the first model and illustrates its strengths and limitations when applied to multicultural education. It can help generate and strengthen teacher interest in multicultural issues; that certainly happened. However, it also allows teachers to pick and choose what they want to learn and change in their own classrooms. As a result, it does not provide a very strong basis for instituting systematic changes in schools.

The project was relatively strong in some characteristics of effective staff development (Sparks and Loucks and Loucks-Horsley, 1989): participating teachers had some input into it (although those who wished to amplify conservative perspectives felt they did not have enough); it was more ongoing and systematic than multicultural education staff development projects usually are; and several sessions focused mainly on curricular and instructional practices. It was weak on other characteristics: it was not school-based nor was it linked with school-wide efforts; it did not have active administrative support; and it did not provide in-classroom coaching with feedback, which has been found effective in changing teaching practices. We were pleased that teachers worked so actively with cooperative learning given the relatively small amount of training provided. The project probably could have produced greater change in the implementation of one or two new teaching skills had its focus been limited to those skills, but we chose not to define multicultural education as one or two skills.

There are limits to the effectiveness of staff development efforts that lack systematic support from central administration, no matter how well conceptualized they are otherwise. William Pink (1990) compared two urban staff development projects, one of which was not well grounded in principles of effective staff development and the other of which was. He found both projects to have limited impact because both lacked strong administrative support that included a sound understanding of the nature of the changes being sought, a willingness to change bureaucratic processes so they support the change and a willingness to commit district resources to institutionalizing the change. The staff development project in this study did not have this kind of district support. Toward the end of the year, I asked a district administrator where it fit in with overall district goals; he responded that the district probably 'is barely conscious that there is such a program' (3 March 1989). But without administrative support, staff development projects in multicultural education, regardless of which model of staff development they employ, provide an illusion of making changes more than they provide its substance. Multicultural education advocates usually know this, hoping that such projects at least produce a pressure group within schools who will press for administrative support.

Theoretical Ambiguities in the Language of Multicultural Education

The language of multicultural education that was used over the two years reflects ambiguities in the field of multicultural education that were discussed in chapter 1. Consider the term 'equality', which is often used in multicultural education discourse and was frequently used in the staff development project. Does this mean equal opportunity and equal rights for individuals, or equal power and wealth across groups? It is usually not defined and therefore subject to the interpretation of the audience, allowing multicultural education to be pushed in different political and theoretical directions without most inductees being of aware of this happening.

The language used in the staff development sessions was either ambiguous in its political perspective or drawn mainly from liberalism; more conservative than radical structuralist language was used. For example, in session #2 on parent involvement, the first speaker articulated a cultural deprivation perspective toward low-income parents; the fact that she was African American would strengthen the credibility of a conservative perspective. The Star Power simulation between sessions #2 and #3 provided an excellent tool for developing a radical structuralist analysis, but language of radical structuralism was not explicitly attached to it and insights from it were not used subsequently. Session #3 on racism, sexism and poverty was packed with information that could contribute to either a liberal or a radical structuralist analysis, but the information focused more on demographic changes than on continued unequal relationships among groups, which lent itself better to liberalism ('We need to do something to address new realities') than to radical structuralism ('Let's examine why the same group inequalities persist'). The visits to community agencies could have examined local examples of oppression and social action agendas, or could have been viewed in terms of state supported programs that attempt to equalize the playing field. And so it went. In addition, over the two years the teachers were given many handouts by different consultants, about half of which articulated 'at risk' discourse.

Multicultural educators may shy away from using radical structuralist language and concepts, not wishing to alienate those with whom they wish to work. This study illustrates, however, what happens when language is either only mildly political or mainly liberal. Teachers who already have insights that can be developed from a radical structuralist perspective do not experience that development and teachers whose own perspective is either conservative or liberal select and interpret what they hear to make it fit their perspective about the nature of society. Were their subsequent actions in the classroom to contribute to a social movement anyway, their beliefs might not matter. But their subsequent actions were fairly limited, and most of the teachers believed they were doing as much as they could.

Summary

What is the potential of staff development for changing schools from a multicultural perspective, when the staff in schools is predominantly White? This study suggests that it is limited when not accompanied by changes in how schools function institutionally, and diversification of the teaching and administrative staff.

Teachers can develop more awareness and interest in multicultural issues. They can learn to respond more positively to students, broaden their repertoire of teaching strategies, and gain more knowledge about race, ethnicity, gender and social class. Within constraints of their work, a few will try new teaching strategies or develop new curriculum quite actively; more will try to make their classrooms a more positive, humanistic place.

As a vehicle for institutional change directed toward racial, class and gender equality, however, staff development is quite limited. Teachers focus on problems they see, wanting solutions. In so doing, they pick and choose what to learn, selecting that which fits in most readily with what they already do and how they already think. Their work conditions and most teachers' personal life experiences limit how they conceptualize ramifications of cultural diversity and social inequality. Teachers tend to see society and its schools as essentially good, although they may be concerned about problems within social and educational institutions. Further, in the context of the late 1980s, their understanding of multicultural education emerged from debates between conservatism and liberalism and most did not recognize radical structuralist impulses in multicultural education or its connection with social movements.

Is that a problem? The answer to this question depends on the changes one wishes to see in schools. As it emerged in the ferment of the late 1960s and early 1970s, advocates of multicultural education envisioned it as meaning changes in schools that would support and work with oppressed groups rather than blocking them and perpetuating White racism and patriarchy. Exactly what those changes might be include extensive curriculum revision; reduction or elimination of tracking; maintaining high expectations for all students, supported with appropriate teaching styles, language policies and parent involvement strategies; and collaborating with oppressed communities.

These changes do not happen through staff development alone. That may seem rather obvious, although many schools approach multiculturalism primarily through staff development. But not only does staff development not bring about institutional changes, it also is not sufficient for educating teachers about the changes that multicultural education should entail, given that people construct a template for understanding diversity and inequality in their daily life experiences. Staff development provides formal instruction; it does not substitute for life experiences. When ideas related to multicultural education are layered onto a conservative or even a liberal conception of human nature, diversity and society, multicultural education takes on meanings that fall short of systemic reform.

This study spanned only two years. Inductees to multicultural education may continue to develop their understanding of issues underlying it. As I reflect over the last twenty years of my own life, I certainly have grown from a starting point much like that of most of the White teachers in this study, although much of that growth has been through life experience. How can people who are interested in changing schools confront the power of life experience, the institutional conservatism of schools, and the limited potential of staff development? I explore thoughts about these questions in the final chapter.

Notes

1 After this study had been completed, he was appointed Multicultural Coordinator for the district. In that role, he actively consumed literature on multicultural education, gravitating enthusiastically toward the social reconstructionist approach (Sleeter and Grant, 1988).

2 Carl Grant and I have discussed the issue of the structure of teachers' work versus their personal autonomy and personal life experience, see Grant and Sleeter (1987a).

3 In other contexts, district administrators told me that teachers had requested a standardized curriculum because so many students moved within the district during the year. None of the teachers in this study discussed that with respect to their own frustrations about the curriculum, although three mentioned student absenteeism as a problem.

4 Both districts had affiliates of the National Educational Association, and the teachers were members of it. None of them mentioned this organization in connection with any of their comments about teacher powerlessness, work conditions, or improvement of instruction. I suspect they viewed the Association as being concerned mainly with salary, pay for extra work and benefits.

5 Similarly, Connell (1985) found teachers to recognize gendered inequalities of access, but not collective unequal relations of power (p. 185).

6 From radical structuralist perspectives, liberalism leaves several problems unexamined and contains some contradictions. First, by stressing the value of careers men of wealth have dominated, liberal feminism tacitly accepts disdain for manual labor and work involving care of the body, thereby reinforcing social class control as well as low status of work associated with physical reproduction. Second, while liberalism traditionally protects the distinction between public and private life, an analysis of sexism inevitably questions family relationships, marriage and family structure, treading into a domain that liberalism regards off-limits for social criticism. Third, as liberal feminists have identified an increasingly lengthy list of 'external' barriers to opportunity for women, they have increasingly recognized 'internal' barriers due to socialization in a patriarchal society: Women often make sex stereotypic and limiting choices due to their prior socialization. Preventing sex stereotypic socialization, however, suggests massive state intervention in childrearing, which contradicts the philosophy of social liberalism. Fourth, liberal feminism does not offer a critique of the economic structure or the relationship between the economy and the state, which leads to naive assumptions about the neutrality of the state and blind to the role of capitalism in women's oppression (Jaggar, 1983, pp. 186–203).

7 I have participated in staff development projects for multicultural education that involve not only a range of teachers, but also a few counselors, librarians, speech pathologists and the school nurse. While multicultural education is relevant to all of their work, its specific applications differ markedly.

Chapter 8

Multicultural Education, Staff Development, and a New American Dream

Changing what teachers do is very difficult, particularly in areas that are informed by deep value commitments and beliefs, and reinforced by taken-for-granted, institutionalized processes and relationships. Teachers will do what they feel they can do, given what they perceive as constraints and imperatives of their work as a whole, and given what they take for granted as valid and important. Staff development can teach them new skills to add to what they do; it can also help them examine those constraints, imperatives, and taken-for-granted beliefs. But given the reforms that multicultural education would entail, the changes brought about by staff development structured around an individual development model are modest and uneven. What, then, does this study suggest to those who want to make schools more responsive to diversity and social justice?

It had been two years since the study ended and I was pondering what to say in this final chapter. Before leaving campus to head home to my computer, I had an appointment with Jill (Janice's colleague) to work on an independent study. My conversation with her helped bring some ideas into focus.

We talked at some length about the development of their teaming, in which they had integrated Janice's general education 'at risk' class and Jill's severe LD class. Since I had visited them last, they had continued to develop and refine several practices, including more cooperative learning, more parent involvement, and teaching higher-level thinking skills. For example, they learned to use brainstorming techniques to help students formulate sophisticated questions to guide their learning, teaching students to pool their knowledge and questions in cooperative groups. Then Jill declared that our staff development project was what started everything they were doing now. Janice, a White woman who had been teaching for years, had been excited by the ideas that were presented and had told Jill, also a White woman, to enroll with the second group of teachers (whom I did not study). The sessions had spoken directly to concerns and beliefs they held, and had given them enough direction to launch a self-sustaining project for restructuring much of their teaching. They believed in the capabilities of children, and were dismayed at experiences children face — including school experiences — that dampen rather than develop those capacities. Jill commented that both of them, being older and experienced, had seen over the years much that children are capable of; they regarded their belief in children as realistic and well-founded rather than as naively idealistic. They approached teaching as experimenters, trying various processes that bring out the best in children; Jill said that she and Janice spent hours critiquing what they tried in order to get better at it. Their colleagues still were not trying to learn from them, but had stopped criticizing them; and the district had adopted some of their thinking skills material (which they were using with 'at risk' and severe LD students) to use in the gifted program.

My conversation with Jill helped me untangle complexities in the relationship between individual teacher agency, school structure, and staff development for multicultural education. Anthony Giddens (1979) explored these complexities in his theoretical analysis of social change. He noted that, '"Action" and "structure" normally appear in both the sociological and philosophical literature as antinomies' (p. 48); theorists concern themselves mainly either with individual subjects who are viewed as relatively free to act as they wish, or with social structures that constrain and overpower individual agency. However, he argued that 'the notions of action and structure presuppose one another' and exist in 'a dialectical relation' (p. 53). Social structures are constituted over time in everyday actions, and imprinted in memory traces of individuals, normally taken for granted as the way things simply 'are'.

> Every process of action is a production of something new, a fresh act; but at the same time all action exists in continuity with the past, which supplies the means of its initiation. Structure thus is not to be conceptualized as a barrier to action, but as essentially involved in its production. (p. 70)

The space in which an individual acts is bounded by structures that limit what a person physically could do, as well as by structures that are socially constructed through routinized action that one takes for granted. Individuals who benefit reasonably well from existing social arrangements are least likely to question socially constituted structures and over time, in their everyday actions, reproduce them. But 'those in subordinate positions in a society might have a greater penetration of the conditions of social reproduction than those who otherwide dominate them' (Giddens, p. 72). Taking fewer existing social structures for granted, such individuals are more likely not to reproduce them, and to question them.

The teachers of color in this study did take fewer social structures for granted than did the White teachers. But some White teachers, such as Janice and Jill, also questioned how schools are structured, and actively engaged themselves in reconstructing specific patterns most teachers accepted as given. In their case, they deconstructed the separation between special and general education, and limitations to learning placed on special education and 'at risk' students. They also questioned the dominance of the textbook, especially in science, and the belief that parents do not care about their children's education.

Giddens' notion of the dialectical relationship between individuals and social structures is important for change agents. It suggests that both levels must be addressed simultaneously. Social structures affect both the conditions under which teachers work as well as conditions under which they live as members of particular social classes, races and genders. But within, and in spite of, structural arrangement, teachers actively create and recreate meanings and patterned activities. They think and make choices.

Advancing an education that is multicultural requires attending simultaneously to the composition of the teaching force and the life experiences teachers bring with them, the long-term processes involved in developing teachers' knowledge and skills, and the structure of the institutions in which they teach. In this chapter I will offer recommendations regarding people who teach, schools as institutions, and the field of multicultural education. Readers may be overwhelmed by my insistence that all of these factors need to be addressed simultaneously. This can only happen if one is working in collaboration with others who are addressing these factors as well.

The People Who Teach

Who is willing to rock the boat? As one ponders the boats that do not get rocked nearly hard enough, it is tempting to succumb to the idea that many boats are simply unrockable, and that individuals accept things as they are rather than challenge them. Much of the literature which examines school structures and the conditions of teachers' work could support this claim. But there are Jills. And as Jill reminded me, some people are quite willing to take on structural change and need only a push and support. As a teacher, I was also a boat-rocker from the first day I student taught (much to the consternation of my cooperating teacher, I am sure). Much of my boat-rocking has been naive, but I, Jill, and many other people have approached 'what is' as if it were a canvas on which to paint 'what could be'. Henry Giroux (1983) argued the need to identify pockets of resistance and politicize the activity there. While those who refuse to accept 'what is' do not automatically construct a political analysis of their resistance, their critical stance toward everyday routines can provide entree to the development of 'strategies in school in which oppositional cultures might provide the basis for a viable political force' (p. 101).

Three groups of teachers emerged in this study as most willing to question and resist some form of domination as it is acted out in school: the teachers of color (although their understanding of racism did not automatically generalize to gender and class oppression), many teachers in special programs that serve students whom the general education program fails or excludes, and teachers in elective, non-academic subject areas whose work was much less controlled than was that of other teachers. Teachers who have been involved in protest politics could constitute a fourth group, since they would have experienced collectively confronting social structures or practices that many people take for granted (Weiler, 1988). The teaching profession needs more people who bring with them a critique of the status quo. We also need to identify and politicize those already in the profession who sense that injustices are at work. The recommendations below address recruiting a more diverse teaching force and helping White educators recognize limits to their own perspectives.

Rethinking Who to Recruit as Teachers

Currently the teaching force is populated by people who self-select to enter teacher education, can pass a growing battery of measures of traditional academic competence (for example, National Teachers' Exam, Pre-Professional Skills Test, grade point average), and can afford to stay in college for an increasing length of time. This recruitment and selection process builds in biases that work against multicultural education.

Of great importance, the teaching force is becoming increasingly White, and given the lengthened time it is taking to complete teacher certification programs, it may also be becoming increasingly middle class. The proportion of teacher education students of color has been gradually declining and predictions hold that by the year 2000 only about 5 per cent of the nation's teaching force will be of color. Several authors have discussed reasons for the declining proportion of teachers of color, including use of culturally biased tests (particularly the NTE), growth in opportunities in other fields, the low status of the teaching profession, a decline in the number of students of color who can afford to attend college and desegregation resulting in teaching positions going to White teachers that earlier would have gone to teachers of color (for example, Dudley and Bell, 1991; Haberman, 1989; Irvine, 1991; Smith, 1984; Tewel and Trubowitz, 1987).

While teachers of color are not necessarily better, more radical, or more knowledgable than White teachers, they do bring life experiences that provide a basis for criticizing practices White people tend to accept and for rejecting culturalist and other simplistic explanations of inequality. The teachers of color in this study brought with them a clear understanding that racism exists and cannot be reduced to individual attitudes, and that the struggles in which people of color have engaged for centuries have not yet been won. They also brought more commitment to serving students of color and to changing schools than most of the White teachers. In addition, teachers of color bring higher expectations for students of color (Irvine, 1991) and more connections with minority communities than White teachers bring (Metz, 1990).

What we need is a highly diverse teaching force, diverse in terms of race, social class background, gender, primary language and disability, in which a wide range of life experiences and perspectives are well represented. This will provide the ferment from which good, radical, multicultural praxis can emerge. Over the past twenty years I have worked with groups of educators that have ranged from all-White to very pluralistic. Generally, the more diverse a group has been, the more richly it has conceptualized what multicultural education means. Predominantly White groups rarely develop the range of insights and commitments they need to address diversity constructively. Allowing the teaching force to become more homogeneous cuts schools off increasingly from their best source of knowledge about their diverse students and about the diverse context within which all Americans will live.

It is vitally important that diversifying the teaching force become a first priority; presently it is not. For the most part schools of education and state departments have first raised traditional standards and then tacked on programs to try to recruit teachers of color. Diversifying the teaching force does not mean sacrificing quality. Rather, it enhances quality. But it cannot be approached as an afterthought.

One step toward diversifying the teaching force is to support and back the actions historically Black institutions wish to take to improve their own teacher education programs, since they are the institutions with the best track records for preparing African American teachers. 'Even though the historically black institutions only represent 5 per cent of the institutions of higher education, the HBIs have produced 66 per cent of the black teachers in the United States' (Clark, 1987, p. 86). Educators should also support the teacher education programs of institutions that belong to the Hispanic Association of Colleges and Universities. In many current discussions of the reform of teacher education, predominantly Black, Latino and Indian institutions of higher education are ignored.

Predominantly White institutions should also seek to diversify their enrollments. Teacher education programs should develop shorter routes to certification for college graduates of color, form partnerships with two-year colleges (Haberman, 1989), channel funds into scholarship programs for students of color (academics can donate their book royalties to scholarship funds, for example) and change or eliminate policies and practices that discourage people of color from entering the profession (such as biased testing). Teacher educators need to design requirements for entrance into teacher education that recognize and reward what teachers of color often bring, such as competency in more than one language or dialect, faith in the ability of students of color to learn, and knowledge of families and communities of their own cultural background.

In addition, the profession must work strongly to educate low-income students of color and prepare them for college, since that is the pool from which most teachers of color will come. Writing about Black teachers, for example, Irvine (1991) noted that, 'The children of the black middle class are preparing for medical, legal, and business careers, and the black community is not likely to encourage them to enter teacher education' (p. 39). Bright students of color from low-income families are more likely to enter teaching, but in order to do so, they first need to be prepared to enter and succeed in college.

Teacher education programs should also seek students who are creative risk-takers, and who have had experience with protest politics and social movements. This recommendation, however, conflicts with the structure of most teacher workplaces, especially those in urban areas. Jobs that are strongly routinized and controlled, and in which employees have little decision-making power, do not attract innovators and risk-takers; quite the opposite (Lortie, 1986). To attract creative people with life experiences in activism, the work of teachers also needs to be restructured, as I discuss later in this chapter.

Educating White Teachers

All teachers, regardless of cultural background, need to be trained in multicultural education. Teachers of color as well as White teachers need to learn about groups other than themselves, how racism works, how oppression is institutionalized in schools and alternative teaching strategies. But based on this study and my own experience as a White educator, I will make some observations about multicultural staff development for White teachers. I must stress, though, that working with White teachers does not in any way substitute for diversifying the teaching force.

As discussed in chapter 2, the literature in multicultural education provides considerable guidance for educating teachers. I will not repeat that guidance here, except to stress the importance of planned, long-term staff development. Multicultural teacher educators have described stages of development: awareness, acceptance and affirmation (Baker, 1983; Burstein and Cabello, 1989; Grant and Melnick, 1978). At the awareness level, teachers are becoming aware of what the issues and problems are; at the acceptance level, they are acquiring basic knowledge about cultural diversity, inequality and teaching implications; and at the affirmation level, they are developing new teaching skills.

At the end of fourteen all-day sessions, most of the teachers in this study were still mainly at the awareness level. That does not mean the fourteen days were useless; it only means that people do not proceed through the stages quickly. As I reflect on my own growth, I know that a White teacher can reach the level of affirmation of multicultural education, but it certainly took me longer than fourteen days! There are many other areas in which we routinely plan for long-term growth, such as in learning to read. School districts and teacher education institutions need to do the same planning for multicultural education.

That education, however, should not be built on the assumption that teachers do not know anything about diversity and inequality. Often multicultural education staff development consists of learning about people of color. But as this study illustrated, regardless of how little experience White teachers have had with members of racial minority groups, they do bring a perspective about the social order that they constructed within the context of their own life experience and use that perspective to self-select what to learn, believe and regard as valid. Joyce King (1991) described the perspective of most White teachers as 'dysconscious racism':

> Dysconscious racism is a form of racism that tacitly accepts dominant white norms and privileges. It is not the *absence* of consciousness (that is, not unconsciousness) but an *impaired* consciousness or distorted way of thinking about race as compared to, for example, critical consciousness. (p. 135)

White teachers need to examine their own life experiences and the perspectives they have developed on the basis of those experiences, in order to come to terms with the limits of those experiences and to recognize alternative perspective about the social order. Whites need to grasp the dual institutional system that has always characterized this society and their own location in it (Ringer and Lawless, 1989).

This is threatening, but less so when built on the premise that what White people know about the social world is generally correct, but only for understanding White people. There are multiple realities; somebody else's reality does not negate one's own, but at time same time one must recognize limits beyond which one's own sense of reality may not reliably transfer. In teaching pre-service students about racism, I begin by having them describe their basic beliefs about how equal opportunity works, why people live where they live, what an ideal student and an ideal parent are like, and so forth. Then they examine their own experiences and communication with people of other racial and social class groups through their schooling, their neighborhoods, their churches, their workplaces and so forth, to identify limits to the context within which their perspectives are valid. I then have them read *The Education of a WASP* (Stalvey, 1988), which is an autobiographical account of a White middle class woman reconstructing her perspective about racism in America, gradually, through interaction with African American people. This provides a framework for validating White people's beliefs about themselves, while at the same time showing graphically that their own experiences do not necessarily generalize to people of color. It also provides a context for critically examining the quality of contact and communication my White students have actually had with people of color. As they come to terms with the limits of their own experiences and their own networks for learning about other people's experiences and perspectives, their receptivity to learning increases. This is not a short process, by the way; it cannot be accomplished in a one- or two-day workshop and provides only the beginning to developing awareness.

Experienced teachers of children who are failing in the mainstream of general education can develop a political consciousness of how institutions oppress and create failure, following a somewhat different mode of analysis. In this study it was a special education teacher who articulated the best radical structuralist analysis of oppression, based on her experience in special education. Jill and Janice both taught special education and 'at risk' students. This kind of teaching experience sensitizes many teachers to the capabilities and basic humanity of 'failures', to the pain of their failure and to inflexibility and injustices built into the education system. This sensitivity can be developed into an institutional analysis, which then can be extended to examine other forms of oppression.

Changing Schools by Starting with Oneself

Over the two years of this study, often 'those other teachers' emerged as a topic of discussion among those participating in the staff development project. After gaining some new insights, teachers would leave sessions wanting to spread the word to their colleagues. At times they reminded me of people who have experienced religious conversion, who then focus their attention on others who have not yet been converted.

Given the popular discussions of multiculturalism in the late 1980s and 1990s, multicultural education can be viewed as an 'in' thing that many people want to be associated with. This increases the likelihood that teachers who are new to the area will leap onto the bandwagon, and before they have reeducated themselves to a significant degree, seek to spread what they know to other teachers, calling it 'multicultural education'.

This is exactly what Jill and Janice did *not* do, which makes them so interesting. Rather than attempting to convert their peers to child-centered learning and high expectations for low-achieving students, they devoted their energies to reconstructing their own practice and learning actually to implement their ideals. At the time of this writing, they have now been teaming for three years, during which time they have become increasingly innovative and skilled. Jill is devoting part of her summer to studying professional literature that can help them expand and develop their praxis. The better they become at acting on what they believe, the more power they have to attract the attention of other teachers and the more they have to share with them.

It is easy to latch onto a new ideology without really understanding it, and without applying it to a reexamination of one's own life and actions. The most effective change agents are those who first learn to live in accordance with the principles they are advocating. I would urge any reader who is wondering how to design a more effective multicultural staff development program, to also spend time developing her or his own understanding of the issues underlying multicultural education, to reconstruct his/her own daily life and work to affirm equality and to engage in support of social movements led by oppressed people.

Multicultural Education as Institutional Change

Many educators and staff developers conceive of multicultural education as something that occurs within classrooms, and as under the control of individual teachers who are assumed to be fairly autonomous. This study has illustrated problems with this conception of multicultural education, which I will summarize briefly.

First, multicultural education historically has been connected with broader struggles for institutional change. Its main advocates and developers have also been concerned with desegregation, tracking and grouping, standardized testing, bilingual education, community involvement and so forth. Most of the literature about multicultural education, however, focuses specifically on classroom practices, enabling educators to disconnect it from broader issues of power and access. Similarly, literature on desegregation, bilingual education, tracking and so forth, tend to be separate bodies, even through they address similar concerns. However, as an orientation to schooling that 'pervade(s) all aspects of educational programs' (Grant, 1978, p. 46), multicultural education cannot be simply reduced to practices that take place within classrooms.

Second, as argued in chapter 7, classrooms are not autonomous units; they are constituted within organizations, and much of what teachers do responds to demands, capabilities and limitations of the organization. Teachers are paid for working a given number of hours, during which time they are to transmit a given body of curriculum to a given number of students. The students themselves are tested and divided institutionally according to how well they master that curriculum in the time allotted and teachers are assigned batches of students within this system of tracks and programs. Multicultural education advocates some practices that can be incorporated into this system, such as calling on students equitably and replacing recitation with groupwork; but it also questions the system, including monolingualism, the content of curriculum, the teaching strategies that are used and the categorization of students into 'winners and losers'. But as long as the context and demands of teaching remain structured as they are, teachers will tend to do little with multicultural education unless they happen to be people who buck the system.

The School as the Center of Change

The school, rather than the individual teacher, needs to be viewed as the center of change. By doing this, we focus on the institutional arrangements, processes and conditions in school buildings, the people who work there and the culture they create, and the institutional context within which the school exists (Sirotnik, 1987).

Michael Fullan (1990b) reviewed research on school improvement projects to develop his discussion of schools as the center of change. He distinguished between innovations which add on programs or change single parts of the school program, and institutional changes which reorganize and reconstruct deep institutional factors. Based on his review, he concluded that,

> Most reform attempts are superficial and/or short lived. Major altera-
> tions are required in structural and normative work conditions of
> teachers and students. We need powerful strategies for powerful
> change. Powerful strategies mean working directly on institutional
> changes over a period of years in the same settings. (p. 252)

Institutional factors include hierarchical structures that stratify both students and faculty, structures that standardize students and teachers and those that emerge from breaking learning into a sequence of decontextualized sub-tasks to be administered by teachers or other staff who specialize in a particular grade level, achievement level and so forth. Skrtic (1991) examined how most schools, as formalized bureaucracies, manage diversity by creating add-on programs that remain marginal to the institution, allowing the insti-tution to remain essentially unchanged. Occasionally, however, schools do undergo fundamental change when,

> someone, some group, or some event increases ambiguity enough
> to cast doubt on the prevailing paradigm and, under conditions of
> increased ambiguity, someone or some group, acting on a different
> set of values, manages to decrease the ambiguity by redefining the
> organization for themselves and others. In fact, it is just this sort of
> organizational phenomenon that one finds in successful schools. Their
> success turns on human agency, on the values, expectations, and
> actions of the people who work in them. (p. 179)

The schools Deborah Meier has reorganized in New York City are an example of institutionally reorganized multicultural schools (Meier, 1987 and 1991).

Much staff development ignores the context in which teachers teach, treating teachers as autonomous individuals. This ignoring of the structural context of teaching is the greatest reason for minimal impact of teacher education in general, and for the persistent similarities in what teachers do (Denscombe, 1982). Staff development for multicultural education needs to be conceptualized as implementation of a broad social policy (Fox, 1981), in which institutional change is the long-range goal. This means that it cannot be a free-floating activity in which teachers are removed from their work context, taught new ideas and skills and expected to return to that same context and do their work differently.

For the past two years, I and two colleagues have been involved in a school improvement project that has approached multicultural education as a process of institutional change. Working in four schools, we have helped core teams that include teachers and the principal to complete a 'do-it-yourself' ethnography on their own schools in order to identify institutional practices that reproduce inequality and that limit what teachers can do from a multi-cultural perspective. Approaching change as an institutional problem is helping staff members generate some of the right observations and questions. For example, teachers are noticing that African American male students occupy a low status in the school in a variety of related ways, such as in their dis-proportionate placement in special education, their disproportionate referral for disciplinary action, their poor representation in the curriculum, and their lack of representation on most school staffs. The analysis is attempting to help educators understand how the school reinforces the broader society's con-struction of African American males into a low-status pariah group who are channeled for self-destruction and incarceration rather than power and self-development. From that analysis, they can then ask how their school can construct a different position and identity for African American male students in school.

The issue of institutional change, however, loops back into the earlier discussion about the people who teach. White teachers tend to rely on their own understanding of the social order and it limits their conception of how racism and classism work. Most teachers, being women whose lives recreate gender relations, have not even critiqued sexism in much depth, as I argued in chapter 7. While teachers are educable and institutions are changable, the school as an institution cannot be changed (from within, at any rate) without simultaneously addressing issues connected with the people who teach and the social structures they take for granted. This problem is becoming quite evident in the school improvement project in which I have been working, as all-White or predominantly-White core teams experience difficulty owning some respons-ibility for problems they have documented through their school assessment.

Probably the one individual whose analysis of institutional discrimina-tion matters most is the principal (who is even more likely than the teachers to be a White male). In a study of high achieving African American schools, for example, Sizemore (1990) found principal leadership to be the single most important factor distinguishing these schools from lower-achieving African American schools. Recruiting principals whose life and professional experience helps them critique institutional discrimination and appreciate strengths of oppressed groups, and educating them to restructure schools for multicultural education is essential.

Restructuring Debates

This study has illustrated the limited power of the teachers in the school districts participating in this staff development project. One may be tempted to address the main problems in the study by arguing that teachers need more power. In fact, much of the literature on staff development in the late 1980s has done exactly that, arguing that schools need to be restructured to empower the people within them to make their own decisions about how to conduct their work.

For example, Roland Barth (1990) compellingly discussed the reform of schools to make them communities of learners and leaders: 'The biggest problem besetting schools is the primitive quality of human relationships among children, parents, teachers, and administrators' (p. 36). He explored conditions under which people will learn and lead, arguing that most schools destroy those conditions by requiring teachers and students to conform to outcomes somebody else expects. His discussion of 'list logic' was similar to Skrtic's (1991) discussion of the standardization of tasks in most bureaucracies. Barth argued that administrators need to provide conditions under which the special talents and capabilities of the particular people in the schools can grow and flourish.

Similarly, Corcoran (1990) concluded his review of teacher work conditions by observing that most schools do not provide good working conditions for teachers by providing sufficient resources, collegiality, opportunities for decision-making, recognition and opportunities for professional development. Other authors have focused more specifically on teacher power, arguing that teachers are closest to students and ought to make the decisions affecting how and what students are taught (for example, Sickler, 1988).

Arguments to restructure schools and empower teachers coincide with my own analysis of the powerlessness teachers experience. Teachers should have more authority, time, and support to design their own classroom practice, and to use their creativity and expertise. However, I am worried about the tendency of many educators to reduce education reform to teacher empowerment. Most arguments about restructuring do not address the identities and social positions of teachers as White upwardly mobile women, whose life experiences usually limit their ability to conceptualize how social institutions function for other people and the strengths and experiences of cultural groups of which they are not members. Michelle Fine (1991) noted that,

> Today, many African-American educators and parents say, quietly, that they are suspect of the rhetoric of teacher empowerment. I've been asked more than once, 'You're suggesting that schools give *more* power to white teachers to wield over our kids?' (p. 153)

Teacher empowerment *should* be part of restructuring schools for multicultural education; usually it is not a topic that is discussed much in connection with multicultural education. As Connell (1985) pointed out in discussing the need of educational reformers to involve teachers in greater decision-making,

The competing ideologies surrounding education give the emphasis to everybody's interests except teachers': the needs of the child, 'parental choice', the needs of industry, the workers, the interests of society. There is constant pressures on teachers to sacrifice their interests to those of the kids, variously interpreted. (p. 203)

But this cannot be done in the absence of recruiting a diverse teaching force and preparing them to teach from multicultural perspectives.

Multicultural Education and the American Dream

The field of multicultural education itself needs to articulate more clearly a new American dream and strengthen its connections with those social movements that are attempting to reconstruct American society. At the 1991 meeting of the American Educational Research Association, Geneva Gay discussed the widening gap in their understanding of multicultural education by those who have been involved actively in it for the past two decades and by those who cycle in and out of the field for short periods of time. Those who are now 'old timers' to multicultural education developed their sensibilities about the field in the civil rights struggles of the late 1960s, and have been developing and broadening their conceptual understanding of oppression and multiculturalism since that time. Many teachers in this study illustrate well those who are new to the field, and whose understanding of it does not develop very far because of their lack of intimate connection with social movements and communities of color, as well as the constraints of their work.

In chapters 1 and 7, I discussed ambiguities in the discourse of many people who are involved in multicultural education. The issues of oppression can be understood best, in their complexity, through radical structuralism. Much of the language of multicultural education is rooted in liberalism. Issues of inequality can be discussed through conservatism, as well as liberalism and radical structuralism. Many educators whose own perspective is conservative dismiss multicultural education, but some, such as Diane Ravitch (1990) manage to translate multicultural education into conservatism, in the process transforming its meaning into something quite different from that which its developers had intended. In the 1990s, as liberals increasingly find themselves on the defensive and conservatism continues to enjoy growing status and legitimacy, there is danger of multicultural education becoming pulled away more and more from its roots in radical social struggle.

Let me emphasize that I am not locating multicultural education in radical structuralism because it is 'politically correct'. Radical structuralist analyses of oppression offer the greatest historical insight into the continued workings of oppression. They push us to consider a wide ranging agenda for social change, and to be cautious against complacency when a few gains have been made. By locating individuals in social groups, they remind us that there is no utopia in which group membership does not matter, and caution us against accepting naive views of individualism that usually mask group conflicts.

The more ambiguous multicultural educators are about their theoretical perspective, the more readily their ideas can be couched in the prevailing perspective, whatever it is, and the less powerfully they have positioned themselves to critique that perspective. Further, the likelihood is heightened that newcomers to the field will conceptualize it in a way that falls short of major change in schools or society. I was dismayed to hear teachers in this study say, for example, that they were 'doing' multicultural education because they had decorated their rooms with bright colors, or used cooperative learning occasionally, or taught a lesson on family heritage. Part of the problem was that they needed more examples of what they could do, but a larger problem was that most of them simply did not see the existence of oppression. Those who adhered to a conservative perspective saw very little about schools or the dominant society that need changing. Those who adhered to a liberal perspective believed that by making adaptations for failing students and offering them more supports, or by celebrating some differences among people, they were creating an even playing field. From my perspective, they were making some starts, but that is all.

To develop the discourse and praxis in multicultural education, and to locate it more directly in a radical structuralist analysis of oppression, we need to rearticulate the American dream and develop more explicit linkages with grass-roots social movements.

Rearticulating the American Dream

Historically, as I discussed in chapter 1, the American dream for most people has meant achieving upward mobility, education and financial security; owning their own home; choosing how and where to live; and being able to construct a personally satisfying lifestyle (Roper Organization, 1987). For most Americans, the dream has been predicated on a belief in individual competition and material accumulation within a hierarchical social and economic structure. Historically pursuit of the American dream was open only to people who were White and male; gradually the right to pursue one's dreams was extended.

Contextualized within a racist, patriarchal, capitalistic society, adherence to the American dream as most Americans view it has legitimated the construction of an increasingly stratified and polarized society. Both conservatism and liberalism offer explanations for people not achieving their dreams that leave unquestioned the stratified, individualistic context and the competitive nature of the pursuit. The 1980s and early 1990s witnessed an increase in competitive individualism and a decrease in concern about the welfare of others, as Americans, and particularly those who are White and male, have been confronted with an increasingly limited and rough playing field for their own personal advancement. A more humane and egalitarian, and a less materialistic American dream, supported by a more egalitarian social and economic structure, would reconnect public with private welfare, greatly reduce rather than increase the gap between the haves and have nots, and free many more people to make genuine choices about how to live within a context that does not promote the control of some groups over others.

These are the kinds of ideals that are embedded in multicultural education. Advancing these ideals requires considerable conceptual as well as political work, including a rigorous analysis of the structures and ideology in our society that militate against them. Too often people who are concerned about equity issues stop short of asking for substantial social change when a few gains have been made, or when placed on the defensive by the growth of conservatism's popularity. For example, Jacqueline Jordan Irvine (1991) discussed how experience with school desegregation transformed and limited how advancement for African Americans is now often articulated:

> Desegregation has altered the concept of the collective whole, the collective struggle, and the collective will. There has been a transformation from valuing collective achievement to valuing individual achievement; that is, the individual is perceived as an independent entity who achieves success through merit and effort. (p. 36)

Within the American public are cultural traditions from which we can learn and rearticulate a more just and egalitarian American dream. I will suggest some examples. I do not wish to be interpreted, however, as suggesting that classical European thought has nothing to offer. Some very worthwhile ideas that should be part of a rearticulated American dream do come from Europe; but compelling and worthwhile ideas come from elsewhere as well. Americans who insist on drawing our national ideals only from classical European bodies of thought are limiting greatly our ability to construct a society that actually embodies the ideals of equality and democracy.

Afrocentric theorists are developing a rich body of thought rooted in African value and social systems, which provide excellent seeds for reconceptualizing what the American dream might mean. Quoting Boykin (1986), Jacqueline Irvine (1991) compared the main dimensions differentiating African and European cultures, shown in table 8.1 (see also, for example, Asante, 1988 and 1990; Shade, 1989). For example, valuing spiritualism over materialism, interconnectedness over separateness, and harmony with nature over its mastery suggest far-reaching ramifications for reordering our social and economic system, that need to be considered.

Native American thought shares many values with Afrocentric thought. Paula Gunn Allen (1986), for example, pointed out that most native cultures distributed goods and power in an egalitarian fashion, placed women in a central position, lived successfully for thousands of years in harmony with nature, and valued spiritual harmony over material gain (p. 211). She further

Table 8.1: Comparison of African and European cultures

African	European
Spiritualism	Materialism
Harmony with nature	Mastery over nature
Organic metaphor	Mechanistic metaphor
Expressive movement	Impulse control
Interconnectedness	Separateness
Affect	Reason
Event orientation	Clock orientation
Orally based culture	Print-based culture
Expressive individualism	Possessive individualism
Uniqueness valued	Sameness valued

Source: Boykin (1986) cited by Irvine (1991) p. 25.

argued that native peoples have contributed to many American ideals, although Whites do not acknowledge their contribution.

> America does not seem to remember that it derived its wealth, its values, its food, much of its medicine, and a large part of its 'dream' from Native America. . . . Feminists too often believe that no one has ever experienced the kind of society that empowered women and made that empowerment the basis of its rules of civilization. The price the feminist community must pay because it is not aware of the recent presence of gynarchical societies on this continent is unnecessary confusion, division, and much lost time (pp. 211–3)

Rather than creating an entirely new American dream or clinging to the old one, we can learn much by remembering and drawing on the dreams and forms of civilization of native peoples in addition to African peoples.

Much feminist thought, especially socialist and radical feminism, shares ideals of African and Native American thought, including a concern for the quality of life of people, value for the body and its connection with the natural world, and a vision of a more egalitarian world. Feminist activity and theory has focused on improvement of life for many of the most vulnerable segments of society, 'organizing and nationalizing movements for public health (mental and physical), poor relief, penal and other institutional reform, education for the previously uneducated, and child welfare' (Sapiro, 1990, p. 36). In her critique of young women's conceptions of the American dream, Ruth Sidel (1990) argued for a new American dream and noted,

> If our society is to be a caring, humane place to live, to rear our children and to grow old, we must recognize that some aspects of life — the education of our young people, health care, child care, the texture of community life, and quality of the environment — are more important than profit. (p. 230)

There are tensions among diverse oppressed groups that cannot be ig-nored or oversimplified. For example, in spite of their common concern with reducing poverty, African Americans and White women compete for power to frame issues and reap rewards. These tensions among oppressed groups arise in a large part precisely from those structural features of American society that most need to be challenged: hierarchy, extreme individualism, competition and materialism. 'The point, then, is to formulate unifying prin-ciples that speak to each of the composite groups and give priority to none, but which can also confront the contradictions of the existing accumulation process' (Bronner, 1990, p. 163).

Rather than taking those structural features as given and advocating extending the American dream to more Americans within the current structural context, those who are involved in multicultural education should explicitly rearticulate the American dream as well as its structural context. It is the latter — its structural context, and particularly its economic context — that the field has addressed most weakly, leaving open a very wide range of interpretations of ideals such as 'equality', including interpretations that justify the status quo.

Connecting with Social Movements

Multicultural education becomes disconnected with social movements that are working toward structural changes that would benefit oppressed groups, when its advocates are disconnected from such movements. In contrast, 'inter-ventions within education can be regarded as effectively radical only when they have the potential to be linked with similar struggles elsewhere to produce transformative results' (Whitty, 1985, p. 168).

Most of the teachers in this study had not been involved in civil rights or other social movements. Though aware that collective movements have existed, several teachers were surprised to learn that the activities of the 1960s had not brought about desired states of equality. Being unconnected to a social movement directed toward equality, most of the teachers in this study could not be expected to advance to a significant degree the interests of oppressed people and to engage systematically in changing institutions that reproduce inequality, including their own educational institutions.

Sivanandon (1985) argued that decontextualized racism awareness training assuages White guilt by making Whites think they are doing something con-structive by engaging in such training and deflects energy from political struggle to psychic self-examination and flagelation. He roundly criticized racism aware-ness training in Britain, pointing out that, 'in terms of the material conditions of the workless, homeless, school-less, welfare-less Blacks of slum city, all this paroxysm of activity has not made the blindest bit of difference' (p. 22).

Social structural change requires collective action. Emancipatory collective action needs to be led by members of oppressed groups: 'If urban school reform is to occur, those most oppressed by these schools must "lead the charge"' (Williams, 1989, p. 52). White professionals can engage and work *with* oppressed groups, but doing so does not come naturally to them. When White professionals who wish to be progressive adopt some of the language and practices of a movement without ever actually becoming a part of or involved with grass-roots struggle, they acquire the illusion of making changes, but not necessarily the substance.

Those who are actively involved in multicultural education should themselves become connected with emancipatory social movements and make those connections explicit. Yes, many educators will find such connections offensive, and will not be attracted to multicultural education because it seems too radical. But others, especially those who are engaged in struggles against oppression, will find multicultural education a welcome rallying point.

Conclusion

I began the study reported in this book wondering the extent to which a staff development project in multicultural education could bring about change in classrooms and schools. I found that it can bring about some limited and uneven changes. Staff development in multicultural education, by itself, barely scratches the surface of the kinds of changes that ought to take place for schools to work more actively toward social justice for oppressed groups. However, this analysis of a staff development project reveals several specific areas in which future work in multicultural education should be directed: greatly diversifying the teaching force, helping White teachers come to grips with limits to their own understanding of social stratification, developing multicultural education as institutional change, rearticulating the American dream and developing stronger and more explicit connections with existing emancipatory social movements. Multicultural education is political work, and these are areas in which we can act.

Postscript

Growth, learning and change do not end with the conclusion of data collection. On occasion I still see many of the teachers who participated in this study and some of them remind me how unpredictable change can be. They also cause me to reflect on the extent to which teacher education is contextualized within other events that may also propel change. Sometimes when I wonder whether my own efforts have accomplished much, I need to consider them in relationship to a constellation of factors.

Michael is now the Director of Multicultural Education for his school district. In that position, he is a strong spokesperson for multicultural education. Over the past year he has invested considerable time and energy developing and deepening his own understanding of the issues so that he might address them more effectively. For him, an unforseen opportunity emerged; he brought to it his own life experience and previous education, sharpened by his participation in the staff development project.

One of the school districts is revising its social studies curriculum to make it more multicultural. While I am not sure exactly what the impetus for that is, I am aware of some factors. Karen, the pre-school teacher, submitted her textbook analysis to a school district curriculum director; about a year later, a graduate student of mine submitted a similar analysis of a different textbook. Both drew similar conclusions about the deficiency of social studies and language arts textbooks. Also during that time, an African American social studies teacher read several US history accounts from diverse cultural perspectives and reviewed some recently-published alternative history materials, which he shared with the same curriculum director. Concurrently, 1990 census data found the local area to have one of the fastest-growing African American populations in the nation.

Serving on the Social Studies Revision Committee is one of the elementary teachers who participated in this study the full two years. Judging from her input into discussions, it appears that her interest and knowledge level in multicultural education has grown steadily since the conclusion of the staff development project.

Postscript

Over the past two-and-one-half years, Susan and I have been working more intensively with four local schools, all of which have teachers who participated in the staff development project studied here, who were instrumental to getting their four schools selected. Although the pace of change in those schools sometimes has seemed very slow, occasionally there are exciting indications of progress. Yesterday, for example, over one-hundred teachers from the four schools, plus two additional schools, attended the first session of a voluntary staff development course about local minority and lower-class White groups in the community and various local advocacy and self-help organizations (such as the NAACP and labor unions). Michael will serve as one of the facilitators; and George was there with most of his current staff.

Perhaps the greatest surprise has been Lee. His colleagues recently told me that although he still verbally does not support multicultural education, he is doing more and more of what was recommended in the staff development sessions. For example, he voluntarily arranged for a Native American speaker for a school program; the teachers found the speaker excellent and the fact that Lee had arranged the presentation astounding. He verbally does not support Women's History Week in March; in response, his colleagues (most of whom are women) make sure women's accomplishments are very visibly celebrated the entire month of March. I gather the relationship between Lee and the women teachers has developed into a source of amusement and possibly affection, rather than one of hostility. And apparently it has developed into an impetus for growth on the part of both Lee and his colleagues.

These developments suggest to me the importance of continuing to do whatever one can to advance education that is multicultural, linking one's efforts as much as possible with other supporting actions and movements in the community. One cannot always see the long-range results of one's actions, even when one tries to assess them through a study. The late 1980s and early 1990s generally did not provide a climate conducive to social change movements, but some events built momentum that coincided with the kinds of changes the staff development project promoted. Local schools steadily became racially diverse, and a new administration in one of the school districts decided to come down in support of some version of multicultural education. Budget cut-backs prompted intense discussions about how to allocate school funds; so far the small amounts of money earmarked for 'multicultural' issues (such as funding for Michael's position) have survived, probably mainly because of demographic changes. The NAACP in Gelegenheit is becoming stronger, and its president recently spoke out loudly against housing discrimination. The war in the Persian Gulf, while generally prompting a highly conservative analysis of the US relationship to the Middle East, also promoted discussion about the capabilities of men and women of color and White women in the military. After the war coverage had subsided from the media, the issue of 'political correctness' emerged, with some analyses featuring multiple perspectives.

In other words, in spite of the conservative tenor of the times, 'diversity' has been quite visible, and has been articulated locally in a variety of ways. If the staff development project planted seeds of awareness in some teachers and nourished seeds in others, the local context has provided some sustenance for growth and action. It is that sustenance that one can work to strengthen, receiving occasional impetus from the unexpected results of one's work.

Bibliography

ACUNA, R. (1972) *Occupied America: The Chicano's Struggle Toward Liberation*, San Francisco, CA, Canfield Press.

ALLEN, P.G. (1986) *The Sacred Hoop*, Boston, MA, Beacon Press.

APPLE, M.W. (1988) *Teachers and Texts*, New York, Routledge.

APPLE, M.W. and CHRISTIAN-SMITH, L.K. (Eds) (1991) *The Politics of the Textbook*, New York, Routledge, Chapman and Hall.

ASANTE, M.K. (1988) *The Afrocentric Idea*, Philadelphia, PA, Temple University Press.

ASANTE, M.K. (1990) *Kemet, Afrocentricity, and Knowledge*, Trenton, NJ, Africa World Press.

ASHTON, P.T. and WEBB, R.B. (1986) *Making a Difference: Teachers' Sense of Efficacy and Student Achievement*, New York, Longman.

BAKER, G.C. (1977) 'Multicultural imperatives for curriculum development in teacher education', *Journal of Research and Development in Education*, **11**, pp. 70–83.

BAKER, G.C. (1983) *Planning and Organizing for Multicultural Instruction*, Reading, MA, Addison-Wesley.

BANKS, J.A. (1984) 'Multicultural education and its critics: Britain and the United States', *The New Era*, **65**, pp. 58–65.

BANKS, J.A. (1988) *Multiethnic Education: Theory and Practice*, 2nd edn, Boston, MA, Allyn and Bacon.

BANKS, J.A. (1991) 'A curriculum for empowerment, action and change' in SLEETER, C.E. (Ed.) *Empowerment through Multicultural Education*, Albany, NY, SUNY Press, pp. 125–42.

BARBAGLI, M. and DEI, M. (1977) 'Socialization into apathy and political subordination' in KARABEL, J. and HALSEY, A.H. (Eds) *Power and Ideology in Education*, New York, Oxford University Press, pp. 423–31.

BARTH, R.S. (1990) *Improving Schools from Within*, San Francisco, CA, Jossey-Bass.

BLOOM, A. (1987) *The Closing of the American Mind*, New York, Simon and Schuster.

BOGGS, C. (1986) *Social Movements and Political Power*, Philadelphia, PA, Temple University Press.

BOXILL, B. (1989) 'Is civil rights legislation irrelevant to Black progress?' in VAN HORNE, W.A. (Ed.) *Race: Twentieth Century Dilemmas — Twenty-First Century Prognosis*, Milwaukee, WI, University of Wisconsin System Institute on Race and Ethnicity, pp. 12–48.

BOYKIN, A.W. (1986) 'The triple quandary and the schooling of Afro-American children' in NEISSER, U. (Ed.) *The School Achievement of Minority Children*, Hillsdale, NJ, Lawrence Earlbaum Associates, pp. 57–92.

BRITZMAN, D.P. (1986) 'Cultural myths in the making of a teacher: Biography and social structure in teacher education', *Harvard Educational Review*, **56**, pp. 442–56.

BRONNER, S.E. (1990) *Socialism Unbound*, New York, Routledge.

BUENKER, J.D. (1976) 'Immigration and ethnic groups' in NEUENSCHWANDER, J.A. (Ed.) *Kenosha County in the 20th Century*, Kenosha, WI, Kenosha County Bicentennial Commission, pp. 1–50.

BUENKER, J.D. (1977) 'The immigrant heritage' in BURKEL, N.C. (Ed.) *Racine: Growth and Change in a Wisconsin County*, Racine, WI, Racine County Board of Supervisors, pp. 69–136.

BURSTEIN, N.D. and CABELLO, B. (1989) 'Preparing teachers to work with culturally diverse students: A teacher education model', *Journal of Teacher Education*, September–October, pp. 9–16.

CARLSON, D. (1987) 'Teachers as political actors: From reproductive theory to the crisis of schooling', *Harvard Educational Review*, **57**, 3, pp. 283–307.

CARNOY, M. (1989) 'Education, state, and culture in American society' in GIROUX, H.A. and McLAREN, P. (Eds) *Critical Pedagogy, the State, and Cultural Struggle*, Albany, NY, SUNY Press, pp. 3–23.

CHAN, S. (Ed.) (1989) *Social and Gender Boundaries in the United States*, Lewiston, NY, The Edwin Mellen Press.

CHERRYHOLMES, C.H. (1988) *Power and Criticism: Post-structural Investigations in Education*, New York, Teachers College Press.

CHIN, R. and BENNE, K.D. (1975) 'General strategies for effecting change in human systems' in BENNIS, W., BENNE, K.D., CHIN, R. and COREY, K. (Eds) *The Planning of Change*, 3rd edn, New York, Holt, Reinhart & Winston, pp. 22–45.

CLARK, V.L. (1987) 'Teacher education at historically Black institutions in the aftermath of the Holmes/Carnegie reports', *Planning and Changing*, **18**, 2, pp. 74–89.

CLYMER, T., INDRISANO, R., JOHNSON, D., PEARSON, D.P. and VENEZKY, R.L. (1985) *Ride the Sunrise*, Lexington, MA, Ginn.

COHEN, E. (1986) *Designing Groupwork*, New York, Teachers College Press.

COLLINS, R. (1977) 'Functional and conflict theories of educational stratification' in KARABEL, J. and HALSEY, A.H. (Eds) *Power and Ideology in Education*, New York, Oxford University Press, pp. 118–36.

COMER, J.P. (1988) *Maggie's American Dream*, New York, New American Library.

CONNELL, R.W. (1985) *Teachers' Work*, Boston, MA, George Allen & Unwin.

CONTRERAS, R. and TERRELL, R. (1981) 'Staff development for desegregated schools', *Educational Research Quarterly*, 6, 3, pp. 65–74.

CORCORAN, T.B. (1990) 'Schoolwork: Perspectives on workplace reform in public schools' in MCLAUGHLIN, M.W., TALBERT, J.E. and BASCIA, N. (Eds) *The Contexts of Teaching in Secondary Schools: Teachers' Realities*, New York, Teachers College Press, pp. 142–66.

CORNELL, S. (1988) *The Return of the Native: American Indian Political Resurgence*, New York, Oxford University Press.

CUSICK, P.A. (1973) *Inside High School*, New York, Holt, Rinehart and Winston.

DELAMONT, S. (1989) *Knowledgeable Women*, London, Routledge.

DELGADO-GAITAN, C. (1990) *Literacy for Empowerment*, Lewes, Falmer Press.

DENSCOMBE, J. (1982) 'The "hidden pedagogy" and its implications for teacher training', *British Journal of Sociology of Education*, 3, 3, pp. 249–65.

DENSCOMBE, M. (1980) 'The work context of teaching: An analytic framework for the study of teachers in classrooms', *British Journal of Sociology of Education*, 1, pp. 279–92.

DUDLEY, T.J. and BELL, M.L. (1991) 'Teaching: The profession Blacks may lose', *Kappa Delta Phi Record*, 27, 4, pp. 108–10.

EPSTEIN, J.L. and DAUBER, S.L. (1991) 'School programs and teacher practices of parent involvement in inner-city elementary and middle schools', *The Elementary School Journal*, 91, 3, pp. 289–305.

ERICKSON, F. (1979) 'Talking down: Some cultural sources of miscommunication in interviews' in WOLFGANG, A. (Ed.) *Nonverbal Behavior: Applications and Cross-Cultural Implications*, New York, Academic Press.

ETHNIC CULTURAL HERITAGE PROGRAM (1977) *Rainbow Activities*, South El Monte, CA, Creative Teaching Press.

FAST, H. (1977) *The Immigrant*, Boston, MA, Houghton-Mifflin.

FENDRICH, J.M. and TURNER, R.W. (1989) 'The transition from student to adult politics', *Social Forces*, 67, 4, pp. 1049–57.

FINE, M. (1991) *Framing Dropouts*, Albany, NY, SUNY Press.

FLOUD, J. and HALSEY, A.H. (1958) 'The sociology of education: A trend report and bibliography', *Current Sociology*, 7, pp. 165–235.

FORDHAM, S. (1988) 'Racelessness as a factor in Black students' school success: Pragmatic strategy or pyrrhic victory?', *Harvard Educational Review*, 58, 1, pp. 54–84.

FOX, G.T., JR. (1981) 'Purpose as context for evaluating inservice programs', *Journal of Research and Development in Education*, 14, pp. 34–46.

FRAATZ, J.M.B. (1987) *The Politics of Reading*, New York, Teachers College Press.

FREIRE, P. (1973) *Education for Critical Consciousness*, New York, Seabury Press.

FULLAN, M.G. (1990a) 'Staff development, innovation and institutional development' in JOYCE, B. (Ed.) *Changing School Culture through Staff Development*, Alexandria, VA, Association for Supervision and Curriculum Development, pp. 3–25.

FULLAN, M.G. (1990b) 'Change processes in secondary schools: Toward a more fundamental agenda' in McLAUGHLIN, M.W., TALBERT, J.E. and BASCIA, N. (Eds) *The Contexts of Teaching in Secondary Schools: Teachers' Realities*, New York, Teachers College Press, pp. 224–55.

GAY, G. (1977) 'Curriculum for multicultural teacher education' in KLASSEN, F.J. and GOLLNICK, D.M. (Eds) *Pluralism and the American Teacher: Issues and Case Studies*, Washington, DC, American Association of College for Teacher Education, pp. 31–62.

GAY, G. (1983) 'Multiethnic education: Historical developments and future prospects', *Phi Delta Kappan*, **64**, pp. 560–3.

GAY, G. (1991) 'The gap between multicultural theory and practice in US schools: A focus on teacher education', paper presented at the annual meeting of the American Educational Research Association, Chicago, April.

GIDDENS, A. (1979) *Central Problems in Social Theory*, Berkeley, CA, University of California Press.

GIROUX, H.A. (1983) *Theory and Resistance in Education*, South Hadley, MA, Bergin and Garvey.

GIROUX, H.A. (1988) *Teachers as Intellectuals*. Granby, MA, Bergin and Garvey.

GITLIN, A. (1983) 'School structure and teachers' work' in APPLE, M.W. and WEIS, L. (Eds) *Ideology and Practice in Schooling*, Philadelphia, PA, Temple University Press, pp. 193–212.

GOETZ, J.P. and LeCOMPTE, M.D. (1984) *Ethnography and Qualitative Design in Educational Research*, New York, Academic Press.

GOODLAD, J.I. (1984) *A Place Called School*, New York, McGraw-Hill.

GORDON, B.M. (1985) 'Teaching teachers: "Nation at risk" and the issue of knowledge in teacher education', *The Urban Review*, **17**, pp. 33–46.

GRANT, C.A. (1978) 'Education that is multicultural: Isn't that what we mean?', *Journal of Teacher Education*, **29**, 5, pp. 45–8.

GRANT, C.A. (1990) 'Desegregation, racial attitudes, and intergroup contact: A discussion of change', *Phi Delta Kappan*, **72**, 1, pp. 25–32.

GRANT, C.A. and GRANT, G. (1986) 'Increasing the educational opportunities of Black students by training teachers in multicultural curriculum development', *Western Journal of Black Studies*, 10, pp. 29–33.

GRANT, C.A. and MELNICK, S.L. (1978) 'Multicultural perspectives of curriculum development and their relationship to in-service education' in EDELFELT, R.A. and SMITH, E.B. (Eds) *Breakaway to Multi-dimensional Approaches: Integrating Curriculum Development and In-service Education*, Washington, DC, Association of Teacher Educators, pp. 81–100.

GRANT, C.A. and SLEETER, C.E. (1985a) 'The literature on multicultural education: Review and analysis', *Educational Review*, **37**, pp. 97–118.

GRANT, C.A. and SLEETER, C.E. (1985b) 'Who determines teacher work: The teacher, the organization, or both?', *Teaching and Teacher Education*, **1**, pp. 209–20.

GRANT, C.A. and SLEETER, C.E. (1986a) 'Race, class, and gender in education research: An argument for integrative analysis', *Review of Educational Research*, **56**, 2, pp. 195–211.

GRANT, C.A. and SLEETER, C.E. (1986b) 'Equality, equity, and excellence: A critique' in ALTBACH, P.G., KELLY, G.P. and WEIS, L. (Eds) *Excellence in Education: Perspectives on Policy and Practices*, Buffalo, NY, Prometheus, pp. 139–60.

GRANT, C.A. and SLEETER, C.E. (1986c) *After the School Bell Rings*, Lewes, Falmer Press.

GRANT, C.A. and SLEETER, C.E. (1989) *Turning on Learning*, Columbus, OH, Merrill.

GRANT, C.A., SLEETER, C.E. and ANDERSON, J.E. (1986) 'The literature on multicultural education: Review and analysis', *Educational Studies*, **12**, pp. 47–71.

GREENBAUM, W. (1974) 'America in search of a new ideal: An essay on the rise of pluralism', *Harvard Educational Review*, **44**, pp. 411–40.

GRUMET, M.R. (1988) *Bitter Milk*, Amherst, MA, University of Massachusetts Press.

GURNAH, A. (1984) 'The politics of racism awareness training', *Critical Social Policy*, **11**, pp. 6–20.

HABERMAN, M. (1989) 'More minority teachers', *Phi Delta Kappan*, **70**, 10, pp. 771–6.

HARMON, M.J. (1964) *Political Thought: From Plato to the Present*, New York, McGraw-Hill Book Co.

HATSOPOULOS, G.N., KRUGMAN, P.R. and SUMMERS, L.H. (1988) 'US competitiveness: Beyond the trade deficit', *Science*, **241**, pp. 299–307.

HAWLEY, W.D., CRAIN, R.L., ROSSELL, C.H., SYMLIE, M.A., FERNANDEZ, R.R., SCHOFIELD, J.W., TOMPKINS, R., TRENT, W.T. and ZLOTNIK, M.S. (1983) *Strategies for Effective Desegregation*, Lexington, MA, Lexington Books.

HECK, S.F. (1989) 'The creative classroom environment: A stage-set design' in SHADE, B.J.R. (Ed.) *Culture, Style, and the Educative Process*, Springfield, IL, Charles C. Thomas, pp. 212–25.

HENRY, W.A., III (1990) 'Beyond the melting pot', *Time*, **135**, 9 April, pp. 28–31.

HIRSCH, E.D., JR. (1987) *Cultural Literacy: What Every American Needs to Know*, Boston, MA, Houghton-Mifflin.

HODGKINSON, H.L. (1985) *All One System: Demographics of Education — Kindergarten through Graduate School*, Washington, DC, Institute for Educational Leadership.

HODGKINSON, H.L. (1988) 'The right schools for the right kids', *Educational Leadership*, **45**, pp. 10–14.

HOLTZ, H., MARCUS, I., DOUGHERTY, J., MICHAELS, J. and PEDUZZI, R. (Eds) (1989) *Education and the American Dream*, Granby, MA, Bergin & Garvey.

HOOKS, B. (1990) *Yearning: Race, Gender and Cultural Politics*, Boston, MA, South End Press.

HOOVER, K.R. (1987) *Ideology and Political Life*, Monterey, CA, Brooks/Cole Pub. Co.

HULSEBOSCH, P.L. (1990) 'Mothering and teaching: Connections and collaboration', *Kappa Delta Phi Record*, **26**, 4, pp. 101–5.

IRVINE, J.J. (1988) 'Teacher race as a factor in Black students' achievement', paper presented at the annual meeting of the American Educational Research Association, New Orleans, April.

IRVINE, J.J. (1991) *Black Students and School Failure*, New York, Praeger.

JACKSON, G. and COSCA, C. (1974) 'The inequality of educational opportunity in the Southwest: An observational study of ethnically mixed classrooms', *American Educational Research Journal*, **11**, pp. 219–29.

JAGGAR, A.M. (1983) *Feminist Politics and Human Nature*, Totowa, NJ, Rowman & Allanheld, Pub.

JIOBU, R.M. (1988) *Ethnicity and Assimilation*, Albany, NY, SUNY Press.

JOYCE, B., BENNETT, B. and ROLHEISER-BENNETT, C. (1990) 'The self-educating teacher: Empowering teachers through research' in JOYCE, B. (Ed.) *Changing School Culture through Staff Development*, Alexandria, VA, Association for Supervision and Curriculum Development, pp. 26–40.

JOYCE, B. and SHOWERS, B. (1988) *Student Achievement through Staff Development*, New York, Longman.

KING, J.E. (1991) 'Dysconscious racism: Ideology, identity, and the miseducation of teachers', *Journal of Negro Education*, **60**, 2, pp. 133–46.

KING, J.E. and WILSON, T.L. (1990) 'Being the soul-freeing substance: A legacy of hope in Afro humanity', *Journal of Education*, **172**, 2, pp. 9–27.

KING, N.J. (1980) *Staff Development Programs in Desegregated Settings*, Santa Monica, CA, Rand.

KLUEGEL, J.R. and SMITH, E.R. (1986) *Beliefs about Inequality: Americans' Views of What is and What Ought to Be*, New York, Aldine de Gruyter.

LAMM, R. (1988) 'The uncompetitive society', *US News and World Report*, **104**, p. 9.

LITTLE, J.W. (1990) 'Conditions of professional development in secondary schools' in McLAUGHLIN, M.W., TALBERT, J.E. and BASCIA, N. (Eds) *The Contexts of Teaching in Secondary Schools: Teachers' Realities*, New York, Teachers College Press, pp. 187–223.

LORTIE, D.C. (1975) *Schoolteacher*, Chicago, IL, University of Chicago Press.

LORTIE, D.C. (1986) 'Teacher status in Dade County: A case of structural strain?', *Phi Delta Kappan*, **67**, pp. 568–75.

McCARTHY, C. (1988) 'Rethinking liberal and radical perspectives on racial inequality in schooling: Making the case for nonsynchrony', Harvard *Educational Review*, **58**, pp. 265–79.

McCarthy, C. (1990) *Race and Curriculum*, Lewes, Falmer Press.

McNeil, L.M. (1986) *Contradictions of Control: School Structure and School Knowledge*, New York, Routledge.

Marable, M. (1987) 'The contradictory contours of Black political culture' in Davis, M., Marable, M., Pfeil, F. and Sprinker, M. (Eds) *The Year Left 2: An American Socialist Yearbook*, London, Verso, pp. 1–17.

Meier, D. (1987) 'Success in East Harlem: How one group of teachers build a school that works', *American Educator*, Fall, pp. 34–9.

Meier, D. (1991) 'Choice can save public education', *The Nation*, **252**, 8, pp. 253 and 266–71.

Metz, M.H. (1990) 'How social class differences shape teachers' work' in McLaughlin, M.W., Talbert, J.E. and Bascia, N. (Eds) *The Contexts of Teaching in Secondary Schools: Teachers' Realities*, New York, Teachers College Press, pp. 40–107.

Mock, K.R. (1983) 'The successful multicultural teacher', *History and Social Science Teacher*, **19**, pp. 87–97.

Mudimbe, V.Y. (1988) *Liberty in African and Western Thought*, Washington, DC, Institute for Independent Education.

Muñz, C. (1987) 'Chicano politics: The current conjuncture' in Davis, M., Marable, M., Pfeil, F. and Sprinker, M. (Eds) *The Year Left 2: An American Socialist Yearbook*, London, Verso, pp. 35–51.

Murray, C. (1984) *Losing Ground: American Social Policy*, 1950–1980, New York, Basic Books.

Nasar, S. (1988) 'America's competitive revival', *Fortune*, **117**, pp. 44–50+.

Nickolai-Mays, S. and Davis, J.L. (1986) 'In-service training of teachers in multicultural urban schools: A systematic model', *Urban Education*, **21**, 2, pp. 169–79.

Oakes, J. (1985) *Keeping Track*, Princeton, NJ, Yale University Press.

Olneck, M. (1990) 'The recurring dream: Symbolism and ideology in intercultural and multicultural education', *American Journal of Education*, **98**, 2, pp. 147–74.

Omi, M. and Winant, H. (1986) *Racial Formation in the United States*, New York, Routledge and Kegan Paul.

Orfield, G., Monfort, F. and Aaron, M. (1989) *Status of School Desegregation: 1968–1986*, Alexandria, VA, National School Boards Association Council of Urban Boards of Education.

Ortiz, F.I. (1988) 'Hispanic-American children's experiences in classrooms: A comparison between Hispanic and non-Hispanic children' in Weis, L. (Ed.) *Class, Race and Gender in American Education*, Albany, NY, SUNY Press, pp. 63–86.

Parenti, M. (1978) *Power and the Powerless*, New York, St. Martin's Press.

Perry, N.J. (1988) 'The education crisis: What business can do', *Fortune*, **118**, pp. 70–3.

PINK, W.T. (1990) 'Staff development for urban school improvement: Lessons learned from two case studies', *School Effectiveness and School Improvement*, **1**, 1, pp. 41–60.

RAMIREZ, M., III and CASTAÑEDA, A. (1974) *Cultural Democracy, Bicognitive Development, and Education*, New York, Academic Press.

RAVITCH, D. (1990) 'Multiculturalism: E plurbis plures', *The American Scholar*, **59**, pp. 337–54.

REDMAN, G.L. (1977) 'Study of the relationship of teacher empathy for minority persons and inservice human relations training', *Journal of Educational Research*, **70**, pp. 205–10.

RESULTS OF SURVEY BRING SUGGESTIONS (1990) *Racine Journal Times*, 26 June, p. 3.

RICH, D. (1988) *Megaskills*, Boston, MA, Houghton-Mifflin.

RICHARDSON, V., CASANOVA, U., PLACIER, P. and GUILFOYLE, K. (1989) *School Children at Risk*, Lewes, Falmer Press.

RINGER, B.B. and LAWLESS, E.R. (1989) *Race-Ethnicity and Society*, New York, Routledge.

ROPER ORGANIZATION, INC., FOR THE WALL STREET JOURNAL (1987) *The American Dream*. Princeton, NJ, Dow Jones & Co, Inc.

SAPIRO, V. (1990) 'The gender basis of American social policy' in GORDON, L. (Ed.) *Women, the State, and Welfare*, Madison, WI, University of Wisconsin Press, pp. 36–54.

SAPON-SHEVIN, M. and SCHNIEDEWIND, N. (1991) 'Cooperative learning as empowering pedagogy' in SLEETER, C.E. (Ed.) *Empowerment through Multicultural Education*, Albany, NY, SUNY Press, pp. 159–78.

SHADE, B.J.R. (1989) *Culture, Style, and the Educative Process*, Springfield, IL, Charles C. Thomas, Pub.

SHIRTS, R.G. (1969) *Star Power*, LaJolla, CA, Western Behavioral Sciences Institute.

SHOR, I. (1980) *Critical Teaching and Everyday Life*, Boston, MA, South End Press.

SHOR, I. (1986) *Culture Wars: School and Society in the Conservative Restoration 1969–1984*, Boston, MA, Routledge and Kegan Paul.

SICKLER, J. (1988) 'Teachers in charge: Empowering the professionals', *Phi Delta Kappan*, **69**, pp. 354–6+.

SIDEL, R. (1986) *Women and Children Last*, New York, Viking.

SIDEL, R. (1990) *On her Own: Growing up in the Shadow of the American Dream*, New York, Penguin Books.

SILBER, J. (1988) 'Education and national survival', *Vital Speeches*, **54**, pp. 215–9.

SIROTNIK, K.V. (1987) 'The school as the center for change', (Occasional Paper No. 5), Seattle, WA, University of Washington Institute for the Study of Education Policy.

SIVANANDON, A. (1985) 'RAT and the degradation of the black struggle', *Race and Class*, **26**, pp. 1–33.

SIZEMORE, B.A. (1990) 'The Madison elementary school: A turnaround case' in LOMOTEY, K. (Ed.) *Going to School: The African American Experience*, Albany, NY, SUNY Press, pp. 155–80.

SKRTIC, T.M. (1991) 'The special education paradox: Equity as the way to excellence', *Harvard Educational Review*, **61**, 2, pp. 148–206.

SLAVIN, R.E. (1983) 'When does cooperative learning increase student achievement?', *Psychological Bulletin*, **94**, pp. 429–45.

SLEETER, C.E. (1986) 'Learning disabilities: The social construction of a special education category', *Exceptional Children*, **53**, 1, pp. 46–54.

SLEETER, C.E. (1987) 'Literacy, definitions of learning disabilities and social control' in FRANKLIN, B. (Ed.) *Learning Disability: Dissenting Essays*, Lewes, Falmer Press, pp. 67–86.

SLEETER, C.E. (1989a) 'Multicultural education as a form of resistance to oppression', *Journal of Education*, **171**, 3, pp. 51–71.

SLEETER, C.E. (1989b) 'Doing multicultural education across the grade levels and subject areas: A case study of Wisconsin', *Teaching and Teacher Education*, **5**, 3, pp. 189–203.

SLEETER, C.E. (1990) 'Staff development for desegregated schooling', *Phi Delta Kappan*, **72**, 1, pp. 33–40.

SLEETER, C.E. and GRANT, C.A. (1987) 'An analysis of multicultural education in the United States, *Harvard Educational Review*, **57**, 4, pp. 421–44.

SLEETER, C.E. and GRANT, C.A. (1988) *Making Choices for Multicultural Education*, Columbus, OH, Merrill.

SLEETER, C.E. and GRANT, C.A. (1991) 'Race, class, gender and disability in current textbooks' in APPLE, M.W. and CHRISTIAN-SMITH, L.K. (Eds) *The Politics of the Textbook*, New York, Routledge, Chapman and Hall, pp. 78–110.

SMITH, G.P. (1984) 'The critical issue of excellence and equity in competency testing', *Journal of Teacher Education*, **35**, 2, pp. 6–9.

SPARKS, D. and LOUCKS-HORSLEY, S. (1989) 'Five models of staff development for teachers', *Journal of Staff Development*, **10**, pp. 40–57.

SPENCER, D.A. (1986) *Contemporary Women Teachers: Balancing School and Home*, New York, Longman.

SPINDLER, G. (1982) 'General introduction' in SPINDLER, G. (Ed.) *Doing the Ethnography of Schooling*, New York, Holt, Rinehart and Winston, pp. 1–13.

SPRADLEY, J.P. and MCCURDY, D.W. (1972) *The Cultural Experience*, Chicago, IL, Science Research Associates.

SPRING, J. (1989) *The Sorting Machine Revisited*, New York, Longman.

STALVEY, L.M. (1989) *The Education of a WASP*, Madison, WI, University of Wisconsin Press.

SUZUKI, B.H. (1984) 'Curriculum transformation for multicultural education', *Education and Urban Society*, **16**, pp. 294–322.

SUZUKI, B.H. (1989) 'Asian Americans as the "model minority"', *Change*, **21**, Nov/Dec, pp. 13–19.

SWADENER, E.B. (1990) 'Children and families "at risk": Etiology, critique, and alternative paradigms', *Educational Foundations*, 4, pp. 17–39.

TAKAKI, R.T. (1979) *Iron Cages: Race and Culture in 19th Century America*, Seattle, WA, University of Washington Press.

TAKAKI, R. (1989) 'The fourth iron cage: Race and political economy in the 1990s', paper presented at the Green Bay Colloquium on Ethnicity and Public Policy, Green Bay, WI.

TAYLOR, B. (1990) 'Grade gap grows as students advance through Unified', *Racine Journal Times*, **134**, 22 April, pp. 4A–5A.

TEENS LESS HEALTHY THAN PARENTS WERE, REPORT SAYS (1990) *Racine Journal Times* **134**, 160, p. 1.

TERKEL, S. (1980) *American Dreams Lost and Found*, New York, Pantheon Books.

TERKEL, S. (1988) *The Great Divide: Second Thoughts on the American Dream*, New York, Pantheon Books.

TEWEL, K.J. and TRUBOWITZ, S. (1987) 'The minority group teacher', *Urban Education*, **22**, 3, pp. 355–65.

TIEDT, P.L. and TIEDT, I.M. (1986) *Multicultural Teaching: A Handbook of Activities, Information, and Resources*, 2nd edn, Boston, MA, Allyn & Bacon.

TROYNA, B. (1985) 'The great divide: Policies and practices in multicultural education', *British Journal of Sociology of Education*, **6**, 2, pp. 209–224.

TROYNA, B. and WILLIAMS, J. (1986) *Racism, Education and the State*, Beckenham, Croom Helm.

TRUEBA, H.T. (1989) *Raising Silent Voices: Educating the Linguistic Minorities for the 21st Century*, New York, Newbury House Pub.

WADE, J.E. (1987) 'Race and raceness: A theoretical perspective of the Black American experience', *The Western Journal of Black Studies*, **11**, 1, pp. 31–8.

WASHINGTON, V. (1981) 'Impact of antiracism/multicultural education training on elementary teachers' attitudes and classroom behavior', *The Elementary School Journal*, **81**, pp. 186–92.

WEILER, K. (1988) *Women Teaching for Change*, South Hadley, MA, Bergin and Garvey.

WEIS, L. (1990) *Working Class without Work*, New York, Routledge.

WELLMAN, D.T. (1977) *Portraits of White Racism*, Cambridge, MA, Cambridge University Press.

WEST, C. (1987) 'Race and social theory: Towards a genealogical materialist analysis' in DAVIS, M., MARABLE, M., PFEIL, F. and SPRINKER, M. (Eds) *The Year Left 2: An American Socialist Yearbook*, London, Verso, pp. 73–89.

WHITTY, G. (1985) *Sociology and School Knowledge*, London, Methuen.

WILLIAMS, M.R. (1989) *Neighborhood Organizing for Urban School Reform*, New York, Teachers College Press.

ZINN, H. (1980) *A People's History of the United States*, New York, Harper & Row.

Index

Ability – 38, 58, 59, 72.
Academic – ability–78; achievements
  –160, 171–4; deficits–60;
  development–57; expectations–
  111; instruction–58.
Acuna, Rodolfo – 23.
Affirmative action – 11.
African American (Blacks) – 16,
  17, 19, 23–5, 27, 68, 92, 106, 120,
  123, 147, 153, 155–6, 192, 211,
  219, 220–1; assimilation–92;
  culture–9, 191; educators 216;
  families–89, 100; history–47, 115,
  153; holiday–117; institutions–209;
  issues–105; learning styles–126;
  leaders–119, 209; low status–9;
  males–62, 134, 215; students–15,
  66, 93, 127, 131, 215.
Allen, Paula Gunn – 219.
American Dream – 6, 7, 9, 10, 12,
  13, 17, 19, 23, 25, 27, 30, 31, 65,
  170–1, 177, 217–22.
American family – 28.
American ideals – 220.
American Indians (also Native
  Americans) – 19, 62, 117, 120,
  123, 152, 155–6, 169, 192, 219–20.
Americanized – 21, 22.
American melting pot – 22, 26, 84,
  138.
Analytic learners – 71, 77, 93.

A Nation at Risk – 26.
Apple, M.W. – 179.
Ashton, Patricia – 58, 84, 197.
Asian American – 27, 29, 123, 155.
Assertive Discipline – 79, 82.
'At risk' – 30, 136, 202, 205;
  children–28, 44, 83, 100, 102,
  138, 148, 167, 178; ideology–28;
  students–43, 45, 46, 104, 206–7,
  212.
Attention – negative–77; positive–
  77; span–71, 73; teacher–78.
Attitudes – assessment–194; biased–
  194; issues–111; multicultural–138;
  peoples'–146; societal–40;
  teacher–33, 35, 88, 178–9, 187,
  192.

Baker, G.C. – 33–34.
Banks, J.A. – 40, 189.
Barth, Roland – 216.
Behavior – classroom–58, 148, 192;
  culturally conditioned–111;
  expectations–61; parent's–105;
  patterns–91; problems–150;
  student–59, 81, 151; style–72;
  teacher–36, 78, 107.
Bias – 107, 120, 133, 208; attitudes–
  110; European–121; gender–77;
  male–120; racial–77; white
  society–122.